MW01105902

American Presidents and Jerusalem

American Presidents and Jerusalem

Ghada Hashem Talhami

LEXINGTON BOOKS
Lanham • Boulder • New York • London

Published by Lexington Books
An imprint of The Rowman & Littlefield Publishing Group, Inc.
4501 Forbes Boulevard, Suite 200, Lanham, Maryland 20706
www.rowman.com

Unit A, Whitacre Mews, 26-34 Stannary Street, London SE11 4AB

British Library Cataloguing in Publication Information Available

Library of Congress Cataloging-in-Publication Data Available

ISBN 978-1-4985-5428-2 (cloth : alk. paper)
ISBN 978-1-4985-5429-9 (electronic)

♾™ The paper used in this publication meets the minimum requirements of American
National Standard for Information Sciences Permanence of Paper for Printed Library
Materials, ANSI/NISO Z39.48-1992.

Printed in the United States of America

Contents

Preface   vii

Acknowledgments   xi

1 The British Mandate: Jerusalem Undivided   1

2 American Zionists Take the Lead   27

3 The Battle for Jerusalem: Bucking the International Consensus   47

4 Planning for Expansion: Overcoming the Limitations of the First
       Borders   71

5 War Unites Jerusalem   95

6 Israeli Faits Accomplis and Jordanian Weakness   129

7 Oslo: The Chimera of a Just Peace   157

8 Clinton's Quest for a Mideast Legacy   177

9 Conclusion   197

Bibliography   209

Index   215

About the Author   221

Preface

The modern history of Jerusalem can be viewed from several angles. There were the Western travelers, the religious and the romantic, who, particularly in the nineteenth century, popularized the image of a great ancient city in ruins. This particular picture fed into the fanciful but unreal impression of Jerusalem as a city awaiting its modern redemption. It was no surprise, then, that when the Mughrabi Quarter was demolished in 1967 to widen the plaza facing the Wailing Wall, Israeli municipal and military officials claimed that the derelict condition of this neighborhood justified its destruction. There was also the image of the Old City as oriental and the New City as the creation of modern and progressive Zionists and no one noticed the Social Darwinian nuances of this binary definition. The US Department of State received feedback after the 1967 War of a city in agony, but managed not to transmit these impressions to the general public. At that time, the mainstream US media, such as *Life* magazine, succeeded in perpetuating the image of a city liberated by brave and youthful citizen soldiers who defeated the Arab horde. Then there was the image emerging from official US documents and government reports, which described the city as an obstacle to any diplomatic settlement of this international dispute. Jerusalem was revealed as the city which defied the solutions of rational policy makers and enlightened presidents. But the one Jerusalem which was hardly understood was that of the Palestinians, whose historic claims were waived and who saw every single one of their ancient neighborhoods placed on the bargaining table in order to ease the way for a comprehensive Israeli-Palestinian settlement.

This study hopes to flesh out this particular image in the interest of providing the missing link in this puzzle, the unacknowledged Palestinian case and the motives which drove them to resist long after resistance was written out of the picture. The story of how the defeated Palestinians defined new forms of resistance is the only key to understanding the dilemma of all Jerusalemites. Whether it was Arafat's advisers, who were smarting under the weight of Arab criticism following the Oslo peace, or Faysal Husseini who struggled to be a peace-maker, institution-builder, and resistance leader all in one, or Arafat himself who was feeling the weight of history on his shoulders, each fought against surrender. This story begins to acquire massive importance beyond the political weakness of the Palestinians when one is reminded of the cumulative burden of the Islamic legacy in Jerusalem. The blindness of American policy-makers to this legacy and their unconcealed admiration for everything and anything Israeli, finally defeated their diplomatic plans. Clinton's diplomacy in particular with its self-assured misconceptions about *realpolitik* and how the weak must obey the strong finally defeated all his plans. This is where this book diverges from the unsubstantiated claims of Clinton's advisers and generations of presidential aides before them by shedding some light on the untold and deliberately submerged Palestinian angle of the Jerusalem dispute.

But why focus on American presidents, almost to the exclusion of any other political actors? These presidents, as are all elected heads of state, are constantly bombarded by myth-makers and peddlers of inchoate ideas in order to force on them favorable policies and decisions. A twentieth-century phenomenon where Jerusalem was concerned, this tendency did not preclude a certain yearning for the holy city in the past. In the nineteenth century, the obsession with Jerusalem was the natural outcome of the missionary century as Christian evangelists and agents of empire crisscrossed the globe in search of souls to save and markets to conquer. Among these were Americans whose influence must have impinged on Abraham Lincoln and infected him with their mystical view of Jerusalem. According to Stephen Mansfield in his *Lincoln's Battle with God* (2012), Jerusalem was on Lincoln's mind when he made his last and fateful visit to Ford's Theatre before his assassination. Reportedly, he said to Mary Todd that he did not intend to return to Springfield but wished to take her to Jerusalem, a place he so desired to visit, a place where the Savior walked.

Later American presidents proved to be more immune to the kind of romantic and spiritual views of Jerusalem which afflicted the tragic president of the Civil War era. As *realpolitik* gradually eroded their ethereal view of the holy city, twentieth-century presidents succumbed to domestic pressures and nascent lobbies bent on changing the destiny of Arab Palestine. Taking their cue from American Zionist leaders following WWI, American presidents were pushed to prioritize the creation of a Jewish homeland, but not necessarily to secure Jerusalem as its capital. The Palestinian Yishuv, or the Jewish community, did its utmost to capture much of the New City of Jerusalem by defying the call for its internationalization in collusion with King Abdullah of Jordan.

Much of this history is well known, deserving minimal summation. But relations of US presidents with Israel began to shift from one theme to the next, without necessarily centering on Jerusalem. John F. Kennedy, for instance, concluded the first massive arms agreement with Israel, while pressuring the ruling Labor party to curb its nuclear weapons program. This study, thus, takes an extended look into the administration of Lyndon B. Johnson simply because of its intersection with the 1967 June War and its impact on the Israeli-captured city. This period became also a study in the expanding role of presidential advisors who began to encroach on the jurisdiction of the State Department itself. Yet clearly, presidents who were distantly engaged in another war zone, such as Johnson and Vietnam, or Nixon's slide into the Watergate swamp led to relinquishing foreign policy decisions to advisors and secretaries of state. Other presidents such as James Carter tried but failed to micro-manage the Camp David talks, only to suffer the determined opposition of Menachem Begin. The most earnest president to seek a resolution of the Israeli-Palestinian conflict, with Jerusalem as the centerpiece of the negotiations was Clinton, but he too failed to make the pacification of the holy city the anchor of his historical legacy. Thus, perforce, this study emphasizes the role of some presidents more than others, depending on the availability of open archives and on the extent of their involvement in the Jerusalem issue as the major determining factor in this complex history. Where some archival collections are still closed, this study has relied on memoirs, secondary sources, and on published accounts in the Foreign Relations of the US documentary series. Hopefully, what this study would reveal is the uncontested prerogative of American presidents to determine the outline of major foreign policy issues. This is also a reminder of the final responsibility of American presidents for these decisions, as has been clearly asserted on July 23, 2013, in the US Circuit Court of Appeals for the District of Columbia. The court affirmed the president's sole power to recognize foreign states by refusing to affix, "Jerusalem, Israel" on the passport of Menachem Binyamin Zivotofsky, a child born in the annexed city.

Acknowledgments

This work which views the Arab-Israeli conflict from its roots in the religious and modern nationalist claims of two communities has been inspired by many authors and experts. Though none have focused exclusively on the impact of American policies on this city, they cleared a path which enabled us to understand the complexities of this ancient and modern place which always served as the embodiment of the history and hopes of communities in conflict. But the story of Jerusalem has always been mired in the distortions of orientalists, amateur historians, ideological pundits, casual travelers, and others. The truth of the matter is that this city had always attracted the gaze of charlatans, race mongers and propagandists, as much as the keen eye of capable diplomats and sharp observation of reporters.

Yet the greatest challenge has always been separating the city from its surroundings and ferreting its distinct story from its larger environment. The task became enormous as the history of this religious center acquired immeasurable relevance to the politics and struggles of twentieth-century Arabs and Jews alike. To focus on Jerusalem alone meant resisting the distractions of its romance and storied past, the layered history of its ancient temples and monuments and the claims and counter-claims of its antagonistic communities. In other words, to understand Jerusalem, one has to balance the lure of the past with the bitter realities of the present in order to grasp the essence of the Arab-Israeli conflict. Indeed, stripped of all of its glory, Jerusalem would always be a witness to the role of the powers, particularly the United States, in strengthening Israel's hand and enabling it to seize by military force what it was unable to grasp by politics and diplomacy alone. So far, most writers have neglected the present in order to focus on the past. But times call for a different approach since Palestinian suffering has finally been revealed in the wake of the 1967 War. As the city's fate has catapulted it to the diplomatic agenda of different powers and political actors, different methodologies and intellectual approaches were called for if one was to understand the core and the context of this issue.

I was greatly inspired by the work of Karen Armstrong and her monumental study of Jerusalem, revealing the human side of Islam and its tenure in this city. Michael Dumper, however, provided a new understanding of the politics of sacred space in this city and the entangled claims and faits accomplis of its various religious communities. Salim Tamari deserved a lot of credit for illuminating unknown aspects of life in the Western and Eastern halves of the city before it became divided and different values of modernity and traditionalism assigned to each side. His studies would always be valued for illustrating the growth and development of Arab neighborhoods in the so-called West Jerusalem. Due to his efforts, the recent history of this city assumed a sociological reality which it was missing in the past.

I am indebted to all of them for inspiring me to study the current realities of this ancient place. I am particularly grateful and indebted to Regina Greenwell, Senior Archivist at the Lyndon Baines Johnson Presidential Library, Austin, Texas, who shepherded me through the maze of valuable material relevant to US policy during the Johnson years. A competent scholar in her own right, Greenwell has already been acknowledged by several scholars focusing on this period. Her custodianship of this valuable repository is unmatched by any other expert with whom I have come in contact.

Finally, I would be remiss if I did not mention the valuable insights and unwavering support of my late husband, Ayoub Talhami, who looked forward to reading the finished product someday. Having spent part of his youth at the Arab College, he too believed that he had a stake in the survival of the Arab heritage of this city.

Chapter One

The British Mandate:
Jerusalem Undivided

No understanding of American policy towards the Jerusalem question is possible without an appreciation of the changes, institutional, communal, and political, wrought by the British Mandate government on the ancient city. Thanks to this administration, Jerusalem was finally detached from its Ottoman and oriental moorings and recast in the mold of twentieth-century colonized cities of the British Empire. For a beginning, this resulted in a reconfiguration of the communal balance among its varied communities. The imperial interests which necessitated these changes were mostly molded by the colonial country's own pugilistic sectoral politics and factionalism which presaged future interplay between the politics of ethnic minorities and mainstream national parties in the United States. The mobilization of the American Jewish community on behalf of the Jewish Yishuv, or community, in Palestine was finalized in the period following WWI, when all eyes were riveted on the British Mandate.

OPENING THE GATES: THE FIRST DOCUMENT

The major document which was to determine the future transformation of Palestine, the former southern extension of the Syrian Province of the Ottoman Empire and its autonomous capital in Jerusalem, was the Balfour Declaration. The document, which was later attached to the Preamble of the Mandate Agreement with the League of Nations, finally changed Palestine from an Ottoman satrapy to an instrument of British foreign policy, though theoretically under the aegis of the world organization. One significant detail of this pronouncement of the British cabinet, drafted and adopted while the major European war was still raging on, was worthy of note. The text of the declaration was drafted by Harry Sacher, a rising journalist on the staff of *The Manchester Guardian*. Foreign Minister Arthur Balfour called upon him to fulfill this assignment due to the former's friendship with Chaim Weizmann. The British chemist and Zionist leader enjoyed the full backing of C. P. Scott, the paper's editor at the time. Sacher pledged to Weizmann that he would strive to produce a statement "at once precise and vague, precise in what it excludes, vague in the means by which what we want is realized."[1] Sacher crafted the final text by synthesizing several drafts penned by other journalists. The declaration, dated November 2, 1917, when it was sent to the Zionist leader Baron Walter Rothschild, finally appeared in the press on November 9. It was a masterpiece of ambiguity and precision, foreshadowing Henry Kissinger's mastery of this diplomatic art. As it turned out, the declaration was silent on the issue of Jerusalem and its destiny. The text merely promised that "nothing should be done which may prejudice the civil and religious rights of existing non-Jewish communities in Palestine." The ill-defined latter groups were actually 670,000 people in 1917, while the Jewish community numbered 60,000, or one-tenth of the total population.[2]

Although opposed to the idea of carving up the territories of defeated empires, Woodrow Wilson approved the Balfour Declaration. He viewed it as a step towards the restoration of the Holy Land to its people. Influenced by his friend Supreme Court Justice Louis Brandeis, Wilson, nevertheless, found himself torn between his Protestant predilection towards supporting Jewish biblical claims and his secular nature which inspired his elaboration on the idea of self-determination, making it applicable to the country's Arab population. To assuage his feelings, the British at one time proposed the idea of an American mandate, or quasi-protectorate over Palestine, which the American President took seriously until it was overtaken by the intensity of the Anglo-French struggle for control of the Greater Syria Province. He then sent the King-Crane Commission to investigate the wishes of the local population, an endeavor easily defeated by the determination of the two European allies to divide the former Ottoman Empire between them. The fate of Jerusalem in particular was settled on the eve of the Paris Peace Conference of January 1919. It was there that Georges Clemenceau, the French Premier, quickly succumbed to demands by British Prime Minister Lloyd George to add Mosul and Jerusalem to his domain.[3] Another British diplomatic victory was scored at Versailles when the powers confirmed the British mandate system over Palestine and agreed to affix the Balfour Declaration to the Mandate agreement with the League of Nations. Britain, already in control of Palestine, initially ignited a firestorm reminiscent of the heyday of the Crusades. The British press later reported that when Allied Commander General Edmund Allenby entered Jerusalem as a conqueror, he proclaimed before a throng of Arab residents, "Now, the Crusader wars are over." This was an astounding statement considering that the Arabs were allied with Britain against the Muslim Ottomans in that war. Several British historians downplayed the statement, attributing it to the imagination of *Punch,* the humorous magazine, but Arab Jerusalemites like Hazem Nuseibeh insisted that it was heard by one of his relatives. An officer in the Ottoman army, Nuseibeh's relative heard Allenby utter words to that effect upon approaching the Church of the Holy Sepulcher when he demanded its keys, historically entrusted to the Muslim Nuseibeh family. Upon receiving them, he said, "Now the Crusader wars are over." Then, after completing his tour, Allenby returned the keys to Abd al-Latif Nuseibeh, saying, "I'm returning the keys to you now, but this time you are receiving them not from Umar or Saladin, but from Allenby."[4]

PALESTINE AND JERUSALEM:
VAGUE MAPS AND ABSTRUSE CLAIMS

The Paris Peace Conference quickly turned into an arena where the claims and counter-claims of those contesting the future disposition of Palestine were played out. The Zionist Organization of America (ZOA) submitted several draft resolutions in February 1919, designed to affirm the historic title of the Jewish people to Palestine and the right of Jews to reconstitute it as their national home.[5] The boundaries of this homeland were outlined in an attached schedule, adding an endorsement of Great Britain as the only sovereign power to be entrusted with this territory under the aegis of the League of Nations. A month later, anti-Zionist figures in the USA, such as Henry Morgenthau, Sr., former ambassador to Turkey, Congressman Julius Khan and *New York Times*'s publisher Adolph Ochs, sent their objections to Wilson in a letter which appeared in *The Times* on March 5, 1919. They argued that the Zionists' plan to segregate themselves in Palestine would lead to unanticipated dangers. The American Jewish leaders then cited the cautionary statement by Sir George Adam Smith, noted expert on the geography and history of Palestine. In his *Syria and the Holy Land* (1918), the Scottish theologian had previously emphasized that the Palestine map had never displayed fixed borders since these fluctuated from time to time. He added, "It is not true that Palestine is the national home of the Jewish people and of no other people." Neither was it correct to describe its non-Jewish inhabitants as "Arabs." He expressed great skepticism towards the designation of "the Jewish race," reminding his readers that the war was fought for democratic principles and that "to unite Church and State, in any form, as under the old Jewish hierarchy, would be a leap backward of 2,000 years."[6]

The American Zionist movement at the time was still miniscule, with only 20,000 members of the total community of 2.5 million Jews, since leaders of the American Jewish Committee (AJC), founded in 1906, remained notoriously opposed to Zionism. Not until Judge Louis Brandeis organized, expanded and headed the ZOA did the Zionists begin to lobby American officials, starting with Wilson. The American president, who admired Brandeis greatly, appointed him to the Supreme Court in 1916 after being cautioned by the AJC against this appointment since the judge's politics did not represent majority opinion in the American Jewish community. Apparently, Wilson had both pragmatic and idealistic objectives in mind when he made the appointment. The American Federation of Labor (AFL), whose support was considered crucial for winning his second term of office had already endorsed the idea of a Jewish homeland in Palestine despite the opposition of several Jewish trade unions. More importantly, his Protestant upbringing as a son of a Presbyterian minister led him to develop sympathy for the Jews as a result of his embrace of biblical teachings. Reportedly, he once remarked, "To think that I, the son of the manse, should be able to help restore the Holy Land to its people."[7]

JEWISH INTEGRATION UNDER THE MANDATE

Upon the establishment of the Mandate Government in Palestine, the Jewish community in that country began to organize its own institutions and interact with the British Government. This made the creation of a political base in Jerusalem, which was declared the capital of the new British regime, mandatory. But the European Jewish disenchantment with the Old City of Jerusalem led to the development of a new modern urban center as their own settlement, or colony. Two unstoppable trends quickly emerged as soon as the British moved into the conquered city: A British effort to foster the establishment of a government and religious and political institutions in the New City, and Jewish determination to build their own demographic centers in order to interact with the British authority. The challenge for European Jews was how to shape a new, urban and clean identity sharply contrasting with that of the diaspora while still maintaining claims to ancient Jewish sites as a confirmation of their historic connection to the land. Thus, they created Tel Aviv as a metaphor of Jewish modernity and Zionist precepts of progress, though built on Arab land and demolished villages. The myth of a city which sprang from the sand in 1909 as a testimony to the courage and toiling efforts of young Zionist pioneers eventually lost ground to an Arab counter-narrative of dispossession and displacement. Zachrot, (Heb. Remembering), an Israeli organization founded in 2002 and dedicated to keeping the memory of the original Arab inhabitants alive, challenged the myth of Tel Aviv and its place in the older Zionist narrative. It declared that Tel Aviv was not just the European streets named after the founding fathers of Zionism such as Herzl, Jabotinsky, Arlosoroff and Ben Gurion, but also the abandoned Arab villages of Summeil, Salame, Jammusin and Shaykh Muwannis.[8] Jews, thus, began to discover that settling Palestine while establishing new claims was not an easy task. It quickly emerged that the home of the *Shaykh* of Shaykh Muwannis village has been serving as the faculty club of Tel Aviv University.[9] The European settlers were, thus, faced with British designs to reshape their colony into their own vision of a perfect settlement, and the relentless resistance of the indigenous population to any effort to erase their memory form the land.

But since the New City of Jerusalem was where the British established their political capital, it beckoned to the Zionists to make a presence for themselves in that location, beyond the myth of Tel Aviv. As soon as Ronald Storrs took over the reins of government in Jerusalem, he brought a British architect to investigate the status of the historic buildings within the area of the Noble Sanctuary, which Jewish writers were beginning to refer to as Temple Mount. The British also founded a group called the Pro-Jerusalem Society, created specifically to work on the preservation and renovation of the city's historic buildings. This resulted in the beginnings of a strict building code for new structures, the use of limestone in all new buildings and the prohibition of high towering units which would interfere with the city's vista, a policy which the Jordanian Government later adopted.[10]

Jerusalem also became the location of the civil administration which followed on the heels of an emergency system known as the Administration of Occupied Enemy Territory. A high commissioner was appointed in 1920 as the top administrator during the Mandate period. Sir Herbert Samuel, a British Zionist politician was the first to fill this position and to hold it until 1925. The British also redrew municipal boundaries, creating 16 predominantly Arab councils and six mixed Arab-Jewish bodies for Jerusalem, Jaffa, Haifa, Tiberias, Safed and Hebron. The status of Tel Aviv as a suburb of the predominantly Arab city of Jaffa was maintained despite the creation of an autonomous Jewish council. By 1934, the British Government empowered the high commissioner to create new municipalities or to alter the boundaries of existing ones when directed to do so by specific commissions of inquiry. Certain Ottoman procedures were retained, such as allowing the top civilian authority, in this case the high commissioner, to nominate the mayor and deputy mayor from within the elected council and to approve or reject any by-laws pertaining to a pre-approved list of items. A network of district commissioners (singular, Ar. *hakem liwa*) who were predominantly British was created, bringing municipal councils under its domain. Voting rights for the municipal council of Tel Aviv were distinct from the others despite the Jewish city's dependence on Jaffa. According to the Municipal Franchise of 1926, only males and workers who held no property qualified for the vote as long as they paid a minimal municipal tax. Tel Aviv, however, came under a different charter, namely the 1934 Municipal Corporation Ordinance which extended the franchise to all residents, regardless of gender or date of arrival. For the Jerusalem Council, the Jewish population which had already achieved a majority status there was allowed six councilors, while the Muslims were confined to four representatives and the Christians given only two. Mayors, however, were always chosen from the list of Muslim councilors, but the deputy mayor was either a Jew or a Christian, with Daniel Auster serving briefly in 1937 in that position. He became mayor again in 1944 and 1949, serving a one year stint each term following the deportation of the Arab mayor, Hussein al-Khalidi, as a result of the 1936 Arab Revolt. [11]

The 1922 census, the first of its kind to be conducted in British Jerusalem, showed a decline in the Jewish population from 45,000 in 1910 to about 33,971 in 1922. The entire city had a population of 62,578, whereas in 1910, the Jews of Jerusalem were about half of all the Jewish population of Palestine. By the end of WWI, Jewish numbers in Jerusalem dropped to 26,600 due to the ravages of war, disease, and expulsions, but rose again after the British supplanted the Ottomans in the Palestine province. The Balfour promise, as expected, was quickly realized by opening the gates to Jewish capital and new waves of human arrivals. Storr's Pro-Jerusalem Society founded a music school and turned it over to the Jewish community as part of its program to introduce cultural refinement to the city. Lord Balfour himself inaugurated Hebrew University in 1925 with great fanfare, which was built on Mt. Scopus in the New City. But on that occasion, the Arabs called for a strike fueled by claims that the land on which the university was built had actually been expropriated Arab land. The Palestine office of the World Zionist Organization (WZO) received permission to establish an elected ten-member community council in Jerusalem, called Va'ed ha-Kehillah, which served as the local branch of the Va'ed Leumi, the national council representing the Ashkenazi and Sephardi communities. This council was first elected in 1918 upon the instigation of the WZO Jerusalem office, but as of 1932, its members were chosen according to regulations adopted by Knesset Israel, the highest representative body, or parliament, of the Yishuv. The British also allowed the ZE which became the Executive of the Jewish Agency (JA), the Keren Hayesod, (later, the United Israel Appeal) and the Jewish National Fund (JNF or Keren Kayemet) to buy land and put down roots in Jerusalem. On the religious front, Jewish personal status courts which used to be attached to the Islamic Shari'a courts, were removed to the Va'ed Leumi. The British then sought to organize and strategize the affairs of the religious communities in 1921 by creating in Jerusalem an office of the Chief Rabbinate and one for the Supreme Muslim Council (SMC). [12]

In addition, great changes were introduced by the Mandate Government in recognition of the rise of the Ashkenazi community. During the Ottoman period and in accordance with the *millet* (community) system which granted autonomy to the empire's major religious communities, the title of *Hakham Bashi* (also *rishon le-Zion*, Heb. the first in Zion) was conferred on the highest religious figure in the Sephardic community. As such, this figure acted as the representative of the entire Jewish population to the Ottoman government. But with the influx of European Ashkenazi immigrants after the middle of the nineteenth century, settling mostly in Jerusalem, Safed, and later in Jaffa, Tel Aviv, Haifa, and the new agricultural colonies in the north and along the Mediterranean coast, Jewish communal ties began to fray. This state of affairs resulted from conflict over issues such as girls' education and the use of *halakha* contributions from abroad. Subsequently, the new Ashkenazi arrivals who were originally under the protection of foreign consuls, organized themselves and appointed a chief rabbi to lead them. At the same time, disputes developed between Moroccan and Sephardi Jews over representation, leading to the outbreak of violent clashes and the eventual creation of a separate committee to speak for the Moroccans. When the British period began, the Mandate authorities eliminated the position of Hakham Bashi, appointing instead two chief rabbis, one Ashkenazi and one Sephardi, to head the Va'ed ha-Kehillah.[13] The first Ashkenazi chief rabbi, Avraham Isaac Kook, was appointed in 1921, and he proceeded to establish Merkaz HaRav seminary in the Old City. Initially unwilling to accept the secularist and socialist Zionist movement, he eventually reconciled with the Zionist state as a main event in the centuries-old redemptive process, resulting in the return of the Jews to Israel. His son, Rabbi Tzvi Yehuda Kook, who succeeded him in that position, was important to the settlement movement which emerged following the 1967 War. It was he who emphasized that Palestine was promised to the Jewish people, concluding that the State of Israel itself was sacred.[14]

When the League of Nations granted Britain a mandate over Palestine in 1922, it made specific references to the "Holy Places" in its Charter. Under Article 13 of the Mandate Agreement, Britain pledged to protect these places and safeguard access and freedom of worship to the various religious communities. It granted the Muslims immunity from interference in the "management of purely Moslem [sic] sacred shrines." But under Article 14, the Mandate called for appointing a special commission, "to study, define and determine the rights and claims in connection with the Holy Places and the rights and claims relating to the different religious communities in Palestine."[15] This amplification of the earlier pledge to the Muslims cleared the way for the adjudication of future demands by the Jewish community, amounting to a severe limitation on the intent of Article 13.

A BRITISH CAPITAL AND TWO CONTENDING COMMUNITIES

In addition to opening the door to more Jewish immigration, the British made Jerusalem more hospitable to a wide array of foreign Christian religious, educational, and charitable institutions. Native Arab Christians were not affected by this trend and lagged behind in grasping these new opportunities since they mostly identified with their fellow Muslim nationals. Repeated attempts by the British to impose a sectarian political representative system failed to gain favor with the Arab community as a whole. Instead, the Arab Higher Committee (AHC), headed by the Mufti, allowed for Christian personalities to gain an equal footing with the Muslims in all Arab councils. Significantly, since the Mandate Charter guaranteed the Status Quo arrangement, dating back to the Crimea War and which protected the various Christian denominations from outside interference, the opportunity to designate a higher Christian council similar to the Jewish and Muslim communities was never realized. The only bow in the direction of tradition was the reinstatement of the Greek Orthodox Patriarch as the acknowledged head of the Christian community by virtue of the historic precedence of his church. The Jewish community in Jerusalem, nevertheless, continued to experience dramatic growth unrelated to increased immigration. One of the far-reaching measures undertaken by the Mandate government was its distortion of the city's boundaries, which reflected on the relative influence of the various groups. Not only did the British stretch the city's boundaries to absorb and incorporate new Jewish neighborhoods which sprang west of the Old City, they also excluded the Arab villages to the east and south of the city. Jerusalem's eastern border, thus, ran very close to the city's walls, avoiding the incorporation of the Arab villages of Silwan, Ras al-'Amud, al-Tur and Abu-Tur.[16]

Jerusalem became the seat of the Mandate Supreme Court, headed by a British judge. Locating this court here was continued by the Israelis after 1948, with grave implications for the Arab population following the 1967 War. A modern infrastructure was provided, such as granting a leading Russian Zionist, Pinhas Rutenberg (d. 1942) a concession in 1928 to provide the city with electricity. Originally, electricity was provided in 1914 by Yarbides Mifrates, who was declared legally insolvent soon thereafter.[17] The British also built a small airport in the nearby suburb of Atarot (Ar. Qalandia) in 1920, and a broadcasting service was based in Ramallah in 1936, though its offices remained in Jerusalem. The city also saw the rise of a vibrant native press, representing most of the communities. The Hebrew-language *Ha'aretz* (The Land) was first published in Jerusalem, later transferring to Tel Aviv. By 1931, the *Palestine Post*, later the *Jerusalem Post,* was also founded in the city.[18] The Arabic press which developed as soon as Ottoman rule ended was mostly in Jerusalem and suffered from British censorship whenever it adopted Arab nationalist positions. Among the earliest in this group was *Souria al-Janubiyah* (Southern Syria) founded in 1919 by Hasan al-Budeiri and a future mayor of Jerusalem, 'Aref al-'Aref. It advocated the views of the Syrian National Congress which convened in Damascus to pursue Prince Faysal's claim to an Arab Syrian kingdom. [19] The paper was second oldest to the Jaffa-based *Filastin*, published in 1911 by 'Isa al-'Isa and Yousef al-'Isa. Another paper, *al-Hayat al-Maqdisiyah* (Jerusalem Life) was published by 'Adel Jabra also in Jerusalem. [20] Quasi-political Arab sports clubs proliferated, among them the Arab Club, the Rowdhah, al-Ahli al-Arabi and al-Islami. Jerusalem also became the site of the largest YMCA in the world, built opposite the King David Hotel. The British encouraged Arab education, building a secondary school system for boys and girls throughout Palestine, as well as a network of elementary schools which covered all Arab villages. Jerusalem became the location of the Arab College, an elite school designed to train the next generation of Palestinian civil servants. [21] Lacking the necessary funds and European backing to build a higher learning institute like Hebrew University, the Arabs called for the founding of an Islamic educational institution in Jerusalem, to be known as al-Aqsa University. This was one of the recommendations of the Islamic Conference of 1931, convened by the Mufti specifically to mobilize Islamic world opinion against Zionist infringement on the Islamic holy places. But other Arab institutional efforts were more successful, such as the Arab Bank in 1930, and an agricultural bank, both in Jerusalem. [22] The city also had a literary café, al-Sa'aleek (the Vagabonds) which became one of the most famous of this urban novelty throughout the Arab world. Among its patrons was renowned Palestinian journalist, educator and poet Khalil al-Sakakini. [23]

RELIGIOUS FESTIVALS MOBILIZE MUSLIMS

The presence of Islam's major holy sites in Jerusalem inevitably served as an effective mobilization magnate for the Palestinian Arab national movement. Mass protests against the Balfour Declaration which opened the door to Jewish immigration materialized as soon as the Mandate Government was established. Secular male demonstrations had their counterpart in women's demonstrations, showcasing the unity of the Christian and Muslim population against the loss of their autonomy. But one religious festival centered on Jerusalem proved to be a great attraction for the Arab rural population and an opportunity to demonstrate fealty to their religious shrines. This was the Nabi Musa Festival (Prophet Moses Festival) which originated in 1263, when Baibars, al-Malik al-Zahir, the Bahri Mamluk ruler of Egypt, launched the usual sanctification and repairs of Jerusalem's holy sites upon the defeat of the Seventh Crusade and its eviction form the city. Baibars' renovation program involving the Dome of the Rock and al-Aqsa Mosque coincided that year with Easter festivities by local churches centering on the Church of the Holy Sepulcher. He ordered the building of a dome over the tomb of Moses, adulated by Muslims and Jews alike, which was located near Jericho. He also revived a religious festival which, legend had it, was started by Saladin. Muslim residents of Jerusalem began to observe this festival annually with a colorful procession, moving from the Dome of the Rock to Jericho where prayers and joyful celebrations were held. [24]

An eyewitness account by a Jewish Polish traveler, Leopold Weiss, who later converted to Islam, captured the ebullient passions unleashed by these events in 1923 and the preternatural rapport generated among the partici-pants. The festival also overwhelmed the Passover celebrations with its own emphasis on Moses. Weiss was informed that the festival was Saladin's own initiative, having absorbed purely religious connotations in the following years. It usually lasted six days, drawing a mix of celebrants who were urban, rural and Bedouin from Nablus, Hebron, and the Jordan Valley, and who chanted religious slogans along the way. The Mufti, Haj Amin al-Husseini, later became the leader of this procession, riding a white steed and sur-rounded by banners. [25] Participation of people from Hebron and Nablus was deemed necessary since the Mufti hoped to encourage these elements to settle in the Old City. Palestinians believed that he wished to bolster Muslim presence in the face of increasing encroachment by militant Jewish groups bent on expanding their rights near the area of the Wailing Wall.

THE WAILING WALL RIOTS OF 1929

The possibility of an assault on the Wailing Wall, or the Buraq Wall, which was always on the Mufti's mind, also aroused suspicions of being a prelude to a Jewish takeover of the Islamic sites in the Noble Sanctuary area. These suspicions were exacerbated by the increased numbers of Jewish immigrants during the late 1920s. Jewish sights were turned on the Buraq Wall, a seg-ment of the Wailing Wall, and an Islamic *waqf* property endowed to the Abu-Midyan family by al-Afdhal, Saladin's son. To Muslims, the Buraq Wall was hallowed ground since it was a place where Muhammad's feet touched dur-ing the Nocturnal Journey. European Jews, on the other hand, being unaware of Islamic history in that part of the world, believed the Buraq Wall to be one and the same as the Wailing Wall, the last remnant of their temple. They, thus, chafed at centuries-old restrictions which limited their right to worship and which the British were now enforcing. In compliance with the Status Quo Regulations which the British pledged to observe, steps were taken to ban the blowing of the shofar on Jewish High Holidays which disturbed Muslim prayers within earshot of the Wall. Responding to complaints by

Muslim worshippers, Edward Keith Roach, Governor of Jerusalem (r. 1926–1945), ordered a raid on the Wall area during the Yom Kippur services and dispersed the worshippers for ignoring restrictions on the use of chairs and the placement of partitions separating men from women. The British also knew that these changes in the Status Quo Law were masterminded by Vladimir Jabotinsky, founder of the Revisionist Movement, and by his quasi-Fascist Betar youth group. [26] To Muslims, the Buraq Wall was also the Western Wall of the Noble Sanctuary. This wall which extended 156 feet and measured 56 feet in height not only was regarded as an Islamic *waqf*, but its provenance was registered in the Office of the Islamic *waqf* in Jerusalem. [27] The Status Quo Regulations allowed Jews to pray along the narrow pavement adjoining the Wailing Wall, but prohibited the use of furniture which might obstruct the passage of Muslim worshippers on their way to the Noble Sanctuary. Recognizing that these Jewish rights were of recent vintage dating to the beginning of the Ottoman period in the seventeenth century, Muslims feared the new Jewish assertiveness greatly. Then there was a militant demonstration by Jabotinsky's followers on August 15, 1929, which sparked opposing Arab riots throughout Palestine, resulting in 133 Jewish and 116 Arab fatalities. By that time, Britain had interceded in another dispute involving Arab Greek Orthodox reformers and the Greek-controlled Patriarchate by upholding the previous system entrusting all leadership positions to Greek nationals. The Arabs regarded this as a defeat for the Arab Orthodox laity and the reform movement headed by Khalil Sakakini, but it was certainly a victory for the Status Quo regime. [28] The British were thus committed to upholding these laws across the board.

The issue of Jewish rights at the Wailing Wall broke out in violence when British police officers removed a screen on September 24, 1928, separating male from female worshipers. Being the high holidays, this act enraged local and international Jewish public opinion leading to fresh demands for Jewish ownership of the Wall and its adjacent area. In reality, placing a screen, as well as the use of chairs were a clear violation of the regulations governing the performance of Jewish religious rites at the Wall area. [29] A British district officer, L. Cust, wrote in 1929 that among certain Jewish communities, presumably newly arrived European immigrants, exercising the right to pray at the Wall became equated with active and real ownership of the site. The secular Zionists, mindful of the powerful symbolism of the Wall, began to exploit it for their own nationalist agenda. [30] The British then appointed an international commission of inquiry which issued its report in December 1930 in accordance with Article 14 of the Charter of the League of Nations. The article called for creating such a commission for the sole purpose of examining conflicting claims to the holy places. The commission charged with arbitrating this particular dispute consisted of three jurists: Eliel Löfgren, a Swiss, Charles Barde, a Swede who served as chair, and C. J. Van

Kempen, a Dutchman. Witnesses from both sides were deposed by the commission, which sat like a British court. The Muslim side was represented by 'Awni 'Abd al-Hadi, a veteran Palestinian nationalist, as well as Ahmad Zaki and Muhammad Ali Alluba Pasha from Egypt. The Jewish case was represented by Dr. M. Alishea, David Yellen and Rabbi M. Blau. Additional Muslim lawyers from several Muslim countries also offered testimony, the rights in dispute being applicable to all Muslims, not only to Palestinians. Additionally, the Muslim side presented twenty-six documents as evidence, while the Jewish side presented thirty-five documents. The final decision was rendered in a seventy-five-page statement which concluded that ownership of the Wall and "the right to dispose thereof," belonged to Muslims. The statement also stressed that the Jewish party did not make any claims to the Wall, the Magharibeh (Mughrabi) Quarter, or any part of the adjacent area, confining itself to seeking permission to visit the Wall.[31] The commission determined that Jews will be able to approach the Wall for devotional purposes at any time, adding that "to the Moslems belong the sole ownership of, and the sole proprietary right to the Western Wall."[32]

The verdicts of British law were provided as an order-in-council, which was signed by King George V and subsequently appeared in Palestine's *Official Gazette*. Upon its ratification by the League of Nations, the judgment became part of international law. The verdicts were no surprise to those who recalled that it was in 1911 when the last attempt to expand Jewish rights by placing chairs and other articles in the limited space next to the Wall was made. Muslims of all nationalities rejoiced in this judgment since it confirmed their contention that the Wailing Wall, which was a small section of the Western Wall of the Noble Sanctuary, as well as the Wailing Place (or hosh al-Buraq) and the Mughrabi Quarter were all Muslim endowments and cannot be alienated. Each time Jews contested these limitations, the judgment, as in the case of Ibrahim Pasha during the Egyptian period in the nineteenth century, assured them of the right to worship there 'ala al-wajh al-qadeem' (according to tradition). Apparently, there was no reference to Jews praying at any section of the Western Wall during the earlier centuries of Muslim rule. For instance, in the fifteenth century, judge and historian Mujir al-Din al-Hanbali (1466–1522), author of *Al-Uns al-jalil fi tarikh al-Quds wa al-Khalil* (The Glorious History of Jerusalem and Hebron, c. 1495) one of *al-Fadha'il* genre (the history of cities) was silent on the question of the performance of Jewish prayers by the Western Wall. Yet, he provided a description of the Jewish Quarter which was situated within the Muslim Quarter. Neither did Arab and Islamic writers of the past mention a Jewish belief that a portion of the Western Wall was a remnant of Herod's Temple. There was no mention of the "Wailing Wall" as such which was known always as the Buraq Wall. Christian pilgrims to the Holy Land also failed to mention such a wall.[33]

PALESTINIAN EXHORTATIONS TO THE MUSLIM WORLD

Palestinian trepidations regarding the threats to their ancient rights over the Muslim holy places and attempts by the Revisionist Zionists to extract more privileges from the Mandate Government finally pushed the SMC and the AHC to look to the rest of the Muslim world for support. By that time, the demise of the Ottoman Empire and the institution of the Caliphate as represented by the Turkish Sultan had transformed the nature of international Islamic relations. The British created the SMC in Palestine in the hope that Palestinian religious autonomy and independence from Istanbul, which translated into control over their vast Muslim resources such as the *awqaf* (pl. of *waqf*) and the Shari'a courts, would prove to be an adequate compensation for the loss of Ottoman protection and Islamic solidarity. But even before Ataturk abolished the Caliphate in 1924, a pan-Islamic modernist campaign known as the Caliphate Movement rose in 1919 in India. The quest for an alternative pan-Islamic system, however, reached a dead end in the 1920s, although its reverberations and the call for Islamic solidarity were still being heard from India to Egypt. It was not surprising, therefore, that the Mufti convened an Islamic congress in 1931 in Jerusalem in order to galvanize the Muslim world around the issue of the holy places. The meetings were held at Rowdat al-Ma'aref College overlooking the Noble Sanctuary. It was attended by a bevy of international dignitaries headed by Mawlana Shaukat Ali of India, leader of the Indian Caliphate Movement.[34] Also in attendance were Muhammad Iqbal, the great Muslim Indian poet; Muhammad Hussein Kashif al-Ghita, a Shi'ite clergy from Iraq; Shukri al-Quwatli, future president of Syria; Muhammad Rashid Ridha, Syrian Muslim leader; Muhammad Ali Alluba and Ahmad 'Azzam Pasha, both among the most ardent supporters of the Palestinian cause in Egypt; and Riyadh al-Sulh, future Lebanese prime minister. The Palestinian attendees included Muhammad Darwaza, Kamil al-Dawudi al-Dajani and Abd al-Qadir al-Muthaffar. The Congress, presaging future meetings of pan-Arab organizations such as the ALS, provided a great platform for highlighting Palestinian Islamic and nationalist issues but failed to achieve concrete and lasting results. Most of its recommendations, such as the creation of an Islamic agricultural company to prevent land acquisition by Zionists, the reopening of the Hijaz Railway since it was owned by the *waqf*, and launching a boycott campaign targeting Zionist goods were never realized. The Palestinians blamed these failures on the unshakable opposition of the British Mandate Government.[35]

BRITISH DESPAIR CHANGES THE FOCUS ON JERUSALEM

Tension over the Wailing/Buraq Wall and Jewish rights to pray there briefly subsided following the adjudication of the dispute by the League of Nations. But fears over the potential loss of Muslim rights over the holy sites persisted and continued to exacerbate other contentious issues pitting Arabs versus Jews. The most prominent among these were increased Jewish immigration and loss of Arab land, both of which leading to declining employment opportunities affecting the Palestinian peasantry. British failure to stem the tide of Jewish immigration, place a moratorium on the sale of land to foreign immigrants, or eliminate or amend the Balfour Declaration, created insurmountable difficulties for the Arab population. British utter unresponsiveness to Palestinian national demands eventually obstructed efforts to encourage Palestinian political participation in the Mandate Government. Fissures within the Palestinian political leadership appeared as early as the 1920s, differentiating the rejectionists from those who exhibited a pragmatic streak and a willingness to cooperate with the Mandate authorities by participating in the proposed Legislative Council (*al-majlis*). But both sides collaborated during the 1936–1939 Arab Strike. The Husseinis and the Mufti's supporters, as well as the opposition, headed by Ragheb Pasha al-Nashashibi, closed ranks and were impelled to cooperate as the flood of immigration from Germany intensified. Most Israeli analysts, like Benny Morris, ascribed these Arab divisions to the clannish roots of Palestinian nationalism, although these were no different than the same phenomenon distinguishing Jewish idealists from realists. When these Palestinian divisions resurfaced later on, the hardliners lined up behind the Husseinis and Khalidis, and the pragmatists behind the Nashashibis, all of whom being members of leading Jerusalem families. The Yishuv, coincidentally, was equally as divided in its response to the Arab Revolt and the recommendations of the Peel Commission which followed. Divisions between Labor Zionism led by Ben Gurion and the Mapai Party, and the Revisionists led by Jabotinsky who claimed Palestine on both sides of the Jordan, were just as pronounced, with the latter group pursuing a hard ideological line. Somehow, Israeli historians never painted these divisions in similar primitive colors.[36]

The rebellion of Shaykh Izz al-Din al-Qassam in the vicinity of Haifa which was brutally suppressed by the British, culminating in the Shaykh's killing in 1935, added more pressure on the traditional Palestinian nationalist leadership. The Arab strike of 1936, which flared up largely in Nablus and Hebron and their villages, as well as throughout the Galilee, also materialized in the Old City of Jerusalem. The rebellion wreaked havoc on Palestinian society, eventually leading to revenge killings within Palestinian ranks. But in Jerusalem, British authorities subjected Arab rebels to imprisonment and torture at the hands of British police, such as Sir Charles Tegart who was specifically relocated from India to deal with the emergency. Another officer who gained notoriety later as the "Bomber of Dresden," Arthur Harris, decimated Arab rebellious villages through his aerial attacks. But the Arabs held out for three years and managed to occupy the Old City for all of two days beginning on October 17, 1938, by executing a sudden attack. Jewish assistance to the British military was coordinated by a maverick officer who was also imported for that purpose, namely Orde Wingate, who had extensive counter-insurgency experience in the Sudan and other places. Wingate proved himself more Zionist than the Zionists, training Jewish fighters from his headquarters near Jaffa Gate, just outside the Old City. When he became an embarrassment to the British he was deported. Although the details of the Arabs' brief control of the Old City are yet to be documented, they demonstrated the powerful symbolism Jerusalem held for all parties, Arab, Jewish, and British, especially in times of war.[37]

Jewish influx in the Jerusalem area continued to alarm the Arabs. According to the last mayor of Jordanian Jerusalem, Rouhi al-Khatib, writing in 1980, between 1918 and 1948, Jewish numbers in Palestine rose from 8.5 percent, to 25 percent of the total population. But in the Jerusalem area, the Jewish population increased from 10,000 in 1918, or 25 percent of the total population, to 100,000 in 1948, or about 50 percent. Jewish land ownership rose from 2 percent for all of Palestine in 1918, to 5.66 percent in 1948. Jewish land ownership in Jerusalem also showed a dramatic increase, rising from 4 percent in 1918, to 14 percent in 1948.[38] Thus, as the British were distracted by a serious Palestinian rebellion covering other parts of Palestine, the situation in Jerusalem and prospects for Arab-Jewish peaceful co-existence continued to deteriorate.

THE GENESIS OF THE IDEA OF INTERNATIONALIZATION

The idea of internationalizing Jerusalem dated back to the nineteenth century but was resurrected whenever all other solutions failed. The French government proposed such an arrangement to the international community in 1840, following the departure of Ibrahim Pasha as a result of a deal brokered by Lord Palmerston. In exchange, the Egyptian ruler of the Syrian Province hoped to gain confirmation of his father's dynastic rule over Egypt. The caveat here was that the French hoped to see Jerusalem become a "Christian Free City," and under their tutelage since France was the patron of the Catholic Church in Palestine. This idea, however, was never taken seriously since the British had already planned to restore their Ottoman allies over all of Syria.[39]

The second time the idea of internationalization surfaced was in 1916, during the Sykes-Picot talks. This was to be a secret undertaking between

Britain and France as the two allies of WWI, but its terms were also known to the government of Tsarist Russia. The French negotiator, Georges Picot, insisted on getting all of Syria, Lebanon, and Palestine. But the British representative, Sir Mark Sykes, was determined to gain territory stretching from the Mediterranean to Iraq and the Persian Gulf. This was one of the chief recommendations of the de Bunsen Committee in 1915 (named after Sir Maurice de Bunsen) when the British and the French began to forecast the fate of the Ottoman territories. In order to deny the French total hegemony over the Greater Syria Province, Sykes proposed that all of Palestine, and not only Jerusalem, be accorded international status. This objective was finally realized only by agreeing to cede Mosul in Iraq to the French as an extension of their mandate over Syria/Lebanon and northern Iraq. This was not one of de Bunsen's recommendations, but Mosul eventually was ceded to the British in the San Remo Agreement in 1920, as the price of evicting King Faysal from Syria. Palestine was also designated as a British Mandate, or protectorate, in that same agreement. The Balfour Declaration, another secret wartime policy, became part of the British Mandate over Palestine. [40] Thus, rather than being internationalized, Jerusalem was declared a state capital for the first time in centuries.

The third internationalization attempt materialized when partitioning Palestine was being considered for the first time by the Peel Commission. This was a royal commission appointed in London and headed by Lord Robert Peel, a former Secretary of State for India, a trained lawyer and grandson of his namesake who served as a British prime minister (1834–1835, and 1841–1846) a century earlier. The commission was charged with investigating the Arab Revolt of 1936 and began by interviewing many people from the Arab and Jewish sides, holding a total of 66 meetings. It also interviewed Prince Abdullah (later King Abdullah) of Transjordan and published its final report in July 1937. But as far as Jews were concerned, it was the first time they were confronted by the question of borders and the prospect of limited sovereignty. In the Jewish memorandum submitted to the commission, as well as through Ben Gurion's oral testimony, the potential for Arab-Jewish co-existence was acknowledged grudgingly despite the ongoing Arab revolt. The memo stressed the Zionist desire to be accorded parity with the other side, "regardless of numerical strength." This was a position articulated during the Paris Peace Conference of 1919 when Zionist organizations argued for holding the principle of self-determination in abeyance until Jewish numerical strength gained through immigration. Ben Gurion stressed before the commission that it was not the Zionists' objective to take over the entire country and dominate the non-Jewish population. Weizmann gave a similar testimony. The Arab side, represented by the Mufti and 'Awni Abd al-Hadi, rejected the prospect of additional Jewish immigration, no matter how limited, reiterating the perpetual demand for overriding the Balfour Declaration.

When the commission at one point realized that partition was unpalatable to either side, it recommended dividing the country into cantons. Eventually, the commission's report opted for a new partition plan, dividing the country into three territories. The commission recommended creating a Jewish state consisting of much of the coastal region and the Galilee, while leaving predominantly Arab Jaffa as part of the Arab state. Being the majority population, the Arabs were offered 80 per cent of Mandate Palestine. The most fertile land, however, was assigned to the Jewish minority. The report also called for creating an Arab Palestine which would be joined to Transjordan, an option soundly rejected by the Palestinians. The third territory was to remain a separate zone under permanent British control and was to include Jerusalem and Bethlehem, to be connected to the Mediterranean through a narrow strip of land. The Zionists accepted the plan, but not without dissension within their ranks reflecting disagreement over the British proposal to limit immigration from Europe. A more serious cause of disagreement was over assigning Jerusalem to permanent British control while converting it into an international city. Weizmann, as head of the WZO, was willing to accept the plan, but Menachem Ussishkin, influential head of the JNF opposed, arguing that the proposed Jewish state would not be viable. Berl Katznelson, who led the Histadrut labor federation, felt that the mini Jewish state would not survive without its head, meaning Jerusalem. He and Golda Meirson (aka Meir) were among the strongest rejectionists of the idea of partition.[41] For the Arabs, the detachment of the two holy cities from the future Arab state, and transferring 250,000 Arabs from the Galilee in order to make it a purely Jewish state pushed them to issue a total rejection. The AHC, as the Arab body which directed the Arab Revolt, succeeded in convening a meeting in September 1937 in Bludan, Syria, in order to mobilize Arab public opinion in countries still under British and French rule against the creation of a Jewish state. "Palestine was becoming an Arab, as opposed to a purely Palestinian Arab issue," wrote Charles D. Smith, a historian of this period.[42]

DISCREPANT JEWISH VIEWS ON JERUSALEM

The debate over the fate of Jerusalem sparked by the Peel Commission presaged later differences among Jewish pragmatists and maximalists which exposed the confusion of Zionism regarding the sanctity and political magnetism of the city. The same debates that were conducted by the political leadership of the Yishuv in 1937, were simply the incubator in which the idea of Jerusalem as the capital of the Zionist state gestated. The same leaders who wrestled with the centrality of the holy city to the ideology and political program of Zionism in the 1930s, found themselves facing identical ideologi-

cal and strategic choices in the late 1940s when statehood appeared to be
more tenable. The Jerusalem issue, simply stated, was being deferred from
one decade to another.

In the wake of the publication of the Peel Commission's Report late in
1937, Zionists finally exposed their disputations over the proposed internationalization of the holy cities of Jerusalem and Bethlehem by the Mandate
authority. What this revealed was that Jewish supporters and opponents of
partition were united over one idea only, namely rejection of any compromise concerning the status of Jerusalem as the future Jewish capital of Palestine. At first, it was Ben Gurion in his capacity as chairperson of the ZE and
of the JA who stated that Jerusalem could be ceded to the British in the
interest of securing a state, no matter how small. When confronted with
fierce opposition, he resorted to declaring fealty to the "heavenly Jerusalem,"
concept. Reportedly, he said, "there was only one issue that will move the
Jewish people," and that is securing the government of Jerusalem. The city's
name, he added, was what attracted the people to the concept of the Jewish
state, just as it had operated in the past in the field of heavenly forces which
secured the survival of the Jewish people. Thus, by magnifying the mystical
Zion, or Jerusalem, Ben Gurion attempted to distinguish between the earthly
Jerusalem and the heavenly city, claiming that bargaining away Jewish rights
in the physical ancient city of yore did not in any way reduce the mystical
role it would always play in the lives of the Jewish people. But that did not
prevent the pragmatists from making other suggestions in light of the unfavorable political picture at the time. Thus, the Peel Report was countered
with a proposal to divide the holy city, with the Western part where Jews
formed a majority remaining within the land area allotted to the Yishuv. The
eastern part of the city within the walls and which contained the holy sites
would be internationalized.[43]

The JA, hence, had no objection to the continuation of British rule in the
Old City, since this eliminated the possibility of surrendering it to the Arab
side. But the JA made a clear and exclusive bid for control over the western
part. There was no mention of ownership of the Wailing Wall since British
rule ensured unobstructed access to Jewish and any other sacred monuments
as defined by the Status Quo Law. For the first time, the JA's plan in response to the Peel Commission's Report demanded that there be no compromise over declaring Jerusalem the capital of the proposed Jewish state. More
importantly, the Jewish position deferred to the British Government in East
Jerusalem, with the implication that this entailed no Arab rights over the holy
places. Both the Arab and Jewish communities, the JA emphasized, would
have no objection to British rule over Jerusalem. The government of the
Yishuv also rationalized confining its proposal to the Western City by explaining to its constituency that Jewish control over the Eastern part of the
city would require a land corridor to link it to Tel Aviv and the coastal area.

This would jeopardize the future capital since it would be surrounded by hostile Arab territory. The Agency also called for granting Jewish citizenship and extraterritorial status to all Jewish residents, no matter their place of residence, including within the Old City. By insisting on Jewish control over West Jerusalem, the Yishuv, thus, was sacrificing the Old City in favor of spreading its control to the outlaying new suburbs, such as Rehavia and Beit HaKerem, originally the Arab suburb of Ein Karem. The Peel Commission had previously proposed placing all of Jerusalem's outlaying areas, as well as the Naqab (Negev) in the south within the Arab canton, while keeping the New and Old Cities internationalized under British control.

Eventually, the Commission's recommendations were turned down by the AHC, but not before the British government itself signaled its rejection of the Zionist counter-proposals regarding Jerusalem. As Motti Golani, one of the early writers on the genesis of the idea of internationalization, summed it up:

> For the Zionists, the policy of "Zionism without Zion," was a brutal national sacrifice that was being made in order to achieve a goal that was then considered far more urgent: The establishment of a Jewish state for the sake of the survivors of the Holocaust in Europe and as a possible solution to the conflict with the Arabs. [44]

Zionist reference to the Holocaust survivors was also deemed a win-win strategy, although Zionist demands for a homeland in Palestine preceded the Holocaust.

Acceptance of the Peel Commission's Report by the JA signaled the tactical abandonment of Jewish sovereignty over Jerusalem, a trend which began a few years earlier. Actually, separation of the Arab and Jewish communities in Jerusalem began when the Arab boycott policy during the 1936 Revolt targeted the economic enterprises of the Yishuv. The policy began in 1927 when riots caused a walkout of Arab workers from Jewish settlements dominated by citrus plantations. This became an opportunity to focus Jewish efforts on hiring Jewish labor exclusively and later to assure the physical and geographic consolidation of the Jewish community. Jewish merchants operating in the Old City and in the Arab sections of the New City and other commercial centers in places such as Haifa and Jaffa also relocated to exclusively Jewish areas. Arabs behaved in a similar manner as the co-mingling of the two communities became fraught with security issues. [45]

Until the eve of the 1947 UN debate on the future of Palestine, the first priority of the Zionist movement abroad and within the Yishuv was Jewish immigration, not the fate of Jerusalem. The preoccupation of the Yishuv in particular with the changing demographic composition of Palestine grew out of the promise of the Balfour Declaration to create a Jewish National Home in that country. By December of 1918, barely twelve months after the British

military government was established in Palestine, the Provisional Council of
Palestine's Jews, or Vaad Z'mani (VZ) held its third assembly and drafted a
plan for the creation of a provisional government, stating the following two
"fundamental assumptions" for consideration by the Paris Peace Conference:
The Jewish people ask that Palestine become its National Home and be given
a "decisive voice" in the government and administration of that country, and
the Jewish People ask that Great Britain be the "trustee power mandated by
the League of Nations" in order to create the National Home of the Jewish
People. The Yishuv demanded that the Zionist Organization be allowed to
appoint a "permanent Under-Secretary for Palestine" in a proposed Executive Council under a British Governor General. The Jewish official chosen to
fill that position should be called upon to provide a list of potential candi-
dates for membership in Palestine's Executive Council. The Yishuv also
called for the creation of a Colonization Association to dispose of state lands,
the exercise of communal autonomy by all groups, and establishing equal
status for Hebrew and Arabic as the official languages of Palestine. Thus,
despite their inferior numbers as 10 percent of the total population at the
time, the Zionist vision for Eretz Yisrael was based on the Jewish population
which aspired to become a majority and to make the Arabs a minority by any
means possible. The Yishuv, using the novel concept of the Jewish People,
still internationally undefined, proposed setting up a representative and democratic government in which the Arabs would enjoy democratic rights as a
minority.

The speakers at the Eretz Izrael Conference, however, quickly realized
that the task of convincing the great powers of the exceptionalism of the
Jewish national case based on the denial of the right of self-determination to
the majority Arab population was a difficult one to pursue. They came to
believe that only after the international community recognized the historic
connection of world Jews to Palestine will they be considered "citizens *in
potential* of that country" and justice will be done. One way of disqualifying
the Arabs immediately as potential citizens, one speaker suggested, was to
subject them to a literacy test. The chair of the meeting voiced vigorous
objection to this idea, as well as to another recommendation which was to
recur throughout Zionist history, namely transferring the Arabs to Mesopota-
mia.[46]

The Yishuv delegates to the Paris Peace Conference, thus, proved to be an
embarrassment to the official Zionist representatives precisely because of
their obsession with demolishing the rights of the Arab majority. But by
1929, Ben Gurion drafted a constitution in the wake of the Wailing Wall riots
after British impartiality led to the acknowledgment of ancient Muslim rights
to the Wall and the *waqf* which owned its surroundings. Realizing that Muslims and Christians of Palestine were able to mobilize and resist Zionist
claims and demands, the Yishuv felt it was time to reassess its vision for

Palestine and its contested holy places. By that time, Ben Gurion was serving as the secretary-general of the Histadrut and was also responsible for the semi-secret Hagana force. In this document, reaching back to the definition of "national home for the Jews" in the Balfour Declaration, Ben Gurion called for equality between Arabs and Jews, regardless of the Arabs' numerical superiority. Zionist leaders were hotly debating the issue of "non-domination" which would render competition for parity among the two communities irrelevant, thereby disabling any British plans to accord the Arabs parity in the proposed representative council at the time. Few years after outlining these secret proposals, Ben Gurion emerged as the new leader of the Yishuv when he was elected chair of the JAE. But this constitution was eventually forgotten as further British studies of the Palestine situation were undertaken, such as the Hope-Simpson Report and the Passfield White Paper of 1930. Both of these were critical of Zionist practices leading to disinheriting the Arab peasants and limiting their employment opportunities while at the same time pushing for unlimited access to land east of the Jordan. British criticism of these practices may explain Zionist willingness to submit to some of the recommendations of the Peel Report. More importantly, the deteriorating condition of European Jews on the eve of WWII called for a Zionist push to open the gates for more Jewish immigration to Palestine, not for a localized effort to assert rights over Jerusalem.[47]

FROM NATIONAL HOME (BAYIT LEUMI) TO JEWISH COMMONWEALTH (MEDINA IVRIT)[48]

The phrase "Jewish Commonwealth" was substituted for "National Home," the terminology in the Balfour Declaration, as early as 1918, but it was not publicly revealed until 1942, when the Biltmore Conference convened in New York. However, gaining solid British support for increased immigration to Palestine was seen as integral to the shift in emphasis in order to eliminate Zionist fear of total Arab domination when the demographics of Palestine change due to the influx of European Jews to the country. When negotiations with leading Palestinian figures ended with the eruption of the Arab Revolt of 1936, Ben Gurion proposed to the ZE the establishment of an independent Jewish state as a member of a larger Arab federation of states. The ZE squashed this idea before it became policy, describing it as a dangerous scheme even though the intention was to convince the British to allow unlimited immigration to the country.

The struggle between pragmatists and hardened extremists within the Zionist movement continued until the convening of the seventeenth Zionist Congress in 1931 at Basel, Switzerland. The official Zionist movement consisting of Labor's alignment with Weizmann accepted the idea of seeking

Arab-Jewish parity in autonomous institutions but Jabotinsky and the Revisionists resisted, promoting instead the idea of achieving instantaneous majority status. While tactics differed, Weizmann's gradualist approach was moving towards reaching the same outcome. Factional strife within the Zionist movement, Palestinian riots, and the uncertainty of British policies in Palestine eroded Weizmann's leadership and he was ousted from office as head of the ZE. Ben Gurion's rise to power as head of the labor movement, which emerged as the dominant faction, placed him second only to Chaim Arlosoroff, Weizmann's successor as the head of the Political Department of the JA. In the years leading to the 1936 Arab Revolt, Jewish immigration increased, swelling the ranks of the Yishuv, from 170,000 in 1929, to 400,000 in 1936, making the Jewish population about one-third of the Palestinian population.[49] These changes and the deteriorating Arab economy finally caused the strike and revolt which formed the background of the Peel Report. Throughout the harshest years of the Yishuv's existence in Palestine, the Zionists fastened their gaze on immigration and how to transfer themselves from a minority into a majority. The fate and future of Jerusalem were still lower on the national agenda.

CONCLUSION

Although the fate of Jerusalem was in Britain's hands, initially the Balfour deal was silent on this issue. The Mandate Agreement with the League of Nations, nevertheless, attempted in 1922 to stake two seemingly contradictory positions: Recognizing Muslim rights to the holy places, and in the following article, calling for the establishment of a commission to examine rival claims to the same places as they occur. The establishment of a national Jewish home in Palestine was also challenged at the Paris Peace Conference when American Jewish leaders themselves disputed the benefits of directing all European Jewish immigrants to Palestine. At the same time, some British biblical scholars disproved the notion that ancient Palestine had specific and known geographic boundaries. When the immigrants began arriving in Palestine in large numbers, they themselves showed a preference for urban space outside of the ancient city and its walls. That was when a new city, Tel Aviv, was constructed in the Jaffa administrative district, specifically over the remains of four erased Arab villages. Tel Aviv quickly earned the reputation of a city rising from the sand and a testimony to the Zionist myth of supporting a progressive culture while at the same time asserting deep roots in the land. The Zionists of this city were also given a boost by the British administration which granted them a special municipal charter, while still part of Jaffa, allowing males and females, citizens or fresh immigrants, to enjoy voting rights to the municipal council.

But Jerusalem was not spared. Extremist Jewish nationalism reared its head in the holy city, creating tension between Arabs and Jews, demonstrating the pivotal role which the holy places played in the solidification of the Palestinian national identity. Attempts by the Revisionist Party to expand Jewish rights in the vicinity of the Wailing Wall, which the British restricted in accordance with the Status Quo Law, aroused the Palestinian masses, leading to the 1929 riots. This was the beginning of the struggle over the holy places when Zionist designs on the Mughrabi Quarter confronted ancient Islamic *waqf* rights, leading to British adjudication of this matter and a victory for Muslim claims and historic customs and practices. The Muslim case was strengthened by citing the absence of any written evidence of the performance of Jewish prayers at the Wailing Wall in previous centuries. The 1929 riots also catapulted the issue of the Buraq Wall as the Western Wall of the Noble Sanctuary plaza to the top of the list of disputed and endangered places.

Arab frustration mounted, however, due to Zionist gains on the economic front and the flood of Jewish immigrants entering Palestine. Failure of the British to stem the tide of land sales which alienated Arab property permanently, or to recognize the autonomy of political and communal Palestinian institutions resulted in the 1936 Arab Revolt. When the British responded with military action, and later, with yet another study commission to determine the cause of this revolt, the result framed the question of the holy places one more time as the pivotal issue leading to instability and riots. The Peel Commission also opened up the entire question of communal and national rights in Palestine. The solution was to divide the country in three zones, one of which, containing Jerusalem and Bethlehem, was to be internationalized under British control. Arabs rejected the Peel report for several reasons, but primarily because the land allotted to them was no match for the fertile coastal plain assigned to the Yishuv, and also because they feared the eviction of the Arab population of the Galilee. Another harbinger of things to come was recommending the attachment of Arab Palestine to Transjordan which Palestinian nationalists rejected.

But for the Jewish side, denying it a role in Jerusalem pitted pragmatists versus extremists, with Ben Gurion rhapsodizing over the eternal mystique of the heavenly Jerusalem and the undeniable advantage of relegating the holy city to British, rather than, Arab rule. This was the position of other leaders who were positing the advantages of securing the rights of European Jewish immigration to Palestine over the ephemeral gains to be made by securing Jerusalem. Among these was Arlosoroff, who succeeded Ben Gurion as the head of the Yishuv, only to lose his life in an assassination attempt blamed on the Revisionists a few years later. The battle for supremacy over Palestine soon shifted to the United States where its imminent entry into WWII energized the American Jewish community and some of the temporarily transplanted leaders of the Yishuv. The battle quickly branched into two theatres, one in British Palestine, the other in the country destined to emerge as the leader of the free world.

NOTES

1. Quoted in: Karl Sabbagh, *Palestine: A Personal History* (New York: Grove Press, 2007): 6.
2. Ibid.
3. Simon Sebag Montefiore, *Jerusalem: The Biography* (New York: Vintage Books, 2012): 448–9.
4. Hazem Nuseibeh, "Al-Quds al-mu'asirah alati a'ref/The Jerusalem I Know," in *Al-Quds wa al-hal al-Filastini wa qira'at fi al-amn al-qawmi al-Arabi/Jerusalem and the Palestinian Condition and a Reading in Arab National Security, ed. Tawfiq Abu-Baker* (Amman: Mu'assasat Abd al-Hamid Shuman, 1999): 140–1.
5. Priscilla M. Roberts and Spencer C. Tucker, eds., *The Encyclopedia of the Arab-Israeli Conflict, Vo. IV, Documents* (Santa Barbara, Calif.: ABC- CLIO, Inc., 2008): 1219.
6. Ibid., 1219–22.
7. Edward J. Tivnan, *The Lobby: Jewish Political Power and American Foreign Policy* (New York: Simon and Schuster, 1987): 16–8.
8. Omer Carmon, "A Palestinian Village in the Heart of Tel Aviv?" Zoghrot.org/en/content/Palestinian-village-heart-tel-aviv. Accessed 5/22/2014.
9. Mark Levine, "Framing Tel Aviv," http://english.aljazeera.net/focus/2009/09/20099892214748263.html.9/17/2009. Accessed 12/18/2009.
10. Ghada Talhami, "Between Development and Preservation: Jerusalem under Three Regimes," *American Arab Affairs*, No. 16 (Spring 1986): 86–7.
11. Fred Skolnik, ed., "Jerusalem," *Encyclopedia Judaica*, Vol. 10 (Farmington Hills, MI: Thomson Gale, 2007): 390–1.
12. Ibid., Vol. II, 174–6. See also: Janet and John Wallach, *Arafat: In the Eyes of the Beholder* (New York: Carol Publishing Group, 1990): 45.
13. Michael Dumper, *The Politics of Jerusalem since 1967* (New York: Columbia University Press, 1997): 197–9.
14. Ian Lustick, *For the Land and the Lord: Jewish Fundamentalism in Israel* (New York: Council on Foreign Relations, 1988): 29–35.
15. Committee on the Exercise of the Inalienable Rights of the Palestinian People, The Status of Jerusalem (New York: United Nations, 1997): 4–5. http://domino.un.org/UNISPAL.NSF/9a798adb.3/21/2005. Accessed 5/21/2005.
16. Dumper, *The Politics of Jerusalem*, 26–8.
17. Skolnik, "Jerusalem," *Encyclopedia Judaica*, Vol. 11, 173–74. See also: Jonathan Kuttab, "Status of Electricity in Jerusalem: It's Complicated." Almonitor (June 6, 2013). www.almonitor.com/jerusalem-electricity-palestine.html. Accessed 5/23/1014.
18. Skolnik, "Jerusalem," *Encyclopedia Judaica*, Vol. 11, 174–5. The Jerusalem airport began as a British base known as Kolundia Airfield, See: Nahed Awwad, "In Search of Jerusalem Airport," *Jerusalem Quarterly*, No. 35 (Autumn 2008). www.jerusalemquarterly.org/pdf. Accessed 5/28/2014.
19. Abd al-Fattah Abu-'Aliyah, *Al-Quds: diraset tarikhiyah/Jerusalem: A Historical Study* (Riyadh: Dar al-Mareekh, 2000): 140. On British censorship laws in Palestine, see: *Aida Najjar, The Arabic Press in Palestine, 1920–1948* (Unpublished Ph.D. Dissertation, Syracuse University, 1976).
20. Bashar Manafeekhi, "Min al-maqahi al-adabiyah fi al-'alam al-arabi; maqha al-sa'aleek fi al-Quds/From the Literary Coffee Shops in the Arab World: al-Sa'aleek Litrary Coffee Shop in Jerusalem" *al-Hurriyah*, No. 1224 (28 February 2009): 22'
21. Nuseibeh, "Al-Quds," 136–7.
22. Abu-'Aliyah, Al-Quds, 142–3.

23. Manafeekhi, "Min al-maqahi," 22

24. Montefiore, *Jerusalem*, 288.

25. Muhammad Asad (Leopold Weiss), "Jerusalem in 1923: The Impressions of a Young European," in *My Jerusalem: Essays, Reminiscences and Poems*, eds., Salma K. Jayyusi and Zafer I. Ansari (Northampton, Mass.: Olive Branch Press, 2005): 221–2.

26. Montefiore, *Jerusalem*, 457–60.

27. Abu-'Aliyah, *Al-Quds*, 141.

28. Dumper, *The Politics of Jerusalem*, 199–200.

29. Avraham Sela, "The Wailing Wall Riots (1929) As a Watershed in the Palestine Conflict," *Muslim World*, Vol. LXXXIV, No. 1–2 (January-April 1994): 68–71.

30. Simone Rica, "Heritage, Nationalism and the Shifting Symbolism of the Wailing Wall," *Jerusalem Quarterly*, No. 24 (Summer 2005). www.jerusalemquarterly.org/ViewArticle.aspx?id=104. Accessed 5/27/2014.

31. Muhammad Hussain al-Farra, "Jerusalem and the Forgotten Documents," in *My Jerusalem*, 93–5.

32. Rica, "Heritage."

33. Abdul Latif Tibawi, "Jerusalem under Islamic Rule," in *Jerusalem: The Key to World Peace* (London: Islamic Council of Europe, 1980): 141–8.

34. Nuseibeh, "Al-Quds," 138.

35. Abu-'Aliyah, *Al-Quds*, 142.

36. Benny Morris, *The Birth Of the Palestinian Refugee Problem, 1947–1949* (Cambridge: Cambridge University Press, 1987): 5–16.

37. Montefiore, *Jerusalem*, 470–3.

38. Rouhi El Khatib, "The Judaization of Jerusalem and its Demographic Transformation," in *Jerusalem: The Key to World Peace*, 111–2.

39. Montefiore, *Jerusalem*, 350.

40. Charles D. Smith, *Palestine and the Arab-Israeli Conflict* (New York: St. Martin's Press, 1988): 47–8.

41. Walter Laqueur, *A History of Zionism* (New York: MJF Book, 1972): 514–9.

42. Smith, *Palestine*, 98.

43. Motti Golani, "Jerusalem's Hope Lies only in Partition: Israeli Policy on the Jerusalem Question, 1948–1967," *International Journal of Middle Eastern Studies*, Vol. 31, No. 4 (November 1999): 578–9.

44. Ibid., 580.

45. Sela, "The Wailing Wall," 85–92.

46. Neil Kaplan, "Zionist Visions of Palestine, 1917–1936," *Muslim World*, Vol. LXXXIV, No. 1–2 (January-April 1994): 23–5.

47. Ibid., 28–34.

48. Ibid., 25.

49. Sela, "The Wailing Wall," 87–90.

Chapter Two

American Zionists Take the Lead

Although President Wilson's support for Jewish self-determination in 1919 originated from his Christian Zionist predilection for interpreting the Bible as a proto-historical document, many historians doubted that he actually included Jews under his broad delineation of this principle. The following statement seemed to have gone beyond his earlier romantic and non-political views on the subject to put the matter to rest. Supposedly, his views were misunderstood only because he made his personal opinion on the matter known as a gesture of approval of his allies' declaration regarding the historical Jewish claim to Palestine. He was told that his own government had approved the Allies' position supporting laying the foundations of a "Jewish Commonwealth" in Palestine. However, during the Paris Peace Conference and upon the request of the Peace Commissioners, he sent a statement on April 16, 1919, via Secretary of State Robert Lansing, clarifying his position. It read:

> Of course I did not use any of the words quoted in the enclosed, and they do not indeed purport to be my words. But I did in substance say what is quoted, though the expression "foundation of a Jewish Commonwealth" goes a little further than my idea at the time. All that I meant was to corroborate our expressed acquiescence in the position of the British Government in regard to the future of Palestine. [1]

This was the first time the term "Jewish Commonwealth" was used during the Paris Peace Conference. However, Wilson had definite plans for the achievement of a lasting peace in the Middle East, but unfortunately, the US Senate turned down his bid for membership in the League of Nations. Just before that, the American president insisted on ascertaining the wishes of the local populations of the former Ottoman Empire before determining their own political future. This idea was defeated by his British and French allies, forcing him to send the American section of the proposed commission to conduct their own investigation separately. This was the King-Crane Commission, named after its eponymous members, Dr. Henry Churchill King, President of Oberlin College, and Charles Richard Crane, Wilson's own commissioner on the mandate system in Turkey. It was the first effort to determine the political wishes of the population of the former Syrian Province, which included Iraq, by plebiscite.[2]

The commissioners' report, based on their interviews of Arabs and Jews, actually excluded Iraq, perhaps because it already had its own Arab government. The final recommendation proposed the reconstituting of the Syrian Province as a single Arab state, to be headed by King Faysal, but remaining as a mandate of the United States. The report added that the second choice of a mandatory power would be Great Britain. Jewish demands for a national home were relegated to a minority community within the larger Arab state. Submitted to the Paris Peace Conference, the commission's final report was not even taken up for discussion and was committed to oblivion as a footnote to the history of post-WWI peace-making efforts. The report remained in the secret archives of the US Department of State, since Wilson failed to win congressional support for the Versailles Peace Treaty or for the League of Nations project. The first time the American public became aware of its existence was upon the publication of *Papers Relating to the Foreign Relations of the United States. The Paris Peace Conference, 1919.* An article by Ray Stannard Baker detailing its contents appeared on August 20, 1922, in the *New York Times.* The isolationist hawks of the US Congress at the time were extremely unlikely to approve such an ambitious plan to intervene in the newly liberated Near East.[3] In addition to ascertaining popular wishes regarding the future governments of this region, the intent of the commission was to assess the Arabs' reaction to the creation of a Jewish homeland in their midst. The idea of the commission itself was a testament to Wilson's ambiguous policy of crafting the self-determination principle as one of his Fourteen Points manifesto, while at the same time approving the Balfour Declaration which denied that same principle to the people of a segment of the former Ottoman Empire.[4] Based on their interviews, the authors of the final report concluded that the Jews would not be accepted by the local Arab population of Palestine who considered themselves custodians of the holy places. The authors added that the Christian holy places associated with the life of Jesus were also sacred to Muslims, but not to Jews who considered these monuments abhorrent and unholy.[5]

WEIZMANN'S AND BRANDEIS' CONFLICTING VIEWS

As the United States entered its isolationist phase following the Great War, a tense battle between American religious and political Jews ensued, with the European Zionists applying pressure in the American arena. This transformation, strangely enough, was due to Arthur Balfour's pragmatist streak which combined with his Christian Zionism to sell the idea of his eponymous declaration to the British cabinet. The foreign secretary assured his fellow cabinet members that American and Russian Jews would welcome this British gesture of support, turning the declaration into a definite British propaganda coup. But excitement generated by this document quickly brought forth a serious division in Zionist ranks, with one faction led by Weizmann, an Anglophile and Herzl's heir as head of WZO, and Brandeis, the well-known Boston lawyer who until 1912 was not officially a Zionist. He was born in Kentucky and educated at Harvard, became a friend of the American president and embraced Zionism when in his fifties. Weizmann rose to prominence in 1904, after Herzl's demise. He befriended Balfour, taking credit for being the inspiration for his famous declaration. Brandeis became a de facto leader of the American Zionist movement until 1918, focusing on gaining Zionist converts in this country. His efforts were challenged, given the European-Jewish-American antecedents of this foreign ideology which advocated the goals of Jewish political nationalism among culturally assimilated Jews. Among his strongest opponents were members of the AJC, who warned of the danger of double loyalties. They also advised Wilson against appointing him to a cabinet post since he belonged to the radical fringe of the Jewish community.[6] Brandeis fought these accusations by addressing the problem upfront, declaring in 1915, in a renowned speech before a conference of American Reform Rabbis:

> Let no American imagine that Zionism is inconsistent with Patriotism. Multiple loyalties are objectionable only if they are inconsistent. . . . Every American who aids in advancing the Jewish settlement in Palestine, though he feels that neither he nor his descendants will ever live there, will likewise be a better man and a better American for doing so. . . . There is no inconsistency between loyalty to America and loyalty to Jewry. The Jewish spirit, the product of our religion and experiences, is essentially modern and essentially American. . . . America's fundamental laws seek to make real the brotherhood of man. That brotherhood became the Jewish fundamental law more than twenty five hundred years ago. . . . Indeed, loyalty to America demands rather that each American Jew become a Zionist.[7]

These remarks which were to become a mantra of American Zionism, aided in anointing Brandeis as the head of ZOA. Since this address, American audiences were never informed of the opinions and wishes of the

Arab majority in Palestine, a lacuna that continued to dominate Zionist advocacy efforts down to the creation of the Israeli state. By the time Wilson appointed him to the Supreme Court in 1916, the American president was quite sympathetic to the Zionist cause. The ideology of American Jewry dovetailed perfectly with Wilson's endorsement of the principle of self-determination, and his embrace of American Protestantism's traditional commitment to Christian Zionism. European Zionists remained suspicious of Brandeis' definition of the new political ideology, referring to him as an advocate of "Zionism without Zion." The American Jewish leader was not only unimpressed with European Zionist conclaves, which seemed to occur annually, but he had never expressed an interest in moving to Palestine. The confrontation between the two representatives of American and European Zionism began in 1921, when Weizmann toured the United States on a fund-raising trip for building Hebrew University in Jerusalem. It did not take long before US Jews forced Brandeis to resign his position in the organization based on Weizmann's distaste for his leadership. Future Zionist leaders such as Felix Frankfurter, Reform Rabbi Stephen Wise, and Abba Hillel Silver withdrew, taking their followers with them.

SPLITS CONCERNING STRATEGY

This leadership gap made room for the rise of another contender for Weizmann's position, namely Vladimir Jabotinsky who pushed for massive migration of European Jews to Palestine. This campaign, he hoped, would stay the hand of British authorities and force them to accept the growing Jewish majority as the main group in the country. Jabotinsky would also be remembered for the phrase, "iron wall" as a military shield for Palestine, surpassing any strength mustered by the Arabs. The focal thrust of the world Zionist movement, was immigration, sources of which were being identified as mainly in Europe. The new role being charted for American Jewry by this movement was that of a pressure group to facilitate this immigration. Jabotinsky tried but failed to push Weizmann out of his leadership position of the WZO in 1925, later creating his own New Zionist Organization in 1935, known also as Revisionist Zionism. He was forced to curtail his plans when Jewish immigration to Palestine continued, not as a flood but as a trickle. British records indicated that 77,063 Jews moved to Palestine between 1920 and 1929. British census figures two years later recorded the number of Jews in Palestine as 175,000, making them roughly 17 percent of the total population. But Jabotinsky's program echoed several of Herzl's classic propaganda lines about redeeming the land of Israel, resurrecting its language, and expanding on both sides of the Jordan River. Another Zionist who emigrated in 1906 from Poland was Ben Gurion, who helped create the Zionist Labor movement, Paoli Zion, later Mapai, or the Labor Party which played a seminal role in the creation of Israel. He became a member of the WZO executive, assuming the role of the head of the Jewish Agency (JA). He moved in 1915 to New York City but was back again in Palestine after WWI. Ben Gurion was not only well-acquainted with Jewish life in the United States, his role as the head of the JA made him the supreme leader of the American Jewish community. He was charged with building a national home with funds from abroad, while still trying to fend off the hostility of Jabotinsky's group.

By 1935, the leadership of the American branch of the WZO passed to Stephen Wise, a well-known reform rabbi. He, too, became a close friend of an American president, Franklin Delano Roosevelt (FDR) and gave the American Jewish community needed prominence in public life which suffered with the withdrawal of Brandeis from the ZOA. When WWII began, Wise struggled to set the right priorities for his community and its operational agenda, particularly its fund-raising efforts. This boiled down to a choice between funding Jewish refugee camps in Europe, or spending it on Zionist building efforts in the United States. Wise focused on the task of rescuing European Jews and directing them to Palestine, using his friendship with Roosevelt to that end. Wise also leaned towards reviving the Herzlian vision of settling Jews in East Africa, reviving the old criticism that this was not what Zionism had advocated. Even his old friend, Rabbi Silver, attacked this idea in 1941, refocusing Jewish American sights on British restrictions on immigration to Palestine. [8]

THE IMMIGRATION AVALANCHE AND SUBSTANTIATING THE BALFOUR PROMISE

European Jewish refugees who were forced out of their homes during the late 1930s galvanized all sections of the world-wide Jewish community. However, while there was general agreement on the nature of the problem, there was little agreement on a solution. German refugees were of particular concern due to their numbers and the gravity of their situation. To deal with this international humanitarian situation, President Roosevelt convened a conference in July of 1938 in Evian, France, which was attended by representatives of thirty-two countries. The British Government objected to designating Palestine as the main recipient of this flood of immigrants, but a parade of representatives declined to receive them, claiming that their countries were unsuitable for settling these massive numbers. The only two areas willing to take in European Jews were the Dominican Republic and Shanghai—the latter being quickly closed to immigrants following the Japanese invasion. Zionist leaders failed to convince the rest of the world of the seriousness of the situation of European Jewry, but remained hopeful of convincing others of the suitability of Palestine as the ultimate place of Jewish refuge.

By 1939, the British Government began to restrict legal Jewish immigration to Mandate Palestine as a result of the White Paper issued that same year. Despite Herzl's projection of a process of gradual Jewish settlement in that country, the impact of the Holocaust and the ambitious leadership of the Yishuv combined to push the flow of homeless Jews in the direction of Palestine. The Zionist leadership continued to make the spurious argument that Jewish material and human capital were bringing prosperity to all of Palestine, with the Arabs making great gains in the process. Successive British commissions of inquiry which documented the devastating economic impact of unlimited Jewish immigration and land acquisition on the Palestinian peasantry were completely ignored. The Zionists continued to popularize the notion that the land which nurtured the orange groves was nothing but sand dunes under the Arabs, a claim casually repeated in the Peel Report. This mendacious logic materialized later as "they made the desert bloom," slogan, a classic social Darwinist distortion of the facts to justify the uprooting of an entire nation. The Palestinians, however, were not only painted as a primitive people, they were also accused of collaboration with Nazi and Fascist powers. Many Jewish apologists for Zionism continued to proclaim these "essential truths" about the Palestinian national movement throughout the post-WWII period.[9]

American Zionists began to consolidate their ranks in the late 1930s and bring various Jewish organizations under their tent. Organizations like B'nai B'rith, initially founded in 1843 by German Jews to combat anti-Semitism on the American scene and act as a service organization dedicated to improving living conditions of Jews, began to focus on Palestine. So did a number of prominent reform synagogues. The AZO increased in numbers, and the American Palestine Liberation Committee (APLC) made up of pro-Zionist Christian scholars was revived and began to call for a Jewish homeland in Palestine. Even though news of the Holocaust reached the United States by 1943, some Jews were reluctant to speak out for fear of being accused of lack of American patriotism. The AJC was still unwilling to join the Zionist camp, until a major American Jewish conference pushed the community to act.

THE BILTMORE CONFERENCE AND BEN GURION'S TRIUMPH

A conference representing most organized Jewish groups was convened in New York from March 6 to 11, 1942, and was attended by 502 delegates. The gradualist approach of Weizmann at first dominated, calling for opening the door to immigration to Palestine, rather than demanding the immediate creation of a Jewish state. Rabbi Silver, however, unexpectedly took to the podium to make a plea for facilitating rescue operations of European Jews, whom he said could only be saved by allowing unrestricted immigration to Palestine. This depended on the exercise of full political rights by members of the Yishuv, he asserted. He then linked this to world recognition of the Jewish people's historic roots in Palestine, allowing for the building of a national home. The result was a wave of enthusiastic support for his program, but also the withdrawal of the AJC. Disputes between Silver, a Republican, and Rabbi Wise, a Democrat, increased. The latter advised that Jews should wait for a diplomatic solution by Roosevelt. As a result, Silver tendered his resignation as of 1944, having failed to persuade the conference to submit a resolution to Congress, by-passing the President and the State Department. Though he returned to office in 1945, he failed to push for a clear Zionist demand for statehood.

Eventually, a bi-partisan resolution was submitted to Congress calling for full endorsement of the Zionist plan. It also demanded opening the gates of Palestine for Jewish immigration, "so that the Jewish people may ultimately reconstitute Palestine as a free and democratic Jewish commonwealth."[10] The resolution was the work of representatives James Wright and Ranulf Compton, who submitted it on January 27, 1944, followed a few days later by its submission to the Senate by Robert F. Wagner and Robert A. Taft. This initiative ran into trouble quickly and was opposed by anti-Zionist Jewish organizations and groups. In addition, Arab diplomats managed to impress on the US Army and the State Department the dangers inherent in these resolutions. The strongest objection was voiced by Secretary of State Cordell Hull who warned that the resolutions, if passed, may result in sabotaging ongoing negotiations with Saudi Arabia over the construction of an oil pipeline. Congress then delayed its hearings for military reasons. When it seemed in October 1945 that the new administration of Harry S. Truman might instigate its congressional allies to support the resolution, the effort failed again when the Anglo-American Commission of Inquiry was created to study the issue.[11]

Emanuel Neumann, who founded the United Palestine Appeal (UPA) in 1925, and who went on to serve as president of the ZOA, testified before the House Committee on Foreign Relations in March 1944, regarding the Wright-Compton Resolution.[12] He was followed by Judge Louis E. Levinthal who offered a clear explanation of the term "commonwealth" for Jews in Palestine. His definition, nevertheless, did not end public debate, Jewish and non-Jewish, on the possible outcome of massive emigration of European Jews to Palestine. He stressed that a Jewish commonwealth did not mean an exclusively Jewish state, adding:

If then we are asked what we mean by the adjective "Jewish" as applied to the future Commonwealth of Palestine, . . . it is a short and abbreviated way of saying that through the repatriation of large numbers of European and other Jews the Jewish people will attain a numerical majority in Palestine and there-by guarantee the open door for others who may follow; so that Palestine shall never cease to serve as a sanctuary and Homeland for any and all Jews . . . The development of the Jewish commonwealth shall take place under democratic institutions and in a democratic spirit . . . . Jew and Arab devoted to their respective cultures and traditions shall co-operate as free and equal citizens and jointly contribute to the prosperity and welfare of a common single unitary state. The Arab citizens of the Jewish commonwealth will be as favorably situated as are the French-speaking citizens of the British Dominion of Cana-da. It will be a free and democratic Jewish state composed of free Moslems, Christians . . . All shall be eligible to public office, even the highest. [13]

The Biltmore Conference, it turned out, was intended to unify the ranks of Jewish American activists behind Ben Gurion's idea of a Jewish majoritarian state in Palestine, unlike Weizmann's preference for gradual immigration and settlement. Events in Europe which aroused great passions among American Jews were now utilized to push against the gradualist approach. The implication of a "Jewish commonwealth" was made irrevocably clear, calling for the absolute necessity of creating a dominant Jewish majority in Palestine, which alone, was entitled to define the rights of the soon to be downsized Arab minority. Although convened by Weizmann, the conference was called in order to accelerate fund-raising in the United States to support the anticipated emigration of millions to Palestine and to pressure it to assist in this endeavor. The commonwealth idea seemed perfectly suited to the Zionist plan at the time as a democratic concept capable of cloaking its intentions to dominate Palestine as a Jewish majority. But the conference itself privately departed from the grand democratic scheme unveiled for the benefit of Congress and the American public. The conference adopted reso-lutions calling for authorizing the JA in Palestine to be placed in charge of the anticipated flood of immigrants and to develop the country as a common-wealth when the war ended. News of the Holocaust which became known in the United States during the second half of 1942, opened the way for the maximalists to determine the outcome of the conference and mobilize large numbers to join Zionist organizations. From that point on, there would be no more talk of a "homeland," it being understood that Jews can never be secure except as a ruling majority in a land with which they had historic ties. The commonwealth idea was touted as a guarantee of the democratic attributes of the projected Jewish state, destined to join the international community of nations. [14] Yet, the term "commonwealth" was not so novel since it had been used in Wilsonian statements but without a defined meaning. The other ob-jective of the conference, namely to produce a unified front favoring directing all immigrants to Palestine so as to achieve statehood, eluded the conveners as the AJC remained outside the official Zionist fold. [15]

ROOSEVELT AND THE ZIONISTS

The wartime president of the United States raised the hopes of many Zionists who sought to convince him to balance the White Paper of Britain on the eve of the war with an American pro-Zionist posture. Roosevelt was also viewed favorably because of his high-level appointment of American Jews to government positions. Several Jewish New Dealers rose to political prominence under FDR, including Henry Morgenthau, Jr., Herbert Lehman, Samuel Rosenberg, Morris Ernest and Robert Nathan.

Then there was Bernard Baruch, a secular Jewish financier, who had the distinction of consulting for five US presidents, from Wilson to Truman. Both David E. Lilienthal and Lewis H. Strauss rose to the position of chair of the Atomic Energy Commission. David K. Niles (aka Neyhaus) became Roosevelt's Executive Assistant following the 1940 elections. Roosevelt placed him in charge of relations with leading Jewish groups, minorities and labor associations. By holding this high position, Niles became the foremost Jewish emissary to the presidency. [16] His ascent to political prominence, however, was astonishingly atypical of the route to similar positions. The child of impoverished Jewish Russian immigrants who settled in Boston where he was born, he never had the benefit of college education but later connected with important liberal Jews like Felix Frankfurter and Stephen Wise. Niles was among those who supported the New Deal and became a protégé of Henry Hopkins in 1933, one of the main architects of Roosevelt's reforms. Hopkins and Niles became responsible in 1940 for managing Roosevelt's third run for the presidency. [17]

Roosevelt's Jewish connections, nevertheless, were unable to blind him to the necessity of maintaining ties to Arab allies. He remained fully aware of the potentially negative impact of certain policies on oil prices and the war effort which pushed him to cooperate with Britain in dampening political and ethnic conflict in Palestine. The two powers, largely on Britain's advice, agreed to postpone any movement on the Palestine issue until after the war. Assurances were made to both sides in this conflict that no decision will be made without further consultation with the two communities. But somehow, the Anglo-American joint statement to that effect was leaked to Zionist circles ahead of time, resulting in wide Zionist protests targeting American officials. When Secretary of State Hull sought the advice of the military, he received assurances from Secretary of War, Henry L. Stimson, that the military situation was not in such dire straits as to require a general statement freezing the Palestine situation. This ended the American-British plan which was hailed as a victory by the Zionists. But the State Department, hoping for a different outcome, was actually acting in response to the first face-to-face meeting between King Abdul Aziz Ibn Saud of Saudi Arabia and Colonel Harold B. Hoskins. The latter was sent to the Arab World in 1943 specifically to seek the Saudi monarch's advice on settling the Palestine issue. Hoskins was also charged with sending feelers for a possible meeting between Ibn Saud and Weizmann. But the Saudi monarch was strongly opposed to opening the floodgates of Jewish immigration to Palestine or the creation of a Jewish state, and a meeting with Weizmann was rejected off hand.[18] But back at home, Hoskins earned the enmity of the Jewish community which branded him an anti-Zionist whom the *Jewish Telegraphic Agency* identified as a president of the Board of Trustees of the American University of Beirut (AUB) and an advisor to the Standard Oil Company of New Jersey.[19]

In the meantime, the State Department was concerned over Arab reaction to the Wright-Compton resolution since it called for the creation of a Jewish commonwealth when the majority of the population was still Arab. Secretary Stimson indicated his displeasure to the House Foreign Affairs Committee Chair Sol Bloom, calling for shelving the resolution since it threatened to harm the American war effort by causing negative ripples in the Middle East. But even though the resolution was not adopted, Zionist influence over the White House managed to stop another attempt at issuing an Anglo-American joint statement calling for freezing the situation in Palestine. Wise and Silver declared to the press that Roosevelt fully supported the Zionists soon after a meeting with the president, thereby forcing his hand. Another demonstration of the extent of Zionist influence was made during the 1944 political campaign, when both political parties included statements supporting Zionist positions in their platforms. Both parties referred to a "free and democratic commonwealth" in Palestine, with Governor Thomas E. Dewey adding the term "Jewish" to the commonwealth in question in his public addresses. Roosevelt continued to caution congressional leaders against introducing additional resolutions on Palestine, but was able to stop such legislation only after it reached the Senate floor. Hostile Arab reaction in the Middle East intensified, contributing in 1944 to the adoption of the Pan-Arab Protocol, or the Alexandria Protocol, which led to the creation of the ALS. By that time, not even King Abdul Aziz was a believer in American good intentions or in the urgency of safeguarding American economic and strategic interests in the Middle East.[20]

In addition, Zionism had already established strong bases of support among non-Jewish American liberal circles, making great inroads into Protestant groups and the liberal press. Among its staunch supporters in the period of the war and after were renowned figures such as Reinhold Niebuhr, the founder of Christian ethicism, and such liberal media as *The Nation, The New Republic* and *The New York Post*.[21] Niebuhr was moved by reports of the demonizing of European Jews and the destruction of their communities by the Third Reich, turning into a strong advocate of a state for Jews in Palestine. He also broke off from the *Christian Century*, prominent voice of liberal Christianity, for cautioning against joining the war. He then created his own journal, *Christianity and Crisis,* and developed his own theology, "political realism," which called on the US Government to fight evil as personified in Nazi Germany. He also recommended that the Arabs be resettled outside of Palestine in order to make room for Jewish refugees, realizing all the while that there will be a great resistance to this scheme. Another Protestant figure of German background was Paul Tillich who eventually joined the call for a Jewish state once news of the concentration camps became public. Both imbibed Zionist allegations regarding the backwardness, underdeveloped state and under-populated reality of Palestine unquestioningly.[22]

Zionists had a great friend in Eleanor Roosevelt, also for the same reasons which won over the support of secular liberals and eminent Protestant theological leaders. She felt admiration for what the Zionists had accomplished in Palestine, believing that they had improved living conditions for all of its population. The president, on the other hand, flew over the country at one time, noting the limited nature of Zionist development which was confined to the coastal area in the western part of Palestine. Eleanor was at first a supporter of the idea of trusteeship but was won over eventually to the concept of Israeli statehood. But the president who felt a great sympathy for Jewish victims of Nazi Germany was not a believer in Zionist plans for statehood. Instead, he had greater concern for protecting American national interests abroad and the looming development of a bi-polar international system heralding the rise of global Soviet power. Apparently, he held definite views on what would be an optimum solution for Palestine. According to State Department documents concerning the Middle East in 1943, which were opened in May 1964, he continued to call for the creation of a trusteeship in Palestine, referring to it as "the Holy Land." He advocated the appointment of three trustees representing Christians, Muslims and Jews to run the country. This plan was proposed on the heels of a fiasco resulting from an attempted bribe to King Abdul Aziz by Weizmann, which the Jewish leader claimed was guaranteed by Roosevelt.[23] Niles commented in retrospect that Israel would never have come into existence as a state had Roosevelt remained at the apex of American government.[24]

Truman Accelerates the Push for Statehood

Zionist supporters in the United States continued to face great opposition from the State Department following Truman's accession to the presidency on April 12, 1945, after Roosevelt's death. If there was ever any time in which this office was focused on the urgent need for Middle East oil, it was at the end of WWII. The gathering clouds of the Cold War necessitated close coordination with the Arab states more than ever. Roosevelt's sudden death came on the heels of his assurances to Rabbi Wise that he did not rescind his earlier letter to Senator Robert Wagner in support of the Jewish common-wealth idea, even though the State and War Departments have succeeded in killing the resolution upon Roosevelt's instruction. By that time, the Arabian American Oil Company (ARAMCO) had acquired an exclusive concession to develop the oil fields of Saudi Arabia and US investors were already the owners of one-fourth of Iraq's oil.

The so-called State Department Arabists began to be subjected to heavy bombardment of anti-Semitic charges. Pro-Zionist forces clashed directly with the State Department as soon as Truman took office, particularly when the new administration sought greater coordination with Britain. On the eve of the Potsdam meeting between Soviet, American and British leaders in July 1945, Truman came under pressure to seek British approval of unlimited Jewish immigration to Palestine and the creation of a Jewish state. The AJC led the way in mobilizing Congress behind these two ideas, resulting in endorsements being presented to Truman by Senator Wagner. Worried lest Churchill suggest certain concessions to the Zionist camp, the State Depart-ment, now headed by Edward Stettinius, warned Truman against broaching the subject of Palestine during the European summit, and the president seemed to agree. [25]

ANGERING BRITISH ALLIES

After the Labor Government of Clement Attlee and Foreign Secretary Ernest Bevin succeeded to power in Great Britain, Truman suggested that they should quickly lift all restrictions on Jewish immigration to Palestine. It appeared that the Zionists, who began to refer to Jewish immigrants as DPs, achieved a major victory over Truman, although the latter began to waver in his commitment upon returning to the United States. He declared in a press conference that if Zionist demands could be achieved peacefully, he would support that outcome, but he had no plans to send American troops to Pales-tine in order to secure a deal. But his aides, like Niles, continued to stress that his support for open-ended Jewish immigration would not be met by violent Arab acts. Yet, even after Truman received the report of Earl Harrison, the Dean of the University of Pennsylvania who headed an American mission to investigate the conditions of Jews in DP camps, the American President maintained his skepticism regarding the need for a Jewish state. The mission was inspired by Weizmann who sent emissaries to persuade Secretary of the Treasury Morgenthau to urge Truman to create such a body. Harrison's report concluded that most of the Jews wished to emigrate to Palestine and not to be forced to go back to their original domicile in Europe. He added that he agreed with the JA's demand that 100,000 of these be allowed to proceed to Palestine, although evidence showed that this number was inflated. Neglecting to consult with the State Department, Truman sent a message to Attlee signifying his approval of Harrison's findings. Attlee's reaction was to warn of harming the two countries' relations if the report was made public. He cited the strong possibility of damaging Britain's relations with the Arab countries and offered to move a large number of Jews to camps in North Africa. When pressure on Truman mounted, he made it clear to Rabbis Silver and Wise that he would no more endorse a Jewish state in Palestine than endorse a Catholic state. But he continued to anger his British allies by declaring his support for allowing 100,000 Jewish immigrants into Palestine. This position, his aides explained, was motivated by his anxiety over Jewish voter pressure during the 1945 New York City mayoral elections.[26]

The Anglo-American Committee of Inquiry

Though apprehensive about American competition for Mid-East oil and the region's export markets, the British Government, particularly Bevin, decided to involve the Americans in the Palestine issue, but on his own terms. Britain at that time was facing a militant Zionist rebellion in Palestine following its refusal to retreat from the White Paper issued after the London Conference. Bevin came up with the idea of an Anglo-American commission of inquiry regarding the future of Jewish DPs in Europe. He was hoping that this would lead the reluctant Americans to assist in putting down the Zionist uprising in Palestine and perhaps prolong the DP issue until the uprising died down. The commission finally received Truman's approval after the New York City mayoral contest was won by a Democrat, putting to rest any anxieties he may have had regarding forcing Jewish voters to abandon the Democratic Party. But Truman continued to stress to American diplomats in the Middle East that he was not committed to the idea of a Jewish commonwealth which would have grave ramifications for US position in the world. He also revealed his preference for endorsing limited Jewish immigration to Palestine, hoping that this would be accepted by all sides as a humanitarian gesture. He continued to declare his opposition to making Palestine a Jewish state. The Anglo-American Committee (AAC), which convened in 1946, ended up producing a proposal close to the position of the two participants, but Truman refused to endorse its findings. Remarkably, the committee included two American delegates recommended by Niles, namely Bartley C. Crum, a lawyer and League of Nations high commissioner on refugees, and James G. McDonald, who jointly supported the idea of a Jewish state and eliminating any restrictions on Jewish immigration. Among those testifying before the

committee in favor of Jewish statehood was Niebuhr, by then head of the
American Palestine Committee. The liberal theologian repeated his well-
known line that the Arabs could settle throughout the Middle East and that
Palestine was the homeland of the Jews, echoing the Revisionist Zionist call
for population transfer, or expulsion by force, as the only way for accommo-
dating the influx of Jewish European Jews in Palestine.[27]

The committee's hearings in Jerusalem in early 1946 were held at the
YMCA building where a parade of witnesses provided testimony. There was
Weizmann who admitted that creating a Jewish state would cause limited
injustice to the Palestinians, but who also insisted that they would easily find
an alternate home in the Arab countries. Ben Gurion, on the other hand,
testified that there was never an Arab Palestine. The committee also heard
from Martin Buber and Judah Magnes of the Ehud Party, with the latter
insisting that both Arab and Jewish claims were equally valid, hence his
organization's preference for opening the door to Jewish immigration until
Jews achieved parity with the Palestinians sometime around 1957. The Arab
side, badly divided at the time, offered uncoordinated testimony. The AHC,
the political arm of the SMC, was reconstituted by the ALS while its leader,
the Mufti, remained in exile. Its leadership now fell to Jamal Husseini who
led all Arab witnesses in rejecting the prospect of unrestricted Jewish immigration leading to statehood. The future leader of the first Palestine Liberation Organization (PLO), Ahmad Shuqeiry, who presided over the ALS office in Jerusalem signifying the new organization's concern for the Palestine
issue, threatened violence if the wishes of the Palestinians were ignored. In
the end, all twelve members of the committee reached consensus by agreeing
to allow 100,000 Jewish DPs to enter Palestine. The committee, however,
was divided over the issue of Jewish statehood and the idea of partition. This
meant living with the status quo, or continued British control of the country.
But Arabs everywhere protested terminating the White Paper's proposed
restrictions on Jewish immigration. Just as in previous British commissions
of inquiry, the AAC added guarantees to safeguard the holy places of all
three faiths, the majority of which were located in Jerusalem. Zionist organizations in Britain, the United States and Palestine continued to reject every
subsequent proposal, including the Morrison-Grady plan and Britain's shift
in favor of a federated Arab and Jewish Palestine. Most modern writers,
however, including John B. Judis in his monumental expose of the Truman
administration's prevarications on the Palestine issue, continued to stress the
rejectionist posture of the Arabs while overlooking similar, if not more violent, reaction of the Jewish side. But Niles did not rest following the failure
of this committee and persisted in pressuring Truman to make public his
disagreement with the British over the immediate admission of 100,000 Jews
to Palestine. Rejecting this recommendation, the American president took the
advice of the State Department which called on him to avoid such a confron-

tation and to support Britain's preference for the continuation of the talks. Truman, thus, settled on former Assistant Secretary of State Henry Grady to represent the cabinet in a new round of discussions with a British delegation headed by Deputy Prime Minister Herbert Morrison.[28]

The Morrison-Grady Plan

Soon after the publication of the report of the AAC in May 1946, the Morrison-Grady Committee began its deliberations in London. Its eponymous plan was issued within the month, reflecting a sharp British departure from the AAC's proposals. The recommendation for a unified Palestine was now discarded in favor of a unitary federal British trusteeship. The Jewish province in the federation was granted 17 percent of Palestine and the Arab province around 40 percent. The remaining area comprised of the Naqab (Negev) Desert and Jerusalem and Bethlehem would continue to be administered by Britain, which would remain the sovereign political power. The two provinces would only enjoy control over local administration. But a big concession was made to the Jewish side by promising the immediate admission of 100,000 Jewish refugees. In return, the Yishuv was asked to accept limited immigration thereafter, subject to the absorptive capacity of the land.[29]

The plan specified that all financial, foreign, and immigration matters would remain under British control. A national legislature would allow for equal representation by Arabs and Jews in the upper house. If accepted, the British indicated openness to granting total independence following a peaceful transitional period. The fact that the plan favored the Jewish side, apparently, did not escape Truman's notice. He complained to Secretary of Commerce Henry Wallace that Jews were being awarded the most desirable part of Palestine, referring to the coastal area. By the time of unveiling the plan, the Arabs were still two-thirds of the total population, yet the committee felt justified in granting the one-third Jewish population equal representation in the proposed legislature. Despite all that, the Morrison-Grady Plan aroused unprecedented furor in Washington when American Jews expressed displeasure with British limitations on their openly stated determination to achieve majority status in Palestine. Rabbi Silver expressed anger at the prospect of confining 100,000 immigrants to their own "ghetto" of a homeland. Congressional pressure began mounting on Truman asking him to turn down the plan, while Senators Wagner and Taft attacked it in the Senate. When warned of the negative impact of the plan on the upcoming elections, Truman protested being bombarded by "Jews and other ethnic groups" about their interests, saying he also wished "to hear from Americans." But while extremely irritated by this pressure, he decided against approving the plan despite prominent backers such as Secretary of State Dean Acheson and Secretary of War James Forrestal. As Judis concluded, Truman's rejection of the plan finally ended his long-held strategy of guaranteeing the admission of the 100,000 Jewish refugees which would absolve him and the United States from acceding to that other Zionist demand, namely the creation of a Jewish state in Palestine.[30]

PARTITION, THE LAST ALTERNATIVE

With the failure of the Morrison-Grady Plan, the idea of partition began to gain traction again. First proposed by the Peel Commission, the idea failed because the Arabs rejected it vociferously. Later, the search was on again to find the right partition framework capable of garnering the requisite support of the American Jewish community. The idea was then advanced by Nahum Goldmann, the chief representative of the JAE in the United States. It turned out he was well-aware of Truman's increasing exasperation with the Jewish vocal preference for establishing a Jewish state in all of Palestine, which both the Arabs and the British rejected off hand. Recognizing the absence of the requisite Jewish numbers in Palestine to constitute a majority, he began suggesting conciliatory moves towards the Arab community. He was also dismissive of the Biltmore program centering on the creation of a Jewish commonwealth. He considered this to be impractical since it required constituting a Jewish majority in the land, an unattainable goal in light of the devastation of the Holocaust. Neither was he optimistic about the chances of survival of cantons, instead calling for the creation of a Jewish state as a member of a larger Middle Eastern federation of states. In essence, his proposal was a return to the Morrison-Grady plan of creating autonomous areas, but this time allocating total control over immigration policy to the Jewish territorial entity, rather than to the British. Only then, he argued before State Department officials, a Jewish ghetto in Palestine would become acceptable. In July 1946, the Zionists dynamited the King David Hotel, the headquarters of the British administration in Jerusalem, demonstrating British failure to achieve total security in the country and the predictable slide of Palestine into a state of chaos. But as Truman was won over to the idea of partition, the question of peaceful implementation of this plan became more elusive than ever. Thus, when the United States switched positions after promoting the UN partition plan in November 1947, then switched again in favor of a "temporary trusteeship" in March 1948 due to the inescapable conclusion that a peaceful solution was untenable, it balked at the prospect of sending troops to keep the peace. The State Department did offer to participate in a joint UN military force but Secretary of War, James Forrestal, fought the idea claiming that if the United States was expected to provide 50,000 troops, this would deplete the country's entire marine and army reserves. But even after the United States speedily granted recognition to the new State of Israel on 15 April 1948, peace in Palestine was a prominent casualty.[31]

Truman decided to support the creation of a Jewish state in Palestine no earlier than the fall of 1947, but the opportunity to do so did not emerge until May 1948 following the brief reversal of policy in favor of a trusteeship. Yet, the speed with which he resolved the extension of recognition, merely eleven minutes following Israel's declaration of independence in May astonished the State Department. Truman was counseled by this department against taking such a step before the Arabs and the Zionists managed to arrive at a settlement. But, it appeared that he was convinced of the Arab side's obdurate resistance to partition, which pushed him to act quickly.[32] In a cabinet meeting on May 12, 1948, which was also attended by a seemingly disapproving Secretary of State, George Marshall, and his undersecretary, Robert Lovett, the pro-Zionist White House Chief Counsel, Clark Clifford made the case for recognition. Not only did he base his case on humanitarian grounds, Clifford also quoted the Book of Deuteronomy in support of the Jewish historical claim to all of Palestine, or as the Bible read, "Go in and possess the land which the Lord sware unto your fathers, Abraham, Isaac, and Jacob, to give unto them and their seed after them."[33] Even though Marshall threatened to vote against Truman in the upcoming elections, Truman took this step without the approval of part of his cabinet, much of the State Department and the military establishment. Commenting on this episode years later, Walter Russell Mead asserted that the use of a biblical quote was proof of the genuine affinity of Protestant America with the Zionist project. He added that the fact that Jews at the time made up only 3.8 per cent of the American population did not deter Americans from identifying with them as the best hope of bringing progress to that unhappy land. Mead claimed that Americans also sought comfort in their parallel conquest of the native Indians and the Israelis' forcible removal of Palestine's indigenous Arabs. This was not the case of Truman being manipulated by a handful of his advisers or a small minority lobby.[34] Mead concluded:

> In the future, as in the past, U.S. policy toward the Middle East will, for better or worse, continue to be shaped primarily by the will of the American majority, not the machinations of any minority, however wealthy or engaged in the political process some of its members may be.[35]

Mead's remarks, which denied conclusive evidence to the contrary, stood as a poor footnote to the current and widely disseminated view of the Zionist manipulation of American presidents, their advisers, the Protestant establishment and the media. Kathleen Christison, a CIA analyst, summed up the net effect of Truman's pro-Zionist advisers on his policies by singling out the trio of Clifford, Niles and Max Lowenthall. The latter was a friend of Truman who supplied Niles with legal advice. These three enjoyed consistent influence over the president which exceeded that of the personal approach of Eddie Jacobson, another long-time friend. The three advisers enjoyed uninterrupted access to the chief executive during the UN debate on Palestine's future, molding his ideas by exercising a monopoly over what information he received in the form of official memoranda. They made Truman receptive to the "fanatical and backward" image of the Arabs. Much of this information came from Niles' and Lowenthall's wide Zionist network, with the latter undertaking the task of contacting undecided member states in the UN to vote in the Zionists' favor, without informing Truman. Finally, not only did Lowenthall escape any responsibility, but he went on to boast of his accomplishment. Truman finally became comfortable in the knowledge that he was making the right policies despite manipulation by Jewish voters and organizations.[36]

CONCLUSION

The genesis of the pro-Israel lobby in the United States dated back to the tenure of two war-time presidents, Franklin Delano Roosevelt and Harry S. Truman, long before 1959 when the American Israel Public Affairs Committee (AIPAC) was born. Once the leadership of the free world began to shift to the Western Hemisphere and the decline of Britain as a great power became evident, the epicenter of the Zionist world movement relocated to the land of the new rising American star. Not only did the Zionist camp begin to prioritize focusing on Washington, the political leadership of the movement began to be assumed by the likes of Ben Gurion and not by Weizmann. Gradualists who articulated the case for a Jewish commonwealth in Palestine, which would be open to its Arab residents and continue under British control, failed during the Biltmore Conference to inspire American Zionists who were frightened by the impact of the Holocaust. These made immigration to Palestine their primary focus and fought the Anglo-American Commission of Inquiry and the Morrison-Grady Plan, both of which opted for a federated state for the two contending communities, but with Jerusalem remaining under British control. American Zionists struggled to keep the attention of the world focused on Jewish DP camps in Europe while demanding opening up the gates of immigration to Palestine. The United States, on the other hand, worried about the survival of the Anglo-American alliance, especially as the Cold War loomed on the horizon. It also see-sawed between withdrawing from the Palestine dilemma in order to nurture its relationship with the Arab Gulf countries, or pursuing greater engagement with its British ally in order to achieve a greater outcome for its political supporters at home. It took a concerted effort of a new phenomenon in American public life, namely pro-

Zionist presidential advisers such as Clark Clifford and David K. Niles, to steer the policies of an exasperated Truman towards recognition of the gestating Zionist entity in Palestine. This achievement entailed confronting hostile American cabinet members, who in addition to their concern for the weakening of the American-British alliance also fretted over the possibility of alienating the Arab oil producers. Zionist efforts bore fruit only because they threatened an American president with the backlash of angered American Jewish voters. Pro-Zionist advisers also continued to predict that the Arab Palestinians will not offer any resistance to the creation of a Jewish state in their midst and to assure the President of the loyalty and cooperation of the Arab oil countries. Thus, when Truman speedily extended official recognition to the new state of Israel, the gesture was recommended to him wrapped in biblical phraseology and presented as an inevitable happening. But the battle for the creation of a Jewish state was not over yet, as events on the ground threatened to wipe out gains in the major halls of power. Zionist objectives in Palestine quickly expanded beyond the issue of immigration, with statehood and a capital in Jerusalem as the prize. The survival of the state, however, became forever linked with Israel's influence in Washington.

NOTES

1. Quoted in: Alfred Lilienthal, *The Zionist Connection: What Price Peace?* (New York: Middle East Perspectives, Inc., 1979): 30.

2. Smith, *Palestine and the Arab-Israeli Conflict*, 62.

3. Wilbur Crane Eveland, *Ropes of Sand: America's Failure in the Middle East* (New York: W. W. Norton and Co., 1980): 33–6.

4. James Gelvin, "The Ironic Legacy of the King-Crane Commission," in *The Middle East and the United States*, David W. Lesch and Mark L. Haas, eds., 5th ed. (Boulder, CO: Westview Press, 2012): 15–6.

5. Eveland, *Ropes of Sand*, 349N.

6. Tivnan, *The Lobby*, 15–7.

7. Quoted in Ibid., 17.

8. Ibid., 17–23.

9. Laqueuer, *A History of Zionism*, 507–10.

10. Ibid., 549–55.

11. Ibid., 554–5.

12. The American Jewish Committee—Committee on Peace Problems Proposed Plans for the Future of Palestine, "Interpretations of Jewish Commonwealth by Leading Zionist Personalities and Groups." www.bjpa.org/Publications/downloadFile.cfm?FileID=1987. Accessed 6/13/2014.

13. See: Louis E. Levinthal, "The Case for a Jewish Commonwealth in Palestine," *The Annals of the American Academy of Political and Social Science*, Vol. 240, July 1945, 89. Government Printing Office, ann.sagepub.com/content/240/1/89.full.pdf. Accessed 6/13/2014.

14. Smith, *Palestine and the Arab-Israeli Conflict*, 117–8.

15. John B. Judis, *Genesis: Truman, American Jews, and the Origins of the Arab-Israeli Conflict* (New York: Farrar Straus and Giroux, 2014): 173–5.

16. Lilienthal, *The Zionist Connection*, 95, 235.

17. Judis, *Genesis*, 197.

18. Lilienthal, *The Zionist Connection*, 36–7.

19. "Col. Hoskins, Anti-Zionist, Named State Department Consultant on Near Eastern Affairs," *Jewish Telegraphic Agency* (March 1, 1951). www.jta.org/.../col-hoskins-anti-zionist-name. Accessed 6/17/2014.

20. Lilienthal, *The Zionist Connection*, 37–9.

21. Judis, *Genesis*, 6, 213–4.

22. Donald E. Wagner, "The Mainline Protestant Churches and the Holy Land," in *Zionism and the Quest for Justice in the Holy Land*, eds., Donald E. Wagner and Walter T. Davis (Eugene, OR: Pickwick Publications, 2014): 146–51. See also: Eric Alterman, "Israel and the Liberal Imagination," *The Nation*, Vol. 266, No. 16 (May 4, 1998): 25.

23. Lilienthal, *The Zionist Connection*, 43–5.

24. Laqueur, *A History of Zionism*, 554.

25. Judis, *Genesis*, 199–201.

26. Ibid., 201–6.

27. Ibid., 206–14.

28. Ibid., 214–27.

29. Philip Mattar, ed., *Encyclopedia of the Palestinians*, Rev. ed. (New York: Facts on File, 2005): 323.

30. Judis, *Genesis*, 224–7.

31. Ibid., 228–35.

32. Ibid., 356.

33. Walter Russell Mead, "The New Israel and the Old: Why Gentile Americans Back the Jewish State," *Foreign Affairs*, Vol. 87, No. 4 (July/August 2008): 28.

34. Ibid., 28, 37, 40.

35. Ibid., 46.

36. Kathleen Christison, "U.S. Policy and the Palestinians: Bound by a Frame," *Journal of Palestine Studies*, Vol. 26, No. 4 (Summer 1997): 54.

Chapter Three

The Battle for Jerusalem:
Bucking the International Consensus

Seeking a moral argument, Truman hued closely to his advisers' biblical rationalization for recognition of the new state of Israel. He also repeatedly added progressive terms to describe Jewish achievements in Palestine, especially when addressing American Jewish audiences. He gloated on May 26, 1952, at a JNF event by taking credit for committing the United States to this policy in the face of strong opposition by members of his own government:

> The growth and progress of the new State of Israel are a source of great satisfaction for me. I had faith in Israel even before it was established. I knew it was based on the love of freedom, which has been the guiding star of the Jewish people since the day of Moses. [1]

His plaudits were occasioned by the JNF's announcement of planting trees in his name at a village renamed Kfar Truman. By October of that same year, he sounded even more ebullient about Israeli deeds, while at the same time willing to gloss over the tragic consequences suffered by the Palestinian Arabs as a result of Israel's expansion beyond the UN partition lines. At another event organized by the National Jewish Welfare Board, he expressed admiration for the way in which Israel dealt with difficult issues, adding:

> Since its creation, it has admitted not 100,000 but 700,000 refugees. This has not been easy. . . . Peace between Israel and the Arab states has been an important objective of our Near Eastern policy . . . . The American people understand the problem of Israel. Part of our sympathetic Interest in the future of Israel stems from the fact that we, too, once proclaimed our own independence. . . . We too, are people of diverse origins. [2]

47

Remarkably, an American president reflected before his audience the sum total of his putative propaganda with nary a single disapproving remark. Bestowing this kind of legitimacy on one of the most controversial minorities in the United States at the time was meant to dispel any notion of the existence of differences between the two countries. In reality, reference to the Jewish refugee issue was meant to minimize the gravity of the Arab refugee crisis which was to haunt successive American administrations. More importantly, omitting any reference to Jerusalem was an attempt to conceal widening differences over the fate of the holy city. This was the time when Israel and the United States prepared to grapple with each other over the two most grievous issues of the 1948 Arab-Israeli War, Jerusalem and the Arab refugees.

JERUSALEM, THE EPICENTER OF THE WAR

According to some experts, Zionist policy on the holy city, or Zion, evolved over a ten-year period dating back to the 1937 Peel Commission. While still occupied with the Mandate's restrictive policy towards Europe's displaced Jewish survivors of the Holocaust, the Yishuv leadership was also determined to prevent the internationalization of Jerusalem and its holy sites. By creating facts on the ground, this battle quickly mutated into a race to blunt the momentum of UN reports and resolutions. If fighting the British and the international community presented Israel with great difficulties, battling other contenders for the physical possession of the city presented substantial opportunities. From the Peel Commission until statehood, the fate of Jerusalem was in Ben Gurion's and Moshe Sharett's hands, the first as head of Mapai and virtually all of the Yishuv, and the latter as head of the JA. The two, destined to be Israel's first prime minister and foreign minister respectively, differed substantially over the pace and military trajectory of the Zionist statehood campaign. Both favored partitioning Jerusalem into the Old and the New City, and separating the eastern, predominantly Arab section of the New City from the predominantly Jewish section. Both preferred detaching Mt. Scopus and its two Jewish sites, Hebrew University and Hadassah Hospital, from the Arab part of the New City, attaching them to the Jewish section. They also advocated the internationalization of the holy places, despite their location within the Arab part of East Jerusalem. But these were inchoate ideas throughout the period of WWII as the Yishuv battled the Mandate over the issue of immigration. The visible marginalization of the Jerusalem question from the Peel Commission until the Morrison-Grady Plan went unchallenged.[3]

UNSCOP DEFINES THE ISSUE

When the UN dispatched its own investigative team, United Nations Special Committee on Palestine (UNSCOP) to that country in May 1947, Ben Gurion was interviewed regarding the Zionists' plans for the city. The Jewish leader was evasive, indicating that the Yishuv approved the partitioning of the city but without specifying any boundaries, while recommending placing the holy places under international sovereignty. The latter preference was seen as a net gain since it would remove the sites from Arab control while there was no hope of ceding them to the Jewish side. What he meant, of course, was that the western half of the city should be joined to the Jewish state, while the entire eastern section of Jerusalem, or the Arab side, should be international-ized. However, the Zionist leadership was fully aware of the coolness of some of UNSCOP's members to the idea of ceding any part of the city to the future Jewish state, leaning largely towards internationalizing the city in its entirety. Fearful lest claiming the New City would jeopardize UN backing for statehood, Ben Gurion dropped any claims to Jerusalem. Convinced that admission to the UN held a higher value than confronting the world body over Jerusalem, the JA quickly yielded to UNSCOP's resurrection of the Peel Commission's call for the internationalization option. But as the UN launched its debate over UNSCOP's majority and minority reports and the call for partitioning Palestine, a parallel debate within the JA, the Yishuv's effective government, broke wide open. Some members raised the cry, "No Zionism without Zion," while others called for a pragmatic approach culmi-nating in statehood. A third option centered on the creation of an Arab and a Jewish Jerusalem, but leaving the holy places under international control. [4]

Since the JA was unable to adopt a unified position, Sharett, its represen-tative to the UN during the statehood debate, was instructed to seek the best possible deal within the framework of internationalization, which the major-ity of UN members favored. Sharett offered the following recommendations to the Sub-Committee on Borders of the General Assembly: (1) A referen-dum after ten years of internationalization to ascertain the residents' views on the city's future, (2) a joint municipal council to be based on the Arab and Jewish population ratios within the city, (3) dividing the city into an Arab, a Jewish and an international municipal zones. The Yishuv was hopeful that if these recommendations were accepted the Jewish majority in the city would eventually be able to control all of Jerusalem. But the sub-committee was not enthusiastic and the JA anticipated defeat and turned to statehood instead. When General Assembly Res. 181 (II) was adopted it was considered a victory for the JA's Jerusalem position since it approved the ten-year referen-dum and the municipal council idea, which was to be based on the population ratios of the respective communities. The General Assembly, however, re-tained for itself the right to name the city's international trustees and to ensure the autonomy of each ethnic zone. But by accepting these conditions, the JA was also banking on rejection by the Arabs which would spell failure of internationalization, making the incorporation of West Jerusalem into the new Jewish state more palatable to the international community. Yet, Israeli historian Motti Golani argued that even then, the departure of the JA's leadership from Jerusalem to Tel Aviv on December 9, 1947, before the battle for the city heated up, should be understood as a genuine gesture of acceptance of the impending internationalization plan. One could also offer the counter-argument that this move, which did not stop Ben Gurion from regularly visiting Jerusalem in order to direct the military battle, was also proof of involvement in military planning in order to seize as much territory as possible. By December 1947, and with mounting anger by the city's Jewish residents over their perceived abandonment, the JA's Situation Committee created a sub-committee called the D Committee, or the Jerusalem Committee. This was charged with creating conditions for establishing an autonomous Jewish section, but within the framework of internationalization. More importantly, during the same month, Ben Gurion turned down a request to declare Herzliya in the north as the capital of the new state while still awaiting a final clarification of the status of Jerusalem.[5]

BEN GURION'S COMMITMENT
TO INTERNATIONALIZATION WAVERS

Ben Gurion's apparent willingness to retreat from Jerusalem and direct the war effort from Tel Aviv where the state's fledgling military forces were being organized, soon changed as a result of a development on the ground. Specifically, Jerusalem became the focal theater of war between the Jordanian armed forces and local Jewish militias as soon as the Yishuv declared statehood. Nevertheless, when the Hagana, the main faction in the future Israel Defense Forces (IDF), attempted to consolidate its control over the Western part of the city by racing to occupy vacated British military positions, this did not mean a rush on the Old City. As Jordanian forces strengthened their military hold on that section, Ben Gurion was reluctant to push the Hagana towards the Old City. Some Israeli historians attributed this to a genuine desire on his part to prevent Israeli desecration of Jerusalem's Christian and Muslim holy places. This claim, however, was contradicted by Ben Gurion's secret contacts with Transjordan to reach an agreement over the only part of Palestine which King Abdullah so desired that he was willing to break ranks with other Arab states in order to add it to his kingdom. The Israeli leader's objective was not only to circumvent General Assembly Res. 181, with its commitment to the internationalization of the city, but also to make West Jerusalem Israel's capital without risking the country's admission to the world body. While this diplomatic battle was quietly waged, Israel appointed Dov (Bernard) Joseph as the city's military governor on August 1, 1948, a move which did not call for a declaration of annexation. Joseph retained this post until March 1949, when it was eliminated after the newly created ministry of the interior appointed a municipal council headed by Daniel Auster, the last deputy-mayor of the Arab-Jewish council under the Mandate.[6]

Once Israel was admitted to the UN in May 1949, the annexation of Jerusalem became inevitable. The occasion was provided by Australia's move to seek the ratification of the internationalization resolution in November 1949, after two years have lapsed since approving the original decree. Fearing that the approval would receive an overwhelming number of votes, Sharett resigned. This gave Ben Gurion the excuse to announce the annexation decree on December 5, 1949. After the General Assembly passed the resolution on December 9, he reacted by declaring Jerusalem as the eternal capital of Israel, adding that this historical fact cannot be altered by a UN vote. One reason for this rushed move was that the prime minister feared that United States and UN conciliatory policy towards the whole Palestine issue would force the surrender of territory in order to accommodate the Arab refugees. Ben Gurion, who harbored a fierce determination throughout his career not to yield any territory, now looked to Jordan to buttress his decision on partitioning the city.[7]

Thus, after only six months of the JA's acceptance of the Partition Resolution (181) with its explicit provision for internationalizing the city, the new state of Israel reversed course. Israelis claimed that military confrontation with the Arabs killed any chance of adopting the General Assembly's recommendations. On September 10, 1948, Sharett, now the foreign minister, sent new instructions to the Israeli delegation at the UN. The memo explained that the inability or reluctance of the international community to enforce the internationalization decree by military means, and Christian silence in the face of Muslim attacks on the holy city in which British officers participated left Israel no choice other than to demand locating West Jerusalem within Israel's borders. But calling on the UN to recognize the new borders meant also recognizing the de facto Jordanian borders emerging from the partitioning of the city. Israel, however, was still unable at that stage to reach a bilateral understanding with Jordan over the status of the city. Israel's only hope was to persuade the UN to adopt the idea of functional internationalization of the holy sites. Since most of these were located within the Jordanian sector, this plan did not threaten Israel with any loss of territory. At the same time, Israel was still hoping to negotiate the annexation of the Jewish Quarter with King Abdullah in order to gain access to the Wailing Wall and to gain control of Mt. Scopus and its cultural sites. Israelis believed that the Jordanians would grant these concessions in return for removing international pressure over their control of East Jerusalem, which included the holy sites and the Arab suburbs.[8]

FUNCTIONAL INTERNATIONALIZATION AND PARTITIONING THE CITY

Proposing a functional internationalization plan limited to the holy sites was supposed to scupper the idea of internationalizing the whole city of all meaning and relevance. The Israelis were also banking on weakening the Vatican's determined opposition to partitioning the city and its preference for placing it under the control of an international council. Thus, they signified verbal acceptance of the Status Quo Law, but the Knesset never passed legislation to that effect until after the 1967 War. Commitment to this law, which safeguarded the rights of all the diverse religions in the city, was believed to open the door to Jewish access to the Wailing Wall, a historic right enshrined in the Law. But despite its public posture as a believer in the sanctity of all holy places, Israel had to contain acts of Jewish desecration of Muslim and Christian places of worship all the way until the 1950s. Jordan, on the other hand, expressed total rejection of the internationalization of any places of worship within its Palestinian territories. Within West Jerusalem itself, the Israelis had to face the desecration of the Mamilla Muslim Cemetery, since neither the UN, nor the Status Quo Law defined burial places as holy places. Jewish charges of Jordanian destruction of synagogues within the Old City, however, were attributed by the British Consul to the nature of fighting within the cramped spaces of walled Jerusalem.[9]

Jordan's fighting capability was already weakened when the British Government, under pressure from Washington pulled out its military officers serving with the Arab Legion in Jerusalem. These amounted to two-thirds of the officer ranks of the Legion. Despite all that, Jewish residents of the Old City finally surrendered to the besieging Jordanian units on 28 May 1948. The Israelis understood that the United States was reluctant to enforce UN resolutions, fearing that the ongoing Berlin Crisis may open the way for possible Soviet intervention. Israeli historians stressed the fact that Ben Gurion's swift annexation of West Jerusalem mainly sprang from his fear of losing ground to the dissident forces of Irgun Zvai Leumi and Lehi which were rushing to fill any security void within sight. He declared on 2 August 1948 that Israeli laws will extend to all parts of the city, an annexation step replicated in East Jerusalem in 1967. The appointment of Joseph as the military governor of the Western part softened Israel's defiance of the internationalization decree by pretending that this was a military occupation in the midst of war. The decree was also made retroactive to 15 May 1948, the date of Israel's declaration of independence. Step by step, Israel was moving towards complete annexation of the area under its military control and pro-claiming it as its capital. Then Transjordan reciprocated by appointing a young officer, Abdullah al-Tall, as the military governor of East Jerusalem, which included the Old City. Establishing facts on the ground, then as now, became Israel's signature policy in Palestine.[10] By that time, according to Avi Shlaim, leading Palestinian figures had already served briefly with King Abdullah after abandoning the AHC and its Husseini connections. Ahmad Hilmi Abd al-Baqi, for example, served briefly as military governor of East Jerusalem under this committee, with a cabinet that included many support-ers of the Mufti, such as Jamal and Raja'i al-Husseini, as well as Michael Abcarius and Anwar Nuseibeh. The Jordanians, however, were determined to control Arab Jerusalem and sever all connections to the Mufti's network. The United States and the UN countered the hardening of positions in Jerusa-lem with the creation of the Palestine Conciliation Commission (PCC), which operated from January to August 1949, with the participation of Tur-key, France, and the United States. The Commission was confronted with Israel's increasing intransigence as it replaced Jerusalem's military governor with a civilian one, followed by an elected municipal council, in effect incor-porating West Jerusalem within the new state. This was followed by conven-ing the first Knesset session in Jerusalem on February 14, 1949, which was another blow to internationalization, all the while claiming that these steps were simply administrative in nature. The State Department reacted by reaching an agreement with Britain and France to bar their representatives from attending the Knesset opening ceremonies in the new capital. But there was no serious reprisal, even after Abba Eban, Israel's representative to the UN, offered the excuse that the Knesset opening was an expression of "an historical motive which had nothing whatever to do with the future status of Jerusalem."[11] In his autobiography, Aubrey Eban reflected sarcastically on the feeble reaction of the PCC, attributing it to the pedestrian credentials of its members. "None of the three governments composing the Conciliation Commission extended itself in the choice of its representatives," he wrote.[12] He explained spitefully that the Turkish representative was a respected jour-nalist but so advanced in age that he had no ability to foresee the future, while the French representative was a non-essential diplomat later assigned the directorship of the Folies Bergére, a position historically filled by the French Foreign Office. As to the American representative, Mark Ethridge, he was a newspaperman who hailed from Kentucky lacking any conception of the complexity of Middle East issues.[13] Additionally, the Commission's plan for dividing the city into autonomous Arab and Jewish spheres and placing a UN commissioner over the holy places, as well as enforcing a ban on immi-gration designed to halt changes in the demographic balance, threatened Zionist plans for the city.[14]

Eban also took note of Ben Gurion's notorious disdain for the Old City
and its typically oriental characteristics of poverty, congestion and general
state of disrepair. In an interview with Cyrus Sulzberger of the *New York
Times,* the Prime Minister had publicly downplayed international concern for
safeguarding the international status of Jerusalem, particularly the holy sites
and the Old City. He insisted that the city should be regarded as no different
than any other Western capital, such as Washington, Paris, or London.[15] His
adherence to the position of "no Zionism without Zion" may have softened
his contempt for the Old City but his military commanders were the ones
who understood the value of seizing Jerusalem once the hostilities of 1948
began. What they feared the most was a linkup between Egyptian forces
advancing from the south and Jordan's Arab Legion which would threaten
the Tel Aviv-Jerusalem corridor, thereby cutting off the flow of supplies,
food and fighters to West Jerusalem. There was no letting down of Jewish
guard over the fate of Jerusalem after that.[16] But Ben Gurion's decision to
defy the UN over Jerusalem had other motives. He felt that yielding on this
important city would only open the way to other UN pressures such as taking
back the Arab refugees and perhaps allowing international control over additional holy places. He saw this as the main test case of international acceptance of Israeli sovereignty. He intended to seize the moment of defiance
over Jerusalem in order to block any attempts to force him to give up the
gains of war in order to achieve peace with the Arabs. Israel, thus, turned
down a chance to yield on the issue of Arab refugees as a price for peace at
the PCC meeting at Lausanne, although contacts with Jordan continued.[17]

ISRAEL'S AND JORDAN'S FATAL EMBRACE

Surprisingly, only Jordan stood in the way of Israel's seizure of the entire
city soon after the declaration of statehood. Relations between the two entities stood out not only because Jordan was the only Arab state which
maintained any contact with the JA, but also because of the latter's complex
strategy of gaining as much territory as possible, including making a run on
the Old City. Failure of the Hagana to take the necessary military initiative
by 19 May 1948, resulted in the Arab Legion's advance on Mt. Scopus and
the Old City, though there was always the suspicion that this was part of a
secret agreement between the two sides. In reality, this was only the natural
outcome of a lack of agreement on Jerusalem, which both sides coveted.[18]

By February of 1949 and in the midst of these developments, the Knesset
convened its first meeting in Jerusalem. This did not take the international
community by surprise since all the signs that Israel was heading in this
direction were in full view. For instance, by September 1948, the Supreme
Court was placed in the Russian Compound in West Jerusalem upon Ben

Joseph's advice. He also recommended that all ministerial departments based in Tel Aviv which can carry out their duties smoothly be transferred to the capital. The appearance of these departments in Jerusalem was taken for granted once a network of roads connected the city to the rest of Israel.[19] Washington and its Western allies were, thus, fully aware for quite a while of Israel's intent to transform the area under its military control into a permanent capital. Although Jordan stopped short of making a similar move until 20 August 1959, it did so only by proclaiming East Jerusalem as its second capital after Amman. The step was taken under mounting pressure by West Bank Palestinians and in response to several years of consolidating Israel's official capital in West Jerusalem. Jordan held only one parliamentary session in the divided city, keeping its change in status symbolic rather than real.[20]

Israel's gradualist, step-by-step approach to the confirmation of the city as its capital finally succeeded in sidelining the UN and the Catholic countries' internationalization plan. The Israeli achievement also defied the recommendations of Folke Bernadotte, UN Peace Mediator, and the PCC. Israel realized its objective by banking on US reluctance to send troops to the region due to rising Cold War tensions, and Britain's apprehension of incurring its ally's displeasure with its continued involvement with Jordan's military forces. But what Israel failed to achieve was maintaining the secret Jordanian alliance which at one time held the promise of reaching an accommodation over the fate of Jerusalem. The JA's contacts with the Jordanian monarch actually had a variegated history. They began in November 1947, when Golda Meir received a verbal notice announcing the King's intention to march on the Arab part of Palestine as soon as the other Arab armies entered the war in defiance of UN resolutions. Jordan's entry into the war, therefore, was not a total surprise to Ben Gurion, the prime minister and defense minister of the new state. But he did not anticipate clashes or bloody confrontations between Jordan's Arab Legion and the IDF over Jerusalem. Relations between the two secret allies reached their nadir when Jordanian units attacked Gush Etzion (Kufur 'Asioun), a stretch of territory marked by four Jewish settlements along the Jerusalem-Hebron road. The Legion's activity was still within the confines of the two entities' secret agreement and the area's designation by the UN as part of the future Arab Palestine.[21]

Many Jordanians, including members of the military, were cognizant of secret pledges by Glubb Pasha (John Baghot Glubb), head of the Legion, to honor Britain's commitment to the partition resolution and to refrain from invading any territory assigned to the Zionist state. According to Abdullah Tall, the Israeli-Jordanian secret pact concluded in a meeting between the King and Sharett near the Rutenberg hydroelectric project outside of Jericho on April 12, 1948, was confined to the partition plan. Still, the pact was in defiance of the unified position of the ALS and had to remain secret, but the

Israelis proceeded to sabotage it by invading the areas designated as Arab. Tall's conclusion was that the Israelis interpreted Jordan's secret acquiescence in the partition plan as a pledge against opposing Israeli forces by military means. This disagreement over the interpretation of the secret pact flared up in a meeting between the King and Golda Meir on May 12, 1948, in Amman. Thus, at the end of the Mandate, Israel sought assurances which the Jordanians were reluctant to give. Meir asked that the King declare a state of peace with Israel and decline sending his troops into Palestine altogether. The King would then be allowed to appoint a governor to rule the Arab part of Palestine, which meant a total commitment to accepting the outcome of the impending hostilities and yielding to Israel's determination of the contours of the new borders. Only under these conditions would the JA be willing to accept Jordan's annexation of what remained of Arab Palestine. After some threats by his Zionist interlocutors, the King was only willing to pledge that the Legion and Iraqi forces would confine themselves to the Arab part as defined by the partition plan. According to Tall, who was the only Arab witness to these talks willing to reveal everything after the war, Meir accepted this deal and sought assurances that the King would keep his promise. Following this encounter, the King never tired of alluding to Meir's rough approach and brutal negotiating method.[22]

It was not surprising, therefore, that Israel rushed to seize any area in New Jerusalem from which the British beat a hasty retreat once the Mandate ended, including as much Arab property as became available. But once the Israelis reached the walls of the Old City, there were no more consultations with their Jordanian ally. Glubb, who headed Jordanian forces in Palestine, was reluctant to engage the Israelis and did not make any offensive moves. He repeatedly asserted later that the Jordanians crossed into Palestine on May 15, 1948, simply to defend territories allocated to the Arabs by the UN, which did not include Jerusalem. But on May 17, the King ordered Glubb to make a stand in defense of the Old City.[23] Meanwhile, Jordanian troops were bitterly opposed to Glubb's decision to uphold the partition plan and the internationalization of the city when Israel openly flouted both. His rationalization was that the ALS itself excluded Jerusalem from the Arab defense lines and adhered to a truce with the Jewish state in this area under the supervision of foreign consuls. To avoid contact with the enemy, Glubb decided to enter Palestine by proceeding to Nablus via the long and increasingly unpaved route of the Allenby Bridge-Jericho-Jiftlek-Nablus road. But Jewish assault on Jerusalem forced Glubb to abandon his original plan and take the direct Jericho-Jerusalem route in order to defend the city. It quickly became apparent that Jewish attacks would not spare areas of Arab concentration, especially as the Hagana directed its fire at the Old City's main gates of Bab al-Amoud, Bab al-Khalil, New Gate, and Nabi Dawud. Home to 60,000 Arabs at the time, most of whom recently arrived from the surrounding conquered villages, the Old City was defended at first by local Palestinian militias under the command of Ahmad Hilmi and Khaled Husseini. The weak defenses of the city and its dwindling provisions prompted local delegations to proceed to Amman and plead for help.[24]

After three days of the Jewish assault on the city, the King was still hesitant to commit his troops to the battlefield due to Glubb's opposition. One of the last delegations to plead with the King was headed by a venerable Palestinian patriot, Dr. Izzat Tannous, who worked for the AHC. The King finally began to send troops under Tall's command on May 18, charging him with joining local defense groups. The battle for the Old City by then was conducted in alleys and narrow streets, barring the use of vehicles. The immediate result was the destruction of old Jewish homes used for observation and the quartering of Jewish militias. When the combatants of the Jewish Quarter finally surrendered, they included a commander of the Hagana and a number from the Irgun, as well as some rabbis who led the negotiations with the Arabs. The Jews, numbering 1,800, surrendered on May 28, 1948, with Tall anxiously guarding them against revenge attacks by the local Arab population. The Jewish defenders and residents knew of the massacre of Deir Yassin, a village nearby, and the arrival of its surviving Arab families to Jerusalem in April, and were fearful of Arab retaliation. Meanwhile, the King was basking in the adulation of the Arab World, a moment of glory squandered by his subsequent decision to keep the Old City under his command. This strengthened the Jewish bid to annex the New City and to defy the UN internationalization decree. Holding on to the Old City, in addition to fortifying the religious legitimacy of the Hashemite dynasty, also presented the King with a strategic advantage. Were it not for the capture of Old Jerusalem by the Jordanians, the entire West Bank would have fallen to Jewish forces which could have easily descended on the Jordan Valley. Since the Old City overlooked the Jerusalem-Jericho route, its capture by the Israelis would have cut off Jordan from eastern Palestine completely.[25]

JEWISH MILITARY INITIATIVES—THE WAILING WALL AND THE CULTURAL SITES OF MT. SCOPUS

As soon as the IDF lost the battle for the Old City, they moved to capture the Latroun Salient which overlooked the Tel Aviv-Jerusalem route. This was within the Arab area according to the partition plan and posed several challenges due to its heavy fortifications. Unlike the Jordanian king who was begged by his commanders to take on the defense of the Old City, Ben Gurion's commanders begged to be released from this dangerous assignment. Part of this was caused by their lack of trust in the secret understanding with Jordan, which did not hold out in Jerusalem, and they feared would not hold out in this case either. Among those expressing public doubt in the effectiveness of these secret contacts was Yigal Yadin, Chief of Operations of the IDF. Indeed, he and others knew of the absence of a well-defined agreement over the fate of Jerusalem, leaving plenty of room for suspicion and misunderstanding. Jerusalem turned out to be the deal-breaker for the JA and the Hashemites. In the absence of a specific agreement with concrete features, both sides proceeded to tighten their grip over the New and Old Cities. The fact that Jerusalem was relegated to an international status, a position neither side favored, led them both to dwell on their fears in secret and ended their trust in each other. [26]

The push to take control of the Jewish state's cultural sites, which were also of strategic value, exacerbated existing tension between the two sides. This was in addition to the Jewish resolve to gain access to the Wailing Wall by any means necessary. At the same time, the Arabs have always resented and feared the rise of Hadassah Hospital and Hebrew University on the slopes of al-Mukaber Hill, north of the city, bestowing on them a strategic advantage. Not surprisingly, the Jordanian forces made these their primary targets in order to protect other locations nearby. Word reached the units around the Old City that the Jordanian Third Division deliberately avoided any clashes with Jewish units on Mt. Scopus. The Jordanian commander, Tall, then received the unusual news of Amman's refusal to attack these installations because they were built with American, not Jewish, funds. But Arab local militias began shelling these buildings from their position within the Augusta Victoria Hospital building, leading to a visit and a reprimand by the American Consul in Jerusalem. King Abdullah eventually ended these attacks, following his usual pattern of yielding to his British commanders by withdrawing from Jewish areas. American pressure to save these buildings from Arab bombardment was also reported by Count Bernadotte in his book *To Jerusalem* (1951). [27]

Arab bitterness towards Jewish commanders who established military positions within these cultural sites was also a reflection of their resentment over the expulsion of the Arab residents of West Jerusalem. As Jewish residents of mixed neighborhoods began to abandon their homes in the midst of fighting, the Hagana Commander in Jerusalem, Israel Amir, began to push the Arabs from their areas in order to make them safe for Jewish habitation. This was the fate of the Arabs of Lifta, Romeima, and Sheikh Badr villages, all of which occupied front positions on the road leading to Tel Aviv. Lifta was singled out for attacks by the Hagana and the Irgun in order to intimidate its residents into leaving, while the Arabs of the two others were pushed out as early as January 1948. The Arab residents sent messages to the Mufti in his Egyptian exile, complaining of lack of weapons and absence of leadership in West Jerusalem. As an example of this, prior to its recent settlement by Jews, the homes of the village of Sheikh Badr were looted by the settlers of Nahlaot.[28] Israeli historians like Benny Morris documented the destruction of many homes in nearby villages by the Hagana and the Palmach militias, even before the war began in a repeat of British practices during the 1936 Arab Revolt. Home demolition, sometimes on suspicion of serving as headquarters of Arab fighters, was believed to be an effective punishment and deterrent. The other anticipated result was easing the eviction of the Arab population from their villages, some fleeing on their own. In several cases, nearby Jewish settlers willingly participated in razing Arab homes, motivated by strategic military considerations and a desire to mete serious punishment on the Arab residents. The "Transfer Committee" of the JA, led by Yosef Weitz, Ezra Danin, and Eliahu Sasson, began to refer to the Arab exodus as a "miracle," with Ben Gurion implementing a policy of blocking the Palestinians' return to their destroyed homes and villages. Therefore, when 143,000 additional Jewish immigrants entered the country between May 1948 and February 1949, they were settled in abandoned Arab villages and the predominantly Arab or mixed sections of Jaffa, Jerusalem, Haifa, and Safed.[29]

It soon became clear that the Jordanian king had no intention of challenging the Israelis in West Jerusalem. The Arab Legion did not have the King's or the British commanders' consent to launch an attack on the New City following its victory in the Old City. Even then, a Jordanian company bombarded Notre Dame Monastery, just outside the gates, until Glubb Pasha ordered it to cease fire. After securing the ground floor of this strategic building, the Jordanians were forbidden from launching additional attacks. This incident, typical of the state of near-insurrection within Jordanian ranks, ended up with the resignation of the Jordanian commanding officer, Lieutenant Ghazi al-Harbi. As a result, the United States held Britain responsible for the intransigence of Jordanian troops and threatened to resume military shipments to Israel unless the British helped enforce a UN truce. Jordanian troops were simply forbidden from undertaking any military operations except for defensive purposes. Major Tall was also refused permission to attack from Jaffa Gate. Some Jordanian commanders sought the release of Iraqi military equipment entrusted to their care in order to facilitate operations beyond the gates of the Old City, but were turned down by their commanding officers and British and American resistance. This left the fate of West Jerusalem in Jewish hands, and by May 1949, Jewish settlers had completed the occupation of most Arab neighborhoods. Governor Joseph reported by early 1950 that looting of Arab properties and non-Jewish foreign buildings such as Notre Dame was rampant. The few remaining Arab families who did not flee West Jerusalem suffered a different fate. These were confined to the Baq'a neighborhood and later segregated in a barbed-wire fenced area of half a square-mile, presumably to protect them from attacks by night-time marauders. Jewish immigrants from North Africa were planted in the border district of Musrara, to eliminate the possibility of re-infiltration by its original Arab inhabitants. By the summer of 1949, even Deir Yassin was not spared, as East European Jewish immigrants were allowed to populate it despite protests by Jewish intellectuals such as the philosopher Martin Buber and Akiva Ernst Simon. Ben Gurion declined to issue a response to these and other protesters, allowing a totally new settlement, Givat Shaul Bet, to rise from the ruins of the village. The number of Arab homes occupied by Jewish immigrants in West Jerusalem alone was estimated to be ten thousand, in a city that Israel always claimed to be totally Jewish built and inhabited.[30]

THE JEWISH CULTURAL LANDMARKS

When the Armistice Agreement between Jordan and Israel was signed on April 3, 1949, signifying merely a cessation of hostilities and not necessarily a final settlement of the Israeli-Palestinian question, negotiations over the fate of the Jewish cultural landmarks inside and outside of the Old City began. The disposition of these sites, which were in Jordanian hands such as the Wailing Wall and the buildings on Mt. Scopus, as well as the Arab neighborhoods of West Jerusalem which were under Israeli control, were all on the table. Tall was already keenly aware of Israel's intention to establish new rights to the Wailing Wall area as soon as the Old City fell to the Jordanians. He received a call on June 19, 1948, from Shaykh Muhammad Shanqity, Minister of Education and Chief Justice of Jordan, advising him to yield to Brigadier Norman Lash's suggestion allowing Jews daily access and visitation rights to the Wailing Wall. Shanqity clarified that the King and the cabinet approved this step and were promised in return a Jewish donation of £50,000 for the general Islamic *awqaf* fund. But Tall reminded the Jordanian official, who was the highest religious authority in the country, that even an offer of £ one million to buy the Wall or change the Status Quo Law had already been rejected by the Palestinian SMC. Lash had already forwarded a list of agenda items suggested by UN mediators after the first truce, intended to facilitate such Jewish visits to the Wall. These included a daily visit of no more than fifty people who would be allowed a one-hour stay at the site. The timing and the route of the visit was to be determined by a UN commission in accordance with Article 8 of the truce agreement. The commission also offered to send an observer to accompany the visitors who would be allowed a two-hour visit on Friday evenings and would be unarmed. Lash justified these concessions by reference to clauses of the armistice agreement which were approved by the ALS. He clarified that he had already consented to visitations by qualified rabbis to the "old temple" (The Hurva Synagogue). The view of Jordanian officers and Arab residents was completely contrary to that of the British commanders, since they demanded some concessions in return. Tall expected Jewish concessions such as allowing Arab visits to

Muslim holy sites in Jaffa, Acre and Haifa, already under Israeli control. Lash did not pursue the matter further, but the question of Jewish visitation rights resurfaced again during the Rhodes Meeting in April 1949, with Dr. Ralph Bunche, Bernadotte's successor, chairing. Again, the Jewish side demanded free access to the Wall, along with visits to Hadassah Hospital and Hebrew University and the removal of military fortifications placed on Mt. Scopus by the Arab Legion. The Israelis made the signing of a final armistice agreement conditional on Arab acceptance of these demands. Upon consultation with his government, Tall requested that the Israeli side should return the Arab neighborhoods of the New City.[31] The conflict over the cultural sites was now locked in place, complicated by the addition of the Arab neighborhoods to the bargaining table. After November 1950, the special UN Commission charged with focusing on these issues following the signing to the Armistice Agreement ceased to exist. Meanwhile, the only concession suggested by Israel was embodied in an informal agreement between the two entities, allowing Israel's Arab Christians to visit Jerusalem during the annual pilgrimage. This privilege, which was denied to Muslims living in the Israeli state, gave rise to accusations of Israeli desire to placate Western Christian public opinion. But the Jordanian King repeatedly argued that he would not be able to guarantee the safety of Jewish visitors when they proceed through the Old City's narrow streets, given the bitterness of the local Arab population as a result of the war.[32] The talks broke down again in May, then picked up again in January 1950, when Israel began to demand that all of the Jewish Quarter be placed under its control. This time, a Palestinian minister in the Jordanian cabinet, Khulusi al-Khayri, echoed Tall's earlier objections and the demand for the return of the Arab neighborhoods of West Jerusalem.[33]

Failure to reach an agreement on Jewish access to the Wall became convenient fodder for Israel's propaganda machine, which presented this as an indictment of Jordan's alleged intolerance of other religions. There was no mention, however, of Israel's refusal to vacate and return the Arab sections of the New City. But Israel did score a meaningful victory over the cultural sites on Mt. Scopus. Despite its overwhelming strategic value as a high location overlooking the entire Old City, the Jerusalem-Amman and Jerusalem-Ramallah routes, as well as some of the Arab neighborhoods of East Jerusalem, such as Shaykh Jarrah, Wadi al-Jouz and several of the city's gates, became demilitarized. During the hostilities, Tall and his Jordanian commanders had always felt that Mt. Scopus could have been easily won had the Jordanian government backed them up. Under pressure by the United States and British authorities, however, Brigadier Lash was allowed by the Jordanian side to sign an agreement with Israel placing the entire Mt. Scopus area under international supervision. Thus, despite the fact that the Israelis were unable to take over this area which was severed from the New City, remaining an island within Jordanian territory, Israel succeeded in neutralizing it completely. Yet, there was no comparable protection for Islamic cultural sites within Israeli territory such as in Jaffa, Haifa, and Acre. Jewish police were permitted to protect the Mt. Scopus sites and a convoy system permitting a periodic changing of the guard by crossing Arab territory with a UN escort was established. Fresh provisions for Jewish guards were allowed to go through the Arab suburbs of East Jerusalem every four weeks. The truce agreement of July 7, 1948, stipulated that the Augusta Victoria Hospital, an Arab institution, as well as the Issawiyah Arab village on the east side of Mt. Scopus, be demilitarized. The agreement, furthermore, limited civilian police in the Jewish section of the area to eighty-five, but the Arab civilian police at the Augusta Victoria were placed at forty.[34] Tall's statement that no distinction existed between Jewish civilian and military police was vindicated in the wake of the June War of 1967, when the Israelis acknowledged sneaking weapons into the Mt. Scopus area via their monthly convoy. Israeli historian Tom Segev revealed that the Israeli motorcade which traveled from Mandelbaum Gate through Jordanian Jerusalem surrounded by UN troops, always smuggled Israeli soldiers dressed like policemen or scientists to report back on the Mt. Scopus area. Additionally, UN personnel often complained about the smuggling of weapons.[35]

THE ISRAELI-JORDANIAN MODUS VIVENDI

The might of the Arab Legion and the Jordanian monarch's flexibility in dealing with the Israelis and the UN peacekeepers alike managed to eclipse the power of the Palestinian militias. This became evident after the death of Abd al-Qader al-Husseini in April 1948, in the battle of al-Qastal. By that time, the Palestinian option had evaporated, especially as a result of the exiling of the Mufti following the 1936 Arab Revolt. Failure of the ALS to overcome its divisions, particularly among those supporting the Egyptian-Saudi axis and those lined up behind the Jordanian-Iraqi axis, weakened Palestinian military resistance. The resultant Israeli-Jordanian accommodation, despite the two sides' severe differences over Jerusalem, could not have been possible without British and American backing, though not always in tandem. The only serious opposition to their plans continued to emanate from the Vatican and its internationalization project, to no avail. After the signing of the Israeli-Jordanian Armistice Agreement on April 3, 1949, neither of the two protested the annexation of one section of the city by the other. By July 1950, King Abdullah's annexation of East Jerusalem became official. At the same time, the King's assassination by a Palestinian did not weaken the kingdom's resolve to retain control of its part of the city. The only way that this mutual understanding was achieved was by overlooking and minimizing the unresolved issues separating them. Israel had to give up its push to attain access to the holy places, while Jordan remained dissatisfied with the terms of demilitarizing Mt. Scopus with its threat to the security of the Old City and its network of roads. Neither had Israel yielded on the issue of granting the Arabs of West Jerusalem the right to return to their homes. Indeed, the Israelis did not seem to mind denial of access to their holy places, despite vociferous protestations to the contrary. As some Israeli authorities pointed out, the JA was willing to forgo control of the Jewish holy places as had been stipulated in 1937 in the Peel Commission's plan. After the dust of war settled in 1948, Israel was more concerned with the loss of Mt. Scopus than the Western Wall in the Old City.[36]

A secret memo by the State Department on 6 February 1951, addressed the issue of Israel's tactics in Jerusalem following the declaration of statehood. It lamented the fact that this issue was dealt with by the international community independently, permitting Israel to pursue any policy unchallenged. The department blamed Jordan and Israel, but not itself, for sabotaging the "corpus separatum" Vatican plan. But the department also recognized the impossibility of implementing the internationalization option at that point in time, claiming to be more interested in a limited scheme which would have ensured the safety of the holy sites and the rights of the international community. Edging towards consenting to Israel's promotion of the idea of functional internationalization as a viable solution, even when it came at Jordan's expense, the United States claimed that it was willing to approve any plan agreed to by Israel and Jordan, as well as some members of the international community. There was no mention of the Palestinians here as a people of interest, and the document, when referring to Israel's activity on this front, portrayed it as still within the international consensus, adding:

> The Israeli Government has proclaimed Jerusalem to be the capital of Israel, an act which, while not specifically prohibited by the UN, is in clear violation of the spirit of the special status recommended for the city by the General Assembly. The Department advised the Israeli Government against moving its capital to Jerusalem, but without effect . . . . A difficult factor in the Palestine dispute is that the Arab states regard anything favorable to Israel as being unfavorable to themselves.[37]

An indication of Israel's well-thought out plan to prevent any serious American undertaking from reversing the decision to move the foreign office to Jerusalem was clarified on July 23, 1952, in a meeting of Eban, Israel's ambassador to the UN, and State Department officers. At the time, Israelis were banking on the US desire to cling to any Arab-Israeli agreement that would save it from a confrontation with the General Assembly. The United States, however, was ready to generate a lot of thunder but no heat if the international status of the holy places was revisited. Henry Byrode, Assistant

Secretary of State for Middle Eastern and South Asian Affairs, assured Eban that no US resolution was forthcoming. He added that the Israeli removal of its foreign office to Jerusalem was "unfortunate," in that it was seized upon with glee by the Arab states. These were apparently convinced, said Byrode, that if Jerusalem became the capital city, it would not be too long before the entire city, east and west, would fall under Israeli sovereignty. The American diplomat asserted plainly that moving the foreign office at that time was not in the US interest. Eban responded by claiming that Israel did not covet Arab Jerusalem, despite the presence of some Jewish holy sites within its confines. He repeated his government's position again calling for the functional internationalization or extraterritorialization of the holy places. He stated that Jordan might even welcome this plan since it promised international protection for its own holy places within the Jewish territory. He promised to work for such an arrangement at the UN which would spare the United States many problems.[38]

A meeting with Arab ambassadors on August 4, 1954, on the same issue finally provided the State Department with a different view. Those participating included the representatives of Lebanon, Egypt, Syria, and Iraq, but the Jordanian ambassador was conspicuously absent. Dr. Charles Malik of Lebanon spoke for the group, stressing the uniqueness of Jerusalem to the three monotheistic faiths and the concern of the Arab states over the relocation of the Israeli foreign office there. He complained that John Foster Dulles, the Secretary of State, seemed to have changed his mind, calling for the internationalization of the "city of Jerusalem," whereas UN resolutions called for the internationalization of the "area of Jerusalem." Malik added that changing the location of the foreign ministry constituted a violation of the Armistice Agreements. These agreements were the only ones which guaranteed peace in this region, and they could not be altered. Malik even complained that the timing of the move coincided with establishing relations with the Soviet Union, a step that emboldened the Israelis to decide on the move. He reiterated the general Arab argument that this relocation, which buttressed the status of Jerusalem as the capital of Israel, could only lead to additional aggression against Arab Jerusalem. He explained that the strategic location of West Jerusalem, which surrounded it with Arab territory, was bound to tempt the Israelis to annex more Arab land. In response, Under-Secretary of State General Walter Bedell expressed his government's strong disapproval of this step, adding that the United States could not be held responsible for this action or any other Israeli moves. He stressed that Israel was a sovereign state and the United States should treat it as it treated the rest of the sovereign Arab states. He also blamed the Arabs for rejecting the UN resolution of 1947 which called for internationalizing the city. The Arabs went to war and must live with the consequences. He emphasized that the United States had no intention of intervening militarily in order to reverse this step. Finally, he declined to comment on this situation being a "violation of the Armistice Agreement."[39]

Whereas, Israel quickly declared West Jerusalem to be its capital in defiance of the UN and the cautionary words of its US ally, the Jordanians proceeded with great hesitation. US diplomats abroad were constantly reporting back on the negative reaction in Arab capitals, threatening to harm America's traditional Arab allies. Byrode recommended to Dulles that Israel should be rebuked publicly in order to mollify Arab allies and reclaim their support. This was carried out when Dulles castigated Israel in his press conference of July 28, 1953, soon after the relocation of the foreign office. But Dulles did not follow his criticism with a public demand for the removal of the office back to Tel Aviv, feeling that his gesture was enough to calm down Arab anger. Indeed, that was exactly how Israel viewed this gesture, not as an official demand, but as a pronouncement meant for the Arabs. Yet, when King Hussein of Jordan convened his cabinet in East Jerusalem on June 27, 1953, American reaction was different. One reason was that the Jordanian foreign office had assured the US embassy that this step fell short of declaring the city as the country's second capital. Whenever Arab representatives in Washington complained to the State Department of contacts between the American Ambassador to Israel and that country's illegal foreign office in Jerusalem, Dulles's evasive reply was that only the UN was authorized to take action on the future of the city.[40]

JEWISH VIEWS ON THE LEGALITY OF CONQUEST

Israeli officials never tired of dismissing the idea of internationalization as basically an isolated campaign mounted by the Vatican. The Roman Catholic Church was said to be only one among thirty other Christian denominations in the city, and owned a mere 17 percent of its holy sites. Teddy Kollek had asserted that this obsession with internationalization lacked the backing of the other Christian denominations within the city itself. Practical considerations and the past experience of other internationalized cities were adequate proof of the impracticality of this policy. Kollek recalled the experiences of Trieste, Shanghai, and Danzig as evidence of the futility and impracticality of this policy, recalling that it even contributed to the outbreak of WWI in the latter's case. A city cannot be administered by an international committee subject to the bureaucracy of the world body, he would emphasize. He also cited the problem of funding, adding that Jerusalem basically relied on donations from the Israeli state, and on education and tourism revenue, but lacked the ability to levy its own taxes.[41]

Hebrew University law professor Ruth Lapidot sprang to the defense of Israel's occupation of many parts of Palestine, but especially of Jerusalem. In her view, the Israelis did not defy international law by annexing the western parts of the city in 1948, since the departure of the British left the whole area without a sovereign. This argument, which morphed into more outspoken support for Israel's conquest later on, always rested on the denial of Palestinian claims as a legitimate sovereign. The argument, furthermore, amounted to a denial of any legitimate Palestinian rights accorded by the UN in the 1947 partition resolution. Lapidot insisted that British departure left a vacuum which could only have been filled by a lawful state, and only Israel exemplified that description. She asserted that the Jordanians seized East Jerusalem by illegal means, ignoring the collusion between it and Israel and casually conflating Palestinian with Jordanian rights. Even the eventual Israeli occupation of East Jerusalem in 1967 was justified as an act of self-defense. By confining the legal equation to Israel and Jordan, Lapidot ended up defending the Israeli case since no Palestinians figured in her analysis. But years later, several arguments rebutting Israeli claims materialized. Among these was the opinion of American professor of international law John Quigley who categorically stated that sovereignty cannot be established over land which had been occupied as a result of a belligerent war. According to the UN Charter, any territory which was occupied as a result of war must be restored to its original inhabitants, and the occupying power was prohibited from changing its sovereignty. Quigley affirmed Palestinian rights in that city, arguing that the internationalization resolution prohibited Israel from exercising free control over its eastern and western parts. In 1979, Jordan's Prince Hasan rebutted both Lapidot's argument and the official Israeli view. He wrote that both the Hague Regulations of 1907 and the Geneva Conventions of 1949 prohibited belligerent occupation, clarifying that Jordan, unlike Israel, did not exercise sovereign control over a part of Jerusalem between 1948 and 1967. Jordan established only a military government, whereas in 1967, Israel imposed an occupation regime.[42]

KING ABDULLAH'S ASSASSINATION

Not surprisingly, Ben Gurion, as well as his military commanders, were dissatisfied with the final transfiguration of the Jerusalem map once the armistice agreement was signed. This became clear as soon as Israel scrambled to "defend" West Jerusalem, and later, seize control of the other piece of the prize, East Jerusalem. Only then did Israel feel satisfied with its boundaries. But another occasion before 1967 revealed the broad outline of Israel's strategic thinking. When King Abdullah was assassinated in 1951 at the courtyard of al-Aqsa Mosque, Ben Gurion could not resist the temptation to display his adamantine posture regarding the holy city. He quickly charged his military aides with drawing plans for seizing all of Jordan's Palestinian holdings, including East Jerusalem. Underscoring what he perceived to be Israel's strategic vulnerability, he felt that this opportunity was too good to miss. His plans, however, were not realized, neither was his other scheme to seize all of the Sinai Peninsula which would lead to the internationalization of the Suez Canal. He advocated opening up Sinai for the establishment of British bases, claiming that the Peninsula's lack of Arab settlement would facilitate this plan, unlike wading through the treacherous and populated territory of the West Bank. He felt that the assassination eased Israel's commitment to the status quo since its tacit Arab ally with whom the Palestinian lands were shared was no longer around, concluding with his familiar Zionist refrain that only force and threats worked with the Arabs.[43]

CONCLUSION

The JA and its successor, the government of independent Israel, had always pursued a strategy based on *realpolitik* and a cold assessment of what was doable and what was not at the time. Accordingly, their priorities and the national programs which they adopted at any given year reflected the realities on the ground both in the United States and in Palestine. These priorities often shifted according to the perceived strengths or weaknesses of their allies. Therefore, during discussions preceding the publication of the Peel Report, Jewish immigration to Palestine and not the fate of Jerusalem topped their list. Despite Britain's insistence on internationalizing the city, the JA favored its partition while retaining control of Mt. Scopus, but later signified its acceptance of the British plan. Then came UNSCOP's cool reception to the idea of ceding territory to a Jewish-controlled West Jerusalem, eventually adopting the British idea of internationalization. This time, the international consensus around this issue headed by the Vatican favored internationalization. Believing that their first priority was the creation of a Jewish state forced the Jewish leadership to mute its push for a Jewish-controlled Jerusalem. Achieving statehood and gaining admission to the UN were now a clear priority.

Deteriorating conditions in Jerusalem, however, opened the way for Ben Gurion to launch a campaign designed to wrest as much territory vacated by departing British troops as was possible. He often justified this action by expressing fear of losing the city to the more militant and extremist Irgun and Lehi forces. He also acted quickly to prevent the encirclement of Jewish-held territory by Palestinian militias and Jordanian troops advancing from the west. Maximizing Jewish control of Arab and mixed neighborhoods within the New City became a strategic necessity. Israel appointed a Jewish military governor in the midst of the battle over the adoption of the partition resolution at the UN. The new Israeli state took every step to camouflage its grand plan for Jerusalem, and speed was of the essence. Civilian bodies were later appointed to secure the annexation of the city, such as a municipal council and a mayor, Daniel Auster, who served as the last deputy-mayor of the Arab-Jewish council under the Mandate. A bizarre and jarring development concerning this appointment became known later, shedding some light on Israeli disregard for Palestinians so rampant during the early years of the state. According to Ilan Pappe, Auster never attempted to shield his former colleague, Hussein al-Khalidi, the Arab deputy-mayor, from expulsion and the loss of his property. Auster also acquiesced in the destruction and erasure of the city's Arab landmarks, such as street names, and the usurpation of abandoned Arab homes by new Jewish immigrants.[44] Yet, the United States and Britain were always quick to condemn any infringement on Israeli rights to Jewish cultural landmarks in the Mt. Scopus area and in the New City. Indeed, United States' later role as Israel's lawyer dated back to the early days of the state.

As soon as Israel was admitted to the UN with a pledge to honor and observe all of its resolutions, particularly the internationalization decree, the annexation of the area which it ceased proceeded apace. In order to deflect international criticism of its unilateral action, the new state came up with the clever idea of internationalizing only the holy places, most of which were in the Jordanian section. Prior to moving its government offices to West Jerusalem, it began building a network of roads linking the city to the rest of Israel. Both the United States and Britain were aware of the significance of these steps and the impending designation of the city as Israel's capital but chose not to take any meaningful steps to defend the internationalization plan. Jordan was emboldened to emulate this move by annexing East Jerusalem to its kingdom, but the weak state limited its defiance of the international community to holding a few cabinet and parliamentary sessions in Arab Jerusalem.

Ben Gurion's greatest fear in addition to being pressured on the Jerusalem issue was to be forced to allow the return of the Arab refugees. If he succumbed to pressure on any of these questions, he feared, a precedent for further pressure would be set. He, thus, made resistance to internationalization his first line of defense. He was also banking on US involvement in the Berlin Crisis and the tensions of the Cold War to discourage any notion of military enforcement of UN resolutions. As expected, international pressure never exceeded the verbal level, leaving the Zionist leadership with much leeway for maneuvering. Israelis also used Jordan's moves in East Jerusalem as a justification, utilizing the Arab state's territorial ambitions for its own avoidance of international sanctions. But Jordanian commanders who were resentful of British withholding of military support continued to contest Israel's push to extend control to the strategic areas outside the Old City. What they feared was the fall of Arab Jerusalem, and with it the fall of the entire eastern part of Palestine. The assassination of King Abdullah in 1951 demonstrated the fragility of the Israeli-Jordanian secret understanding, although the Arab state managed to hold on to East Jerusalem, new and old.

The fallout from the Israeli and Jordanian entrenchment in Jerusalem only set the stage for later and more extensive confrontations. The United States, or at least the Department of State, became woefully aware of the diplomatic cost of its acquiescence in Israel's annexation of West Jerusalem and the permanent change of its status. Its Arab allies became confirmed in their suspicion of the one-sided nature of US Middle East policy, fearing that Israel's next move would be the absorption of East Jerusalem. Byrode recalled years later being threatened by Dr. Nahum Goldman with the sinking of his career if he persisted in his public exhortation of Israel to surrender the attitude of a conquering state and end its misplaced faith in the politics of force.[45] The State Department was being increasingly viewed as hostile to Israel, which, soon after the establishment of the state, became a visible player on the American scene.

NOTES

1. Harry S. Truman, "Address at a Dinner of the Jewish National Fund," May 26, 1952. Foreign Relations of the United States, FRUS, Public Papers of the Presidents, 1952–1953, 374.

2. Harry S. Truman, "Address Prepared for Delivery before the Mobilization Conference of the National Jewish Welfare Board," October 17, 1952. FRUS, 1952–1953, 860.

3. Motti Golani, "Zionism without Zion: The Jerusalem Question, 1947–1949," *The Journal of Israeli History*, Vol. 16, No. 1 (Spring 1995): 39–44.

4. Ibid., 41–2.

5. Ibid., 42–4.

6. Motti Golani, "Jerusalem's Hope," 580–1.

7. Ibid., 581–2.

8. Uri Bialer, "The Road to the Capital: The Establishment of Jerusalem as the Official Seat of the Israeli Government in 1949," *Studies in Zionism*, Vol. 5, No. 2 (Autumn 1984): 273–6.

9. Alisa Rubin Peled, "The Crystallization of an Israeli Policy Towards Muslim and Christian Holy Places, 1948–1955," *Muslim World*, Vol. 84, No. 1–2 (January–April, 1994): 95–115.

10. Yossi Feintuch, *U.S. Policy on Jerusalem* (New York: Greenwood Press, 1987): 38–50; Avi Shlaim, *Israel and Palestine: Reappraisals, Revisions, Refutations* (London: Verso, 2009): 42.

11. Feintuch, *U.S. Policy*, 60–2.

12. Abba Eban, *An Autobiography* (New York: Random House, 1977): 149.

13. Ibid.

14. Bialer, "The Road to the Capital," 287.

15. Ibid., 169.

16. Dan Kurzman, *Soldier of Peace: The Life of Yitzhak Rabin, 1922–1995* (New York: Harper Collins, 1998): 129–32.

17. Avi Shlaim, *The Iron Wall: Israel and the Arab World* (New York and London: W. W. Norton, 2000): 60.

18. Golani, "Zionism without Zion," 46.

19. Yossi Katz and Yair Paz, "The Transfer of Government Ministries to Jerusalem, 1948—49: Continuity or Change in the Zionist Attitude to Jerusalem," *Journal of Israeli History*, Vol. 23, No. 2 (Autumn 2004): 233.

20. Feintuch, *U.S. Policy*, 119.

21. Avi Shlaim, "Israel and the Arab Coalition in 1948," in *The War for Palestine: Rewriting the History of 1948, Avi Shlaim and Eugene L. Rogan*, eds. (Cambridge: Cambridge University Press, 2001): 90.

22. Abdullah Tall, *Karithat Filastin: Muthakarat Abdullah al-Tall/The Palestine Catastrophe: The Memoirs of Abdullah al-Tall* (Cairo: no publisher, 1999): 35–9, 65–8.

23. Shlaim, "Israel and the Arab Coalition," 90–1.

24. Tall, *Karithat*, 78, 96, 99–100.

25. Ibid., 100–42. On the massacre of Deir Yassin, see: Nathan Krystall, "The Fall of the New City, 1947–1950," in *Jerusalem 1948: The Arab Neighborhoods and Their Fate in the War*, Salim Tamari, ed. (Jerusalem and Bethlehem: Institute of Jerusalem Studies and Badil Resource Center, 1999): 92–146.

26. Shlaim,"Israel and the Arab Coalition," 91–2.

27. Tall, *Karithat*, 156–61.

28. Krystall, "The Fall of the New City," 100–02.

29. Benny Morris, *The Birth of the Palestinian Refugee Problem, 1947–1949* (Cambridge: Cambridge University Press, 1991): 155–96.

30. Krystall, "The Fall of the New City," 115–6, 121–3.

31. Tall, *Karithat*, 223–5, 473–4.

32. Ghada Talhami, "The Modern History of Islamic Jerusalem: Academic Myths and Propaganda," *Middle East Policy*, VII, No. 2 (February 2000): 125–6. See also: Gabriel Padon, "The Divided City: 1948–1967," in *Jerusalem*, Msgr. John M. Osterreicher and Anne Sinai, eds. (New York: The John Day Co.,1974): 87, 91–2, 97.

33. Krystall, "The Fall of the New City," 127.

34. Tall, *Karithat*, 234–7.

35. Tom Segev, *1967: Israel, the War, and the Year that Transformed the Middle East* (New York: Henry Holt, 2005): 170–1.

36. Golani, "Jerusalem's Hope Lies Only in Partition: Israeli Policy on the Jerusalem Question, 1948—1967," *International Journal of Middle Eastern Studies*, Vol. 31, No. 4 (November 1999): 584–5.

37. Department of State Policy Statement, 6 February 1951, Israel, FRUS, Vol. V, The Near East and Africa, 575–6.

38. Memo of Conversation by the Officer in Charge of Palestine—Israel–Jordan Affairs (Fred Waller), July 23, 1952. FRUS, Vol. IX, Part II, The Near and Middle East, 1952–1954, 967–8.

39. Memo of Conversation by Deputy Assistant Secretary of State for Near Eastern Affairs (John D. Dernegan), August 4, 1953. FRUS, Vol. IX, Part II, 1266–8.

40. Feintuch, *U.S. Policy*, 111–5.

41. Teddy Kollek, "Introduction: Jerusalem—Today and Tomorrow," in *Jerusalem: Problems and Prospects*, Joel L. Kramer, ed. (New York: Praeger, 1980): 1–5.

42. David Hulme, *Identity, Ideology, and the Future of Jerusalem* (New York: Palgrave Macmillan, 2006): 45–8.

43. Avi Shlaim, *Lion of Jordan: The Life of King Hussein in War and Peace* (New York: Alfred A. Knopf, 2008): 38; Shlaim, *The Iron Wall*, 67–8.

44. Ilan Pappé, "The Window Dressers: The Signatories of Israel's Proclamation of Independence," *The Link*, Vol. 48, Issue 1 (January–March, 2015): 6.

45. Harry S. Truman Presidential Library and Museum. Oral History Interview with Henry Byrode. www.trumanlibrary.org. Accessed 1/30/2015.

Chapter Four

Planning for Expansion: Overcoming the Limitations of the First Borders

In a rare revelation of how Zionist leaders planned to circumvent Muslim attachment to the holy sites of Jerusalem, Herzl replied to the inquiries of Sultan Abd al-Hamid II in 1896, in these words:

> We could get around that difficulty. We shall extra-territorialize Jerusalem, which will then belong to nobody and yet to everybody—the holy places which will become the joint possession of all believers—the great condominium of culture and morality. [1]

Clearly, Herzl's successors, the leaders of the JA, were always inspired by his tactical approach to eventual usurpation of the Old City. It was also Herzl who planted the idea of Europeanizing the Old City by demolishing all the derelict and filthy secular buildings and by surrounding the holy sites with a sanitized new city. He even considered erecting the new Jewish capital on Mt. Carmel, in Haifa, though he never abandoned the prospect of detaching Jerusalem from its medieval moorings. [2]

THE ARMISTICE AGREEMENT AND ITS LOOSE ENDS

After the signing of the Rhodes Armistice Agreement of 1951, secret meetings between the Israelis and the Jordanians resumed. The United States was definitely involved through its own diplomats in Amman. For instance, the American Chargé d'Affaires, A. David Fritzlan, reported to the State Department in a secret memo that Jordanian Prime Minister, Samir Rifa'i, and Reuven Shiloah, Israeli foreign ministry adviser, met at Shuneh in the Jordan Valley to streamline the latest agreement. The Israelis demanded that Jordan comply with specific articles, particularly Article VIII, concerning access to Jewish cultural sites. When Rifa'i demanded the evacuation of certain areas in exchange, Sir Alec Kirkbride, British Minister in Amman, intervened by providing American diplomats with some of Rifa'i's anticipated demands in the next meeting with Shiloah. These included allowing displaced Palestinian villagers to access their fields beyond the armistice lines in order to harvest their fields even if these lands fell within Israeli territory. Jordan also sought the opening of the Latrun-Jerusalem road, restoring the shorter connection between Bethlehem and Jerusalem which existed before the 1948 War. If these demands were met, the Jordanians promised to allow the Jewish cultural institutions on Mt. Scopus to resume their normal activities but under Jordanian military supervision. There were also promises of allowing Jewish visits to the Wailing Wall, all of which remained contingent upon compensating the Arabs of West Jerusalem for their lost properties. Rifa'i also promised to reopen the file of Jewish properties in the Old City. But during the second secret meeting in the Jordan Valley, Shiloah sprang to the offensive. He asserted that Israel had always viewed Mt. Scopus to be part of Israel, discounting any possibility of acceding to Jordan's demands. But even though Rifa'i chose not to refer to the map attached to the Armistice Agreement which clearly placed Mt. Scopus within Jordanian territory, he demanded to learn the basis of Shiloah's assertions. The Israeli official later promised to provide an answer. He did, however, affirm his government's inability to compensate the Arabs of West Jerusalem.[3]

American efforts to bridge the gap between the Israeli and Jordanian positions continued in Washington. In a meeting at the State Department on 23 July 1952, headed by Fred E. Waller who was in charge of Palestine-Israel-Jordan affairs, an attempt to ascertain Israel's future plans for the city was made. Eban suggested that if the United States intended to take up the issue of Jerusalem's holy sites at the next UN General Assembly meeting, it should consider encouraging Israel and Jordan to reach an agreement first. He said that it would be advisable not to pursue the same strategy of 1950, when moving the foreign office to Jerusalem was debated at the UN before reaching an understanding by the parties. Byrode commented, however, that the foreign office move was an ill-guided step since it provided the Arabs with a convenient issue with which to whip up the enemy during the UN debate. He stated that the Arabs were now certain that Israel would soon annex Arab Jerusalem. But Eban denied that this was being planned, reiterating Israel's well-known preference for establishing a UN regime over all of the holy places.[4] American Ambassador to Jordan, Lester D. Mallory, wrote to the State Department in 1954, contrasting Jordan's position on the internationalization of the city with that of the other Arab states. He explained that since the city was under Jordan's political control, any attempt to separate it from the rest of the kingdom by peaceful negotiations was unrealistic. This meant that the prospect of Jordanian acceptance of functional international-ization was also slim, especially in light of the fact that other Christian and Islamic holy places existed in Nazareth and other locations which were part of Israel, and subsequently not included in this plan.[5]

THE AFTERMATH OF THE 1948 WAR

Much of the difficulty of reaching an Arab-Jewish accommodation over the Jerusalem question was a function of the lingering bitterness following the end of hostilities. Benny Morris, who documented the forced flight of Pales-tinian refugees, also wrote on the brutality of both sides characterizing the conduct of the war. He highlighted especially the inevitable excesses of Jewish fighters, attributing these to their quick and overwhelming victory on the battlefield. He wrote that not unlike other wars fought within other settled areas, the number of civilian casualties was unexpectedly high. The Irgun and Stern gangs in particular failed to discriminate between regular combat-ants and women, children, and other civilians. Neither did the Arabs. He did not exempt members of the IDF from these atrocities, accusing them of committing rapes in various locations despite frequent reference to "the pur-ity of arms" by their leaders. He added:

> In truth, however, the Jews committed far more atrocities than the Arabs and killed far more civilians and POWs in deliberate acts of brutality in the course of 1948 . . . the war itself afforded the Arabs infinitely fewer opportunities to massacre their foes.[6]

This perverted logic, nevertheless, did not explain the tragic and massive loss of Arab life and the predictable bitterness of future generations for many years to come.

As Jordanians, Palestinians, and Israelis settled down to sharing their forced domicile in close proximity of each other, contacts across the Jerusa-lem armistice lines became regularized. These lines left Israeli Jerusalem an isolated enclave which was connected to the rest of Israel through a narrow and unsecured land corridor. Additionally, its population boasted a strong religious identity compared to the secular Zionists who settled in Tel Aviv. Orthodox Jews whose ranks dominated the population were openly hostile to Zionism as a political creed. On the eve of the 1967 War, Jewish inhabitants of West Jerusalem had increased to 200,000, making it the third-largest ur-ban center after Tel Aviv and Haifa. Meanwhile, the Jordanians presided over a precarious modus vivendi with the Israelis and regularly admitted Jewish pilgrims who held foreign passports to the Wailing Wall area. The crossing point between the two sides of Jerusalem was established on a site known as the Mandelbaum Gate. This was a road block painted in black and white on the Israeli side and in red and white on the Jordanian side, with a small open square in the middle. The gate was named after Yakov Mandelbaum who built a home there years earlier. The Jordanians at one point demanded a change in name but were undecided whether to call it Salah al-Din or the Gate of Return (Bab al-'Awdah), in memory of the refugees who were yearning to be repatriated.[7]

The house was built by a Jewish merchant (in one account, his name was given as Simcha Mandelbaum) who hoped to encourage other Jews to move out of the Old City and expand the city's northern boundary near "the Third Wall." The land around his house was owned by the Islamic *awqaf*, which forbade selling it to anyone, Muslims or Jews. Thus, the Mandelbaum house was the only remaining structure in the area, which later became a no-man's land. His widow, Esther Liba, and her family left the house during the 1948 War upon the Hagana's request since it stood between the Jewish and the Jordanian-controlled areas. The house was demolished in a Jordanian attack in 1948, leaving only part of the front wall with its gate standing. Soon after the 1967 hostilities, Kollek ordered it demolished. Asked by a journalist to justify this order in which, in all probability, exceeded his authority, Kollek said he did not wish to leave the landmark standing since no one knew under whose responsibility it fell. When asked if he knew the identity of the owner, Kollek said carelessly that he thought he was a certain German doctor.[8] Although traffic from the Israeli side, which required a case-by-case approval by the two governments, favored Christian religious functionaries and Christian Arab citizens of Israel, UN personnel who managed this crossing point rarely reported any breakdown of the rules. For most Palestinians in Israel who endured under a military government from 1948 until 1967, the gate was a harbinger of their restricted movement and uncertain identity whenever they attempted to link up with members of their divided families across the Green Line with the help of the International Red Cross. These crossings were mainly the privilege of those Christian Palestinians who were allowed to visit the holy sites in Jerusalem and Bethlehem during the Christmas holidays.[9]

The issue of Mt. Scopus and who had a right to exercise full control over its institutions remained unsettled. The American ambassador to Egypt, Jefferson Caffrey, responded in 1953 to a State Department query regarding the status of Jerusalem by referring to a Swedish resolution originally submitted in December 1950 to an ad hoc committee of the General Assembly. He doubted whether the Catholic Church would consent to such a draft since it confirmed the primacy of the Greek Orthodox Church in the city and its claim to specific holy places. Other commentary on the draft regarded it as an opportunity to force Israel's clear renunciation of any claims to the Old City. But other US diplomats feared that the revival of the Swedish proposal would be viewed by the Arabs as a confirmation of Israel's fait accompli in

Jerusalem.[10] Unrestricted access to Mt. Scopus, however, continued to be the main objective of the Israeli state. When the Suez War (referred to by Israelis as The Sinai War) of October-November 1956 began, Israel saw an opportunity to change the borderline on the Eastern Front, specifically by launching an operation in Jerusalem to seize the road leading to Mt. Scopus. It hoped to justify this action by referencing Jordan's denial of free access to the Scopus hill. The Operation Branch of the IDF General Staff, thus, came up with a plan which seemed workable at the time and received the approval of Chief of Staff Dayan. The proposed plan of attack targeted not only the road but also all of Arab East Jerusalem, as well as the Jordanian-held area west of the River, meaning the West Bank. All that was needed was a Jordanian provocation which eventually materialized when word was received form the Israeli ambassador to France, claiming that an Iraqi Division was about to cross into Jordan. Ben Gurion activated the plan on October 17, beginning with taking the road to Mt. Scopus. But this was never implemented since the plan threatened to unleash a war with Jordan which some believed to be counter to Israel's best interests. In reality, the military plan was abandoned due to the dissipation of the rumor of Iraqi military advance on Jordan. Israel's eastern neighbor, apparently, had no intention of turning its temporary military pact with Egypt at the time into a more permanent political agreement.[11]

Israel's desire to turn the Suez War into an opportunity to redraw the regional map was also expressed by Ben Gurion in his initial contact with the French government in order to plan the war. In a secret meeting just before the attacks began and prior to the arrival of British Foreign Secretary Selwyn Lloyd, Ben Gurion announced that in his view Jordan was no longer a viable state and should be divided between his country and Iraq. The Arab state, however, should undertake the task of settling the Palestinian refugees in the East Bank before being allowed to take over this territory, as well as agree to the signing of a peace agreement with Israel. He was so confident of victory that he openly made a bid for the entire West Bank to be ceded to his state, but as a semi-autonomous area separate from the Israeli entity. While at it, he also revived one of Zionism's oldest dreams first unveiled during the Paris Peace Conference, namely expanding north up to the Litani River in order to protect Lebanon from its Muslim majority and stabilize it as a Christian state. All of these changes, as he hoped, were inspired by the imminent victory of the tripartite British, French, and Israeli alliance, leading up to the final internationalization of the Suez Canal.[12] While Israel was aggressively touting its victimization and eviction from its cultural institutions on Mt. Scopus, which sat over an enclave within Jordanian territory, it did not always fulfill its obligations under the terms of the Armistice Agreement. Israel, as became known later, sent hidden military supplies and disguised military personnel to boost the defenses of the area, receiving university books smuggled out on the return trip. Neutrality and any semblance of abiding by the rules of the game were the farthest things from Israel's mind.[13]

MULTIFARIOUS CONQUEST TO ABSORPTION PLANS

While the United States continued its resistance to Israeli removal of its political institutions to West Jerusalem, the Israelis persisted in their supercilious moves. American Chargé d'Affaires, Francis H. Russell, captured Ben Gurion's resolute fixation on gaining world recognition for these changes by quoting him as saying:

> When is your government going to stop boycotting Jerusalem? Your present policy is blasphemy. Christ himself came to Jerusalem. So did Dulles, a religious man. Other religions to be sure, have interest in Jerusalem but those who launched them were Jews. Reason given by Western powers for not wanting move of Foreign Ministry to Jerusalem was that it would increase tension. That would mean Arabs would determine Jerusalem policy. Jews have been in Jerusalem for thousands of years and government is thereby right. Government of Israel, not just particular ministries or branches of the government, but government itself, has been in Jerusalem since 1949. Therefore, no basis for change in Western powers policy because of move of Foreign Ministry.[14]

The prime minister's assertion of absolute sovereignty over this conquered city, evoking biblical claims and rejecting any need to submit to pre-approval by "Arabs," was not lost on the American diplomat. The same attitude which led Ben Gurion to assert his right to change the status of Jerusalem unilaterally also led to enunciating other rights to change the boundaries of the region, also unilaterally, following the Suez War. According to Wilbur Crane Eveland, one-time adviser to the CIA, Israel had actually renounced the terms of the 1949 Armistice Agreement by joining the tripartite attack on Egypt during the Suez War, which rendered the status of its own borders rather problematic.[15]

This did not deter Israel from hatching several military plans to expand its territory when another armed confrontation with its neighbors developed, making the period of 1956 to 1967 a prelude to such an event. It was commonly known that the armistice lines of 1948, referred to as the Green Line, were hardly the ideal demarcation anticipated by the early Zionists when envisaging their future state. In June 1963, for instance, Prime Minister Levi Eshkol who also held the defense portfolio, broached the idea of enlarging the state in order to meet projected defense needs of the coming few years with Chief of Staff Zvi Zur, whose deputy was Rabin. Zur revived the idea of the old boundaries which fired the imagination of the Zionist leadership of 1919, such as running parallel to the course of major bodies of water, namely the Jordan and the Litani, as well as the Suez Canal. Should the opportunity of conflict arise, these borders would be capable of protecting the state. The IDF developed a military plan, not merely a trajectory for the ideal borders, called Operation Whip, which would entail taking over not only East Jerusalem but the entire West Bank.[16] But the IDF limited itself for the time being to a more limited plan dubbed Mozart which called for seizing only specific areas to enhance Israel's defenses. These included the headquarters of the UN Commissioner on Mt. Scopus and the Latroun area which sat astride the Bethlehem-Jerusalem road. A third plan which was approved, referred to as Sons of Light, was intended to facilitate the defense of the state against a possible Arab, not only, Jordanian attack, by going on the offensive inside these countries. There were also discussions concerning the disposal of the West Bank once it fell under Israeli control. Believing that the main prize under these circumstances would always be Jerusalem, the question arose whether to join the West Bank to a Jewish-dominated Jerusalem, or retain it as a buffer state between Israel and Jordan. Among the doubters of this traditional geographic plan of defense was Peres, then the deputy minister of defense, who always emphasized the primacy of maintaining a nuclear deterrent. As the main originator of Israel's nuclear program, he was always consulted on matters of defensive strategy, but in this instance did not discount the possibility of taking preemptive action designed to avail the state of defensible borders. These military and strategic discussions predominated from the mid-1960s until the eve of the 1967 June War, despite Eshkol's disavowal of any intent to seize land beyond the 1948 armistice borders. But, not unlike many Israelis, he too fastened his sights on the Litani River as a possible substitute for the 1948 borders.[17] Thus, Israel's assertion that the Jordanian attack of June 1967 was a premeditated act of war did not approximate the whole story.

SAMU': A PUGILISTIC BLOW AT THE JORDANIAN ALLY

From 1966 until the eve of the 1967 War, the United States regarded the Palestinian refugees with some sympathy. It often reminded Israel of its duty to address the humanitarian wreckage resulting from its founding. This policy began to change following the Suez War when the refugees became politicized, transforming themselves from helpless victims to militant guerrilla fighters. The changing refugee political disposition began to send shock waves along the lengthy Israeli-Jordanian border with its bitter front-line Palestinian villages. Jordan was still an ally of some value, at least based on its position as a buffer zone between the Jewish state and Syria. The latter, in the meantime, had become one of the most ardent supporters of Palestinian guerrillas and the PLO.

King Hussein, who was always conscious of his vulnerability to plots, coups, and assassination attempts by various local and regional actors, pursued a double-pronged policy during the early 1960s: Establishing personal contacts with Israeli leaders to secure his western flank, and reinventing himself as a member of the emerging Arab alliance against Israel's endeavor to divert the headwaters of the Jordan River. He was also motivated to cement his secret ties to the Arabs' traditional enemy by fear of a potential realignment of the US position in order to accommodate Nasser's brand of Arab nationalism which would leave Hussein out in the cold. In order to survive these dangerous currents in the Arab region, he also needed to shore up his credentials as a legitimate Arab nationalist leader. This led him to play a central role in the ALS summit meeting of January 13–17, 1964, during which the first PLO under the leadership of Ahmad Shuqeiry was given the Palestine seat, vowing to fight Israel, not the Arab regimes. Shuqeiry aligned himself with Syria, and the PLO's military strategy placed it on a collision course with the one country featuring the longest borderline with Israel, namely Jordan.[18]

Palestinian farmers, most of whom became refugees after 1948, had lived in Syria and Jordan, among other countries, and continued to maintain contact with their original villages. But for those who remained within their former communities along the West Bank border, reliving the trauma of dispossession as their land came under the Israeli plow on a daily basis was an increasingly bitter experience. Much of their land had been lost to the Israeli side mostly through the demilitarized zone created by the Rhodes Armistice agreement which separated villages from their fields, and through the steady encroachment of the Israelis on these lands. The villagers proved to be ready recruits to PLO ranks, which also enrolled residents of Syria's refugee camps. Syria, which joined Egypt as part of the United Arab Republic (UAR, 1958–1961), became the fulcrum of the ideology of armed resistance, spread not by Shuqeiry's timid army but by the militias of new formations such as Fateh. The first PLO attack occurred on January 1, 1965, which targeted the Israeli Water National Carrier on the west side of the Jordan River. This illegal scheme to divert the flow of the river all the way to the Negev Desert was feared to be a preparation for settling more Jewish refugees in the irrigated area. Other attacks followed, some presumably originating from Jordan despite the latter's known opposition to such activity. The most famous act of retaliation by the Israeli state occurred on November 13, 1966, when the source of the attack was traced to Samu', a village south of Hebron in the West Bank. The village was assaulted during daylight hours by a large military force resulting in dozens of Jordanian military and Palestinian civilian casualties, as well as the demolition of forty-one houses. The IDF justified its action by claiming that acts of sabotage were committed by Palestinians who came from Samu' on the Jordanian side. Surprising in its ferocity, the attack was disproportionate to the original Arab incursion and barely elicited any notice from the Israeli public at large.[19]

Israel was aware that the most serious attacks were launched from the Syrian side, particularly after the 1966 coup which was fueled by outrage over the discovery of an embedded Israeli agent, Eliahu Cohen, within the highest levels of the government of Amin al-Hafez. Cohen was secretly relaying information on Syria's plans to fortify its installations near the headwaters of the Jordan, and its strengthening of military fortifications around the Golan Heights. These disclosures enabled Israel to score its stunning victory in 1967 and to capture the heights. The new Syrian government was willing to allow Palestinian guerrillas to transit from its territory in order to gain legitimacy for its coup. Thus, on April 18 and May 16, 1966, two Israeli farmers were killed by a mine suspected of being planted by Palestinians who infiltrated from Syria. Israel responded by launching air attacks on Syrian territory, and destroying equipment used to change the course of the Banias River, one of the tributaries of the Jordan. Failure of the Security Council to condemn the Israeli attack fueled Syria's anger. Skirmishes between the two countries accelerated on August 15, with both sides resorting to aerial, land, and naval attacks. Another incident involving Syrian land mines killed four Israeli policemen in the Galilee, leading to a heated war of words between the two sides over who was responsible for Fateh's attacks. Israel was also angered at the reluctance of the Security Council to act on its complaint against the Galilee attack. That is when Israel decided to target Samu' in response to another landmine incident, although the entire Israeli-Syrian and Golan areas were already inflamed. The guerrillas' attack which destroyed an Israeli military vehicle, killing three soldiers, and wounding six others, thus, was immediately avenged by Israel in order to serve as a deterrent to further acts of sabotage. The retaliatory raid on Samu' took place during daytime hours, leading UN observers to report it quickly, expressing astonishment at the number of casualties involved. According to the UN report, fifteen Jordanian soldiers and three Jordanian civilians were killed, as well as fifty-four wounded, of whom seventeen were farmers. The Israelis planted explosives which blew up 125 homes, a health clinic, and a school after ordering the evacuation of the civilian inhabitants of these structures. This was a formal military operation involving Israeli tanks and armored personnel carriers, supported by Mirage fighter planes. Israeli losses, however, amounted to one soldier killed and ten injured.[20] This disproportionate response to a minor incident signaled Israel's new decision not to permit the UN or any other international body to dictate the size of its response to future attacks.

A BEWILDERING CHOICE OF TARGETS

Despite Israel's attempt to soften the impact of the raid on the West Bank village, the mastermind of the operation, Chief of Staff Rabin, feigned surprise at the extent of the damage it had caused. He claimed that the original plan which received cabinet approval was not intended to be so destructive, adding that he was convinced of the innocence of Jordanian authorities. He explained that the attack plan was merely meant to warn the villagers against cooperating with guerrilla fighters and saboteurs in the future. It was clear, nevertheless, that the damage inflicted far exceeded the plan of action which the cabinet approved. Israel's response to military activity on its Syrian border, thus, initiated the country's uncontrollable slide towards a major confrontation resulting in the June 1967 War. Ample evidence existed that it was Israel which constantly provoked the Syrians over expansion in no-man's land and diversion of the Jordan River following the failure of the American-sponsored Jordan Valley Unified Water Plan. The extent of Israel's determination to gain a military advantage in the conflict with Syria emerged from some of Dayan's posthumous interviews. Rami Tal, a reporter for *Yediot Aharonot*, published several of these in 1997, in which Dayan expressed regret that he did not maintain his original disapproval of invading the Golan Heights in the 1967 War. Dayan confessed that 80 percent of the provocations in this area originated with Israel. The incidents usually began when Israel sent farmers with tractors to plow in the demilitarized zone, knowing full well that Syrian response would involve military action. These "farmers" would be instructed to keep moving until the Syrians began to shoot. That was when Israel would retaliate by using heavy weapons, such as artillery, and later, the air force. Dayan said that all previous Israeli commanders, including Rabin, enjoyed playing this game, particularly David Elazar, who, until 1969, headed the Northern Command. Dayan explained that he, along with most responsible officers, did not look on the armistice lines along the Syrian border as final. Similarly, neither did they view the armistice lines along Jordanian Jerusalem as permanent in nature. [21]

King Hussein was almost toppled from his throne because of his failure to score a victory at Samu'. Demonstrators in major Jordanian and Palestinian cities protested the government's policy of denying arms to front-line villages which would have enabled them to protect themselves. The Israeli attack also exposed the Jordanian army's lack of preparedness and ability to stand up to such an assault by its traditional enemy. Israel's reaction to these popular explosions threatening the friendly regime to the east turned into a convenient occasion to air its own pent up expansionist views. Tom Segev captured the policy makers' quixotic way of thinking when they were caught fantasizing over another opportunity to expand their borders. Peres, at the time the Deputy Defense Minister, responded in a secret cabinet meeting to a question regarding Israel's options should the King be toppled by suggesting that he should be replaced by an Israeli Arab, who would take his orders from Israel. This suggestion did not emerge in a vacuum since the cabinet had already determined the unreliability of Hussein's brother and heir, Prince Hasan, to rule in his place. Eban, on the other hand, worried about the future of the West Bank should the monarchy fall, speculating that it might declare itself a republic and invite Syrian or Egyptian troops to be stationed on its soil. But the more prescient view which also vocalized one of Zionism's long-held secret wishes came from Mordechai Gazit, a foreign ministry official. In a lecture on October 13, 1966, at the National Defense College, he answered a question regarding Israel's chances of annexing the West Bank.[22] He emphasized that such a move would not be approved by the international community. Israel itself had no interest in such a development based on its small size and vulnerability, adding: "What do we do if the population in the West Bank, our sworn enemy, did not flee across the border?"[23]

SAMU' THROUGH AMERICAN LENSES

Jack O'Connell, CIA station chief in Jordan and a close confidant of King Hussein, was apparently unaware of the extent of the King's contacts with Israel at the time. O'Connell was surprised by the intensity of Hussein's disappointment since he had just received an amicable communication from Israeli officials. The monarch explained in a confidential conversation with the CIA official and American Ambassador Findley Burns, Jr., that he had enjoyed a three-year contact with Yaacov Herzog to ascertain Israel's conditions for signing a lasting peace agreement. Hussein believed that anything could be settled through diplomacy and was shocked by the severity of the attack. He also felt that the Israeli military operation was a prelude to the annexation of the entire West Bank.[24]

During that same time, a bureaucratic battle was brewing in Washington over Jordan's request to buy US military arms. President Johnson, as was well-known, had the Vietnam War on his mind, but occasionally took time out to override State Department recommendations on Israel. Based on his official communications which were later published, and even more importantly, on his 1967 telephone conversations, his bias towards Israel and his lack of a serious interest in the Arab allies were palpable. He rarely involved lower-level experts in his discussions of Middle East issues, choosing to confine himself to officials of the National Security Council (NSC), such as Secretary of State Dean Rusk and Secretary of Defense Robert S. McNamara, as well as NSC Adviser McGeorge Bundy.[25] Although mostly uninterested in face-to-face discussions with foreign dignitaries, he made an exception for Israeli Prime Minister Levi Eshkol when the latter visited Washington in 1964, expressing full backing for fulfilling Israel's defense needs. Johnson, however, feared alienating his Arab allies if he authorized the arms deal requested by Israel, preferring to pressure newly elected West German Chancellor Ludwig Erhard to sell the Israelis 150 M-48 tanks, with more to follow later. But Erhard proved just as sensitive to alienating the Arab states as the American president, agreeing to perform this favor only if the deal was kept under wraps. Johnson's closest adviser at the time was Abe Fortas, whose ties to the Jewish state were publicly known and who handled the President's case when he ran in 1948 in a hotly disputed race for the office of Democratic senator from Texas. Johnson repaid him in 1965 with an appointment to the Supreme Court. In addition, Johnson's position as a Senate majority leader and his role in setting up the Democratic Senate Campaign Committee placed him in touch with Jewish donors in order to raise funds for some embattled states. Through some of these contacts, such as entertainment industry lawyer Arthur Krim and his wife Mathilde, a Jewish convert who lived in Israel earlier, Johnson was sold on the image of that country as a frontier state, not unlike Texas, and on Nasser as the Santa Ana of Mexican history. However, a lot of maneuvering was necessary to get congressional approval for selling arms to Jordan so as not to acquire them from the Soviet Union. Johnson also saw this as facilitating larger shipments of arms to Israel in the future. This role of working through Congress was delegated to Robert Komer, a NSC staffer who was expected to get approval for selling arms to Israel in order to induce Eshkol and the Israel lobby to approve the smaller arms' deal for Jordan.[26]

Recently released archival recordings of Johnson's years in the White House exposed his dismissive attitude towards Jordan, whose alliance he viewed through the Cold War prism. He said:

> Our judgment is we oughtn't to let this little king [Hussein] go down the river. He's got a million–and-a-half people and he only controls a third of them—two-thirds [are] against him. But he is the only voice that will stand up there. And if you want to turn him over and have a complete Soviet bloc, why, we'll just have to—and we'll all get out of the arms business. . . . We'll all have to get out of supplying Jordan with money. . . . We'll deprive Jordan of their aid. . . . If that's what they [the Israelis] think. We think it would be better to give them [Jordan] as little as possible, and control it. . . . The only reason I'm helping Jordan is on account of Israel. . . . My judgment is, and it's Rusk's judgment . . . that this little king has some value to us and we ought to keep him as far away from the Soviets and Nasser as we can. The Israelis, though, don't think so. Well, if they don't, we'll just pull out; we won't sell him a damn thing. But we want it to be clear it's their decision.[27]

When Israel launched its attack on Samu', resulting in Arab anti-regime demonstrations throughout the East and West Banks, Washington's view was that the Eshkol government mounted the attack in order to defend itself against accusations of weakness by Israeli hawks such as Ben Gurion. Washington felt that Eshkol responded adequately to terrorist attacks on its soil. In turn, the Israelis, seeking to attract media attention, dubbed the military act "Operation Shredder." Yet, the United States responded quickly to what it perceived to be an attack on one of its client Arab states. Upon instructions from his government, US Ambassador to Israel, Walworth Barbour, declined Eshkol's request to transmit an apology to Hussein. But at the same time, Johnson declined a request from the Joint Chiefs of Staff to deny Israel military aid in protest. More importantly, the United States joined a Security Council Resolution condemning the raid in a unanimous vote and one abstention. Security Council Resolution 228 accused Israel of unleashing a well-planned and deliberate attack by its own military forces on Jordanian territory. The CIA contributed to solidifying the American decision by concluding that Jordan, rather than Syria, was Israel's chosen target so as not to threaten its own relations with the Soviet Union, Syria's main international patron.[28]

Actually, Johnson attempted to pacify the Jordanians and dampen their fear that the raid was a prelude for more Israeli expansionist moves in the West Bank. In a letter to King Hussein dated November 23, 1966, Johnson claimed that it was highly unlikely that this would take place, or that Israel had become more militarized. The US Government, he wrote, was opposed to changing the armistice lines along Near Eastern borders by the use of force and had made this clear to all sides. He concluded that, "There is no doubt in my mind that our position is fully understood and appreciated by the Israelis."[29] The Jordanian monarch may have felt assured by these words, but nothing could have protected him against the rising tide of nationalist dissatisfaction with his transparently weak military response to Israel's act of aggression. All these assurances notwithstanding, the United States was fully aware of at least one thing, namely Israel's greater designs on Arab Jerusalem in particular.

A MILITARY PARADE AND THE
AMERICAN-ISRAELI ALLIANCE

The annual Israeli military parade in Jerusalem has never ceased to aggravate relations with the United States, and 1966 was no exception. On the occasion of Israel's creation, referred to as its independence day, a misapplication of the term since Israel could not claim prior existence as a nation or a state, it asserted its claim to West Jerusalem, declaring it its capital. Any militarization of this commemoration, however, violated the terms of the 1948 ceasefire agreement with Jordan, which permitted the entry of a limited number of

Israeli troops to the city, but not the presence of tanks and other heavy military equipment. Since the international community still upheld the international status of the city and its implied demilitarization included in the General Assembly's partition plan, Res. 181, a military parade was considered an act of open defiance of that consensus. While no comparable event ever took place on the Jordanian side of the partitioned city, Israel continued to assert its right to call it its capital. The last parade to take place in the New City prior to 1966 was in 1961, eliciting a strong Security Council rebuke. Later parades were held in various locations to avoid a confrontation with the major powers such as the United States, Britain, and France which always faced the dilemma of allowing their representatives to participate and be seated on the main stage. For instance, when Barbour was permitted to attend the opening ceremonies of the Knesset building in 1966, Secretary of State Rusk wrote an internal memorandum asserting the singular nature of this divergence from the rules while affirming US unchanging position of rejecting Israel's claim to the city. [30]

No one understood the gravity or serious implications of this decision better than Walt Rostow, member of the NSC. He reminded the president that keeping the American ambassador from attending the parade may lead to "trouble," meaning an unpredictable eruption of Israeli nationalism since the issue was the status of Jerusalem, not the military parade as such. Rostow, who was considered a pro-Israel supporter, referred to Israel's approach as "salami tactics," or asserting its claim to Jerusalem one slice at a time. Heeding this warning, Johnson settled for a compromise: Forbidding the ambassador from sitting with the rest of the dignitaries, but allowing his attendance at a sound and light show on the grounds of Hebrew University. [31]

The 1966 parade proved to be contentious not only in the context of US-Israeli relations, but also within Israel itself. Prime Minister Eshkol's clear effort to minimize its significance, allowing no tanks or heavy weapons in strict observance of the armistice agreement was noted by the country's nationalist hawks. Many began referring to the event as "Eshkol's mini-parade," and Ben Gurion declined to attend, calling on the prime minister to seize the moment by displaying Israel's military power as an assertion of its claim to Jerusalem. In reply, Eshkol insisted that the modest parade was enough of a reminder of the country's claim to the city. Yet, all foreign representatives kept away lest their attendance was used to assert Israel's sovereignty over Jerusalem. The international community persisted in locating its offices in Tel Aviv, which it regarded as the official capital. Israelis, nevertheless, did not abandon their claim to the Western Wall in East Jerusalem, which beckoned to them from the city's storied skyline. Much to the chagrin of the powerful new state with its population of 200,000 Jews in the New City alone, the smaller and less-populated East Jerusalem with its 70,000 Arab residents continued to ban their access to the Wall. Thus, all of the unresolved issues of 1948 and the Israeli state's unfulfilled desire to bring the entire city under its domain were magnified during the parade. On May 15, 1967, Israel celebrated the establishment of its capital in one half of the city and the relocation of its parliament and government offices there for the last time before the June War of 1967 erupted. News of rising tension along the Sinai Peninsula, which drove the Egyptians to demand the dismantling of the last of the remaining Suez War international barriers, began to reach the country. Other news followed, such as the entry of Egyptian troops into Sinai. Pretending not to be rattled by these events, the Israelis carried on with their parade, a mere three weeks prior to the outbreak of the war.[32]

ISRAEL'S GAME OF DECEPTION

The parade's momentum was not affected when top cabinet leaders such as Eshkol and Eban recently moved from the UN to the Foreign Office, and Rabin, the new chief of staff, did not take part in the celebrations. The Israelis had to determine whether Egyptian military maneuvers were a show of force to relieve pressure on Syria, which was undergoing its worst season of bombardment and clashes with Israeli troops, or a definite step towards the liberation of Sinai. That the Egyptians were within their right to ask for removal of UN troops from territory considered theirs by any count did not decrease Israel's rising alarm at the prospect of another military confrontation. Therefore, it was felt that it was in Israel's interest to exaggerate this threat in order to justify its impending pre-emptive attack, which would play out in a manner similar to the Samu' incident. Even when the Indian commander of the UN Emergency Force (UNEF), Major General Indar Jit Rikhye, indicated in some statements that he did not think the winds of war were blowing, Israel began to prepare for the outbreak of hostilities.[33] In addition, it felt it had to make an iron clad case for its future moves, presenting them as defensive acts in order to escape the charge of initiating the attack. This became an urgent matter after President Johnson, who was feeling the burden of the Vietnam War, warned all sides in the Middle East conflict against ushering in a new phase of open violence. In a letter to Eshkol, the American president who was already aware of Israel's recent intransigence against Syria, wrote the following:

> I would like to emphasize in the strongest of terms the need to avoid any action on your side which would add further to the violence and tension in your area. I urge the closest consultation between you and your closest friends. I am sure that you will understand that I cannot accept any responsibilities on behalf of the United States for situations which arise as a result of actions on which we are not consulted.[34]

Taking no chances, Eban responded by seeking confirmation of US pledges to protect Israel against any future attacks, as well as suggesting that the Soviet Union be informed of how America lined up on this issue. The United States declined such a request since no formal guarantee of Israel's security had been issued. Rostow wrote to Johnson, suggesting that an answer should refer to President Kennedy's summation of this commitment in a press conference on May 8, 1963, which read "We support the security of Israel and its neighbors." Johnson then wrote to Eshkol on August 2, 1966, affirming "U.S. support for the territorial integrity and political independence of all countries in the Near East." He also repeated President Kennedy's statement to Israeli President Zalman Shazar. [35]

As tension mounted in the Middle East, the pressure on Johnson escalated. Yet, the official assessment of the CIA was that Israel was the favored military power in the region. Eleven days before the hostilities began, the CIA concluded that Israel would be unbeatable by any combination of its Arab foes, adding that the Jewish state was expected to maintain this military qualitative edge for the following five years. The CIA also reported that Israel was on its way to producing an atomic bomb and that its military leaders were anticipating an Egyptian attack on the Demona atomic reactor in the Negev. Feeling confident about its superiority of arms versus the other Arab armies, the Israeli cabinet began to make war plans. In a cabinet meeting just before the war, Yigal Allon, a self-declared strategist, suggested moving to the Suez Canal, and while seizing it, all of the Palestinian refugees in Gaza be pushed over the canal to force them to proceed westward. Only Dayan's objection to this inhuman operation scuttled the proposal. But Peres, who presided over the fulfilment of Israel's nuclear ambitions a few years before, recommended conducting a nuclear test which would act as a powerful deterrent and force the Arabs to cease pursuing their own plan of attack. [36]

Israel, however, developed several plans to secure the approval of the United States for its planned pre-emptive attack. While Johnson promised to organize an international fleet to force open the Suez Canal to Israeli shipping, the Israelis were relying on old friends in the American intelligence community to sell him on a different plan. Richard Helms, CIA chief, was persuaded to convey to the President the tremendous cost Israel was incurring by keeping a state of military mobilization for two weeks. He was to point out the staggering impact this would have on the economy while at the same time reminding the chief executive that Israel would not seek any help from the United States. But it was an Israeli Mossad insider like Yossi Melman who was able to reveal this story, which demonstrated the close links of this agency to the CIA. According to the rest of the account, Meir Amit, director of Aman, Israel's Military Intelligence, was sent to Washington just before the war to tell Helms and Johnson that war was unavoidable. He was also charged with blaming Nasser for bringing Israel to this stage of military confrontation and expressing confidence that Israel would be victorious. This Israeli account also mentioned that the United States made no objection to the pre-emptive nature of the planned attack, thanks to the high view the CIA held of its Israeli counterpart, an agency with which it had secretly cooperated for years.[37] Walt Rostow sent a memo to Johnson on May 25, 1967, which he copied to various NSC members and State Department officials, giving an assessment by Mossad based on various pieces of information. The latter agency conveyed its belief that Egypt was about to declare war and that a small window of opportunity remained for Israel to strike first and save itself from disaster. The Israelis also asked the United States to think about the possibility of the entire Middle East falling under Soviet hegemony if Egypt was allowed to win the war. Rostow, however, attached his own reaction to the Israeli assessment by doubting the seriousness of its conclusions, adding, that it was probably "a gambit," intended to push the Americans to choose one the following options: increase military aid to Israel, declare their commitment to Israel's survival, acquiesce in any Israeli pre-emptive attack, or go as far as pressuring Nasser directly. Rostow then spelled out the basis for his disagreement with this Israeli assessment by stressing his own view that Egyptian maneuvers in the Sinai Peninsula were defensive in nature, intended to pressure Israel but without having to take the next radical step of directly attacking its enemy. He confirmed current evaluations by adding his voice to the rest of the skeptics who were convinced that Egypt would never be capable of destroying Israel. He also disputed Israel's thesis that the Egyptians were ready to use chemical weapons on Israel's urban centers, arguing that the latter's superior air power would make this feat impossible to execute.[38]

Another indication of US conviction that Israel would prevail in any military confrontation with the Arab states was revealed in a Memo for the Record, summarizing a discussion on May 26 at the White House. The meeting was attended by Rusk and General Earl Wheeler, Chair of the Joint Chiefs of Staff, among others. It was the latter's opinion that Israel would win in any confrontation and that it had the ability to survive even two months of military mobilization without suffering measurable economic damage. He also asserted that there were no signs of an impending Egyptian attack and that Israel would win in any area of war. Rusk reported on a meeting with Eban the previous day, who reiterated Eshkol's view of an imminent Egyptian attack, a view contradicted by Rusk, clarifying that Israel would be on its own if it decided to initiate an attack. Rostow elaborated on this by explaining that according to the doctrine of "first strike," Egypt was already guilty by imposing a blockade on the Gulf of Aqaba. Joseph Sisco confirmed the seriousness of this issue for Israel and its lack of faith in the effectiveness of any action by the UN, based on its experience in the recent past.[39] Some NSC officers, however, still favored coming to Israel's rescue.

Harold Saunders, writing to Rostow on May 25, seemed sympathetic to Eban's charge that the attack on Samu' was the result of Israel's despair over UN wrangling when Israel and Syria were skirmishing, blaming the United States for forcing Israel to hit Jordan instead. The situation in 1967, Saunders added, was different since the United States was again trying to prevent the outbreak of war and jumping into uncharted territory. He did not question the cost in terms of losing Arab allies if the United States approved an airstrike soon after Eban visited the President. Saunders wrote: "So it has been our natural inclination to work for peace at all costs." He then added: "However, if Eban feels only a strike can solve Israel's problem, we ought to think long and hard before we reject this out of hand."[40]

When hostilities began after King Hussein rejected Israel's request to stay out of the war, the situation in the West Bank demanded as much attention as the Egyptian and Syrian fronts. It quickly became clear when Israel raced to take over the eastern part of Jerusalem that the city's fate assumed the dimension of a major crisis because of its contested holy sites. But as far as the United States was concerned, the dilemma of neutrality quickly emerged once it found itself caught between the Jewish Congressional lobby and its own Arab allies in the Middle East. Secret records of Johnson's conversations revealed a beleaguered White House coming under pressure from domestic political allies after failing to persuade the Israelis against carrying out their implied pre-emptive attack. When informing the President of the launching of the war, Rusk again reiterated his strenuous efforts to prevent this deteriorating situation from escalating. His initial objective, he explained, was to have the Security Council bring the hostilities to an end. He suspected that the Israelis initiated the attack disregarding all advice to the contrary, while maintaining that a large Egyptian military formation was advancing on their territory. But when deputy spokesperson of the State Department, Robert McClosky, told reporters of his government's intent to remain neutral, Joseph Califano, special assistant to the President, remarked that these words were "killing us with the Jews in this country."[41] President Johnson made an effort early in the crisis to replicate Kennedy's handling of the Cuban Missile Crisis in 1960 by forming an ad hoc committee of the NSC to focus on the specific Middle East situation. But the so-called Special Committee, or Control Committee of the NSC, did not always achieve consensus on the first try. Its members included the following: Secretary of State Rusk; Under-Secretary of State Nicholas Katzenbach; Secretary of Defense Robert McNamara; Chair of the Joint Chiefs of Staff General Wheeler; Secretary of the Treasury Henry H. Fowler; CIA Director Richard Helms; Under-Secretary of State for Political Affairs Eugene Rostow; former Ambassador to the UAR Lucius Battle who was serving as Assistant Secretary of State for the Near East and North Africa; Walt Rostow of NSC; White House Counsel Harry McPherson; NSC Adviser McGeorge Bundy, who served as the executive secretary of the committee; Chair of Foreign Intelligence Advisory Board Clark Clifford; Special Assistant to the President Marvin Watson; NSC Middle East Specialist Harold Saunders; member of Policy Planning Council of the Middle East and North Africa William R. Polk; and Senior staff member of NSC Howard Wriggins. Saunders declared later that the main achievement of this committee was developing the government's position after the war stopped, which was summarized on June 19, 1967, in a presidential speech.[42]

When the United States was pushed to situate itself in the eye of the hurricane, Walt Rostow reflected on Dean Acheson's memorable assessment as he "looked back on the whole history of Israeli independence and, in effect, said that it was a mistake to ever create the State of Israel."[43] Former President Eisenhower was also consulted on the occasion of convening this committee, telling Johnson that the two main problems in the Middle East which needed attention were the division of water, presumably the Jordan River, and the Arab refugees. The latter problem was a reminder of the principal concern of the previous Republican administration. Johnson began to assess the views of the committee on certain issues, such as whether committing to the preservation of the territorial boundaries of various states could be enunciated without insisting on returning specifically to the pre-June 6 lines. He also wanted them to feel out King Hussein and his needs in an attempt to insure his political survival. Yet, when prodded to remain engaged with West Bankers and with Jordan, the Israelis feigned lack of a crystallized position on the war.

Rusk then warned Israel through Eban that any misstep over Jerusalem could have dire consequences in the United States, leading to a rise in anti-Israel sentiment. He added that the fate of Jerusalem after the war was critical to the United States which needed to pursue a diplomatic resolution of the issue without upsetting its Arab allies in the Gulf region. He was referring to King Faysal of Saudi Arabia who was already sending messages calling for branding Israel as the aggressor. Walt Rostow also transmitted to Johnson some pressure by the Arab states, calling for Israel's return to the 1949 armistice boundaries. Faysal's views and those of the conservative Muslim states were quickly adopted by major US oil companies in the region. They all agreed that if Jerusalem fell in Israel's hands, public opinion in the Arab World would be inflamed and would stir up rebellions against pro-US monarchies. Everett Dirkson, Republican Senator from Illinois, was more direct in his warnings by transmitting a message to Johnson from the executive vice-president of Mobil Oil, which, according to Dirkson, owned 10 percent interest in ARAMCO. Apparently, ARAMCO had reported on a meeting convened by Faysal with Arab ambassadors present, who blamed the United States for encouraging Israel to start the war. The same views, Johnson responded, were conveyed to him via several intelligence reports. Dirkson added that British Foreign Secretary George Brown also favored adopting a tough stand to force the Israelis to retreat to their positions before the war. [44]

THE UNITED STATES DEFINES THE ISSUES AT WAR'S END

Johnson's address at a State Department Conference for Educators on June 19, 1967, turned out to be a coherent summation of views expressed in the Special Committee's meetings. His remarks were also a crystallization of inchoate US policy positions on issues emerging from the June War. He began by declaring the Palestine refugee issue as the most important human requirement for reaching a settlement of the war. He referred to it as "justice for the refugees," emphasizing that a new wave of Palestinian refugees had already lost their homes as a result of the latest hostilities. He renewed US commitment to freedom of navigation of the waterways and decried the widening arms race in the Middle East, for which he blamed external weapons merchants. But he rejected the call by many groups for the return to the defense lines of June 4 as the only solution, quoting US Ambassador to the UN Arthur Goldberg as saying that this was a call for an escalation of the war. Troops must be withdrawn, Johnson said, but only in the context of freedom of maritime passage, and a solution for the refugees must be found, as well as limiting the arms race. He called for respect for the political independence and recognized boundaries of existing states, which would end living under the protection of a shaky truce and would make room for permanent peace arrangements. He also emphasized that there must be special recognition for the concern of the world community for Jerusalem and the holy places of the three great world religions. [45] Thus, the broad outline of the emerging United States position on the post-war settlement seemed to indicate a preference for a humanitarian, rather than a political, solution for the latest wave of refugees. The US position also leaned towards a new, though unspecified, security arrangement leading to more secure boundaries for all, which would result in a permanent peace arrangement. The issue of refugees was not new to American presidents and was a focal point of concern for Eisenhower and Kennedy, Johnson emphasized. It was Kennedy who attempted to link Ben Gurion's request for Hawk anti-aircraft missiles in 1961 to accepting an American plan allowing Palestinian refugees a choice between settlement abroad or returning to their original homes. [46] Johnson's message would have mollified Arab feelings of discontent, but limiting the new US position on Jerusalem to respect for the rights of all faiths in the city was clearly a departure from previous policy. Lumping the fate of the holy city with that of the rest of Israel's new territorial acquisitions was a bow to pro-Israel pressure. The United States was now moving away from its long commitment to the internationalization of Jerusalem.

CONCLUSION

Israel set a pattern of resistance to relinquishing captured territory or compensating the refugees as early as the 1948 War. It was common then to take this stand whenever Jordan negotiated for the return of Arabs to their homes in West Jerusalem. Always bristling with rage under the weight of its unrequited demands for the annexation of Jewish cultural sites on Mt. Scopus and access to the Wailing Wall, Israel never yielded to a *quid pro quo* arrangement with its secret Arab ally to the east. Thanks to Ben Gurion's doctrine of war, not an inch of captured territory could be alienated, even in the context of a comprehensive settlement with Jordan. For the Palestinians who remained in their villages, the focus of their anger was the Rhodes Agreement which finalized the armistice lines at the end of the war. Having lost their land, the Palestinians became internally displaced and continued to exist on the Jordanian side of the border and within a bird's eye view of their former orchards and fields. Thus, the bitterness was mutually shared by Arab and Jew.

Arab bitterness was also enhanced due to the early practice of dynamiting their homes by Jewish militias in West Jerusalem in order to prevent their return. Home demolition, begun by the British during the Arab Revolt of 1936, became a favored tactic of the Hagana and Stern militias and an effective punishment against Palestinians after 1967 whenever these attempted to resist the occupation regime. But any chance of arriving at a decent *modus vivendi* with the Jordanian entity following the establishment of the Israeli state dissipated when the latter found itself entangled with the Ba'ath Government in Syria over the diversion of the Jordan River to the Negev Desert. Relations were also aggravated due to the Israeli practice of sending farmers to plow no-man's-land of the Golan Heights, which the Syrians regarded as a flouting the clauses of the Armistice Agreement and a step-by-step annexation of their territory. Tension along the heights demanded a collective Arab military response, which pushed Egypt, and eventually Jordan, to enter an Arab security pact. All of these tensions later materialized along the Israeli-West Bank border as Palestinian farmers pursued the practice of infiltration to avenge the injustices of the Rhodes Agreement and Jordan's passive response to Israel's border attacks. The Rhodes Agreement, as well as the Israeli-Syrian Armistice Agreement, therefore, did not lead to conditions of peace. Instead, they both contributed to the intensification of bitterness at the unresolved issues of the 1948 War. Given this reality, it should have been easy to foreshadow Jordan's increasing inability to maintain its secret alliance with Israel, particularly following the Israeli punishing attack on Samu'. Contrary to the Israeli narrative claiming that King Hussein betrayed them and declined their peace offer by joining the Arab Defense Alliance on the eve of the 1967 War, his hands were actually tied.

Until the outbreak of hostilities, Israel sought excuses to enlarge its territorial hold over Jerusalem on several occasions, particularly when the armistice agreements with the Arab states seemed to be imperiled. The Suez War, for instance, served as such an occasion in the past, and so did the tension resulting from the struggle to control the headwaters of the Jordan River. Israel drew secret military plans to change the borders in anticipation of the gathering of war clouds as King Hussein's openness to joining the Arab Defense Pact heightened its suspicion of his goodwill and its own intolerance of Palestinian border raids. The attack on Samu' turned out to be the trigger which pushed Jordan to adopt a more militant stance and accelerated Israel's slide towards war. Samu' also magnified the rising influence of the Israeli military and its unchallenged role as the arbiter of the country's strategic priorities.

The US response to the Samu' incident pushed it to make amends to Jordan and to expedite military assistance to the kingdom. The aid, however, was still within the congressional parameters of maintaining Israel's qualitative military edge in the region. The Israeli attack also netted a motion of censure by the Security Council which adopted Res. 228, in which the United States participated. But even these consequential events did not weaken the Israeli military's resolve to adopt punitive pre-emptive measures designed to generate a shock and awe effect among its enemies. Hoping to teach the Israelis a lesson in curbing their appetite for revenge and territorial gains, President Johnson's only available weapon was to raise the issue of the Palestinian refugees. This was also upon pressure by American oil men in Saudi Arabia. Following a common theme pursued since the Eisenhower administration, the United State reminded Israel of its obligation to abide by UN resolutions allowing the refugees to return or offering them compensation for lost properties. The last president to articulate this theme was Kennedy, who linked Israel's request for arms to providing a humane settlement for the refugees, as well as opening up the Dimona nuclear reactor for inspection. Israel, however, persisted in following Ben Gurion's opposition to these demands and his well-known resistance to offering any friendly gestures to US allies in the Middle East region. The United States apparently did approve of, or at least acquiesce in, Israel's planned attack on Jerusalem and the West Bank on 6 June, by demanding that the Israeli action must be based on a semblance of American consent, regardless of how this was defined. Therefore, a great deal depended on securing the silence of the United State in the face of a pre-emptive attack on several Arab fronts simultaneously.

NOTES

1. David Hulme, *Identity, Ideology, and the Future of Jerusalem* (New York: Palgrave Macmillan, 2006): 71. Herzl's quote was based on: Raphael Petai, ed., *The Complete Diaries of Theodore Herzl*, 5 volumes (London: Herzl Press, 1960): 745.

2. Ibid., 72.

3. From Chargé in Jordan, A. David Fritzlan, to Department of State, March 19, 1951. FRUS, Vol. V, The Near East and Africa, 601–4.

4. Memo of a Conversation by the Acting Officer in Charge of Palestine—Israel—Jordan Affairs (Fred E. Waller), July 23, 1952. FRUS, Vol. IX, Part I, The Near and Middle East, 967–8. On the open hostility of Byrode to Israel's extravagant immigration to Palestine policy and Nahum Goldman's (head of WZ0) threats to end his political career, see: 'Interview with Henry Byrode,' www.trumanlibrary.o...HarryS.TrumanPresidentialLibrary&Museun.Oral History Interview with Henry Byrode, Potomac, Maryland, September 19, 1988, with Neil S. Johnson. Accessed 1/30/2015.

5. Lester D. Mallory, Ambassador to Jordan, to Department of State, December 23, 1954. FRUS, Vol. IX, Part I, The Near and Middle East, 1736–7.

6. Benny Morris, *1948: The History of the First Arab–Israeli War* (New Haven, Conn.: Yale University Press, 2008): 404–5.

7. Tom Segev, *1967: Israel, the War, and the Year that Transformed the Middle East* (New York: Henry Holt, 2005): 166–7, 171.

8. https://en.wikipedia.org/wiki/The_Mandelbaum_Gate. Accessed 6/22/2015.

9. See: Seraj Assi, "Memory, Myth and the Military Government: Emile Habibi," Collective Autobiography.www.palestine-studies.org/JQ-52-Assi-Me...

10. Jefferson Caffrey, Ambassador to Egypt, to Department of State, August 30, 1953. FRUS, Vol. IX, Part I, The Near and Middle East, 415.

11. Motti Golani, "Jerusalem's Hope Lies Only in Partition: Israeli Policy on the Jerusalem Question, 1948–1967," *International Journal of Middle Eastern Studies*, Vol. 31, No. 4 (November 1999): 594–6.

12. Avi Shlaim, *Lion of Jordan: The Life of King Hussein in War and Peace* (New York: Alfred A. Knopf, 2007): 117–8.

13. Segev, *1967*, 171–4.

14. Chargé d'Affaires Francis H. Russell, U.S. Embassy in Israel, to State Department, October 7, 1953. FRUS, Vol. IX, Part I, Near and Middle East, 1339–40.

15. Wilbur Crane Eveland, *Ropes of Sand: America's Failure in the Middle East* (New York: W. W. Norton, 1980): 351. See also: Muhammad Nimer al-Hawari, *Asrar al-Nakba/ Secrets of the Catastrophe* (Nazareth: no publisher, 1955): passim.

16. Segev, 1967, 175.

17. Ibid., 176–7.

18. Shlaim, *Lion of Jordan*, 194–207.

19. Shlaim, *The Iron Wall: Israel and the Arab World* (New York: W. W. Norton, 2000): 100–01, 232–5.

20. Donald Neff, *Warriors for Jerusalem: Six Days that Changed the Middle East* (New York: Simon and Schuster, 1984): 37–41.

21. Shlaim, *The Iron Wall*, 233–6. See also: Fred J. Khouri, The Arab-Israeli Dilemma (Syracuse, N.Y.: Syracuse University Press, 1968): 227–45.

22. Segev, *1967*, 180–3; Neff, *Warriors for Jerusalem*, 42.

23. Segev, 185.

24. Jack O'Connell, with Vernon Loeb, *King's Counsel: A Memoir of War, Espionage, and Diplomacy in the Middle East* (New York: W. W. Norton, 2011): 39–40.

25. Robert David Johnson, "Lyndon Johnson and Israel: The Secret Presidential Recordings," Tel Aviv University Research Paper No. 3, July 2008. Published by the Daniel S. Abraham Center, with a preface by Itamar Rabinovich. www.tau.ac.i/humanities/abraham/publications/johnson_Israel. Pdf. Accessed 5/30/2013.

26. Ibid.

27. Ibid.

28. Ibid.

29. Neff, *Warriors for Jerusalem*, 49–50.

30. Segev, *1967*, 194, 218–19.

31. Ibid., 219–20.

32. Neff, *Warriors for Jerusalem*, 61–3.

33. Ibid., 63–4.

34. Ibid., 74. A secret cable to Eshkol, dated May 17, 1967.

35. Ibid., 77. This was in a memorandum to Johnson, titled, The U.S. Commitment to Israel.

36. Segev, 1967, 253–64, 326–30.

37. Ibid.; Dan Raviv and Yossi Melman, *Every Spy a Prince* (Boston: Houghton Mifflin, 1990): 161–2.

38. Memo from Special Assistant Walt Rostow to President Johnson, May 25, 1967. FRUS, Vol. XIX, 104–5.

39. Memo for the Record, May 26, 1967. FRUS, Vol. XIX, 127–8.

40. Memo for W. W. Rostow from Hal Saunders, "Reflections pre-Eban," May 25, 1967. NSF Country File, Box 12, Folder 7, LBJL.

41. R. D. Johnson, "Lyndon Johnson and Israel."

42. Special Committee of NSC, or the Control Committee, Box 1, Folder 1, LBJL.

43. R. D. Johnson, "Lyndon Johnson and Israel."

44. Ibid.

45. Lyndon Johnson, Address at the State Department's Foreign Policy Conference for Educators, June 19, 1967. FRUS, Vol. I, Public Papers of the Presidents of the US—Lyndon B. Johnson, 632–4.

46. Motti Golani, *The Road to Peace: A Biography of Shimon Peres* (New York: Warner Books, 1989): 70.

Chapter Five

War Unites Jerusalem

The June 6 War started with a Jordanian attack on West Jerusalem, an event of somber significance to Israel. Yet, the Israeli military were well aware of the relative insignificance of Jordan's attack capability. The Israeli narrative, as was often the case in the past, played up both Israel's victimhood and bravado in its national version of events. In Eban's recounting of rising tension in Jerusalem on the eve of the war, he was quick to point out that the official assessment of Jordan's capability was that its army numbered anywhere between 50,000 and 60,000 men who relied heavily on 250 Patton and Centurion tanks. The army's weakness, in his view, resided in its air force which consisted of twenty-four British Hunter fighter bombers and some American Starfighters recently arrived in Jordan but quickly and discreetly withdrawn to the United States. There were also rumors of an Iraqi division already advancing towards Jordan. But as soon as this country launched its attack and inflicted more casualties than what Israel suffered on the Egyptian front, the decision was made to destroy its aircrafts on the ground at Amman's and Mafraq's airfields. Eban then justified targeting the Old City of Jerusalem at the beginning of the war. Prime Minister Eshkol followed this by announcing that seizing the Old City was for the purpose of defending West Jerusalem since the Jordanians were bombarding the Knesset building. At that point, officials had no interest in distinguishing the Old City from the rest of Jordanian Jerusalem, since they eyed both for quite some time. Eban amplified his government's official position by coming up with a preliminary statement prior to the fall of the eastern section of the city. He declared that once Israeli troops entered the Old City, it would be impossible to return it to Jordanian rule due to the emotional and historical appeal it held for the majority of Israelis. A warning and a prediction all in one, the statement was supposed to prepare international public opinion for the predetermined hard-ening of the Israeli position. [1]

AMERICAN DIPLOMACY AND THE ART OF SIDELINING OFFICIAL ESTIMATES

If official Washington was seemingly perturbed by the uncontrollable slide towards war, it was fully aware of Israel's unmatched regional strength in any imminent war with the Arabs. President Johnson had already received a CIA estimate in early June which predicted an Israeli victory within a period of two weeks, later adjusted to one week. Yet, Goldberg, who was already representing the United States at the UN, warned against the strong possibil-ity of an Arab massacre of the Israelis. At a follow-up White House dinner which he attended, along with Fortas who was already seated in the Supreme Court, the President was again forewarned of dire consequences for Israel. Fortas told Johnson that war was imminent, a remark quickly directed to McNamara who was among the few predicting that no war would take place. Johnson had actually agreed with this view since it was based on CIA intelli-gence reports. But in less than six hours, he received a phone call from Walt Rostow announcing that Israel attacked and that the war had begun. Follow-ing the decimation of the Egyptian air force, Rostow gleefully reported that the one-sided casualty count was "the first day's turkey shoot." Upon the advice of people around him, Johnson authorized the transfer of a prepack-aged weapons' shipment to Israel despite the destruction of Jordan's air force in the evening hours of the same day. The destruction of two-thirds of the Syrian air force on the second day of the war, according to McPherson, caused an outburst of joy in the State Department Operation Room. This led Rostow to caution jokingly that the United States was still officially neutral. Yet, McPherson related later how Israel deliberately attempted to deceive his country through an incident involving him personally when on a visit to Tel Aviv. He described how he was pushed into a bunker, with sirens wailing, upon touching down at the airport even though the Egyptian air force was already totally eliminated in order to create the illusion that the war was continuing. [2]

Additionally, CIA experts who evaluated Arab and Israeli military strength on the eve of the war had already concluded that it would not only defeat any combination of Arab forces, but would maintain this military qualitative edge for the next five years. The United States was also expecting Israel to build its first atomic bomb within five years, following a long period of wrangling with the Kennedy administration over this development. Yet, while the Israeli military establishment had always contended that the atomic reactor at Dimona would be Egypt's first target in a situation of war, this prediction was not realized.[3]

THE CONQUEST OF THE OLD CITY BECAME THE DEFINING ISSUE OF THE WAR

Israel hesitated before launching its attack on Egypt, maintaining its state of mobilization for two weeks. Two reasons accounted for this: Waiting to obtain American approval, and at the same time hoping to give Eshkol enough time to assemble a coalition cabinet with the Rafi Party. Known locally as the nuclear party, this was a faction of the Labor Party which exited the parent group under Ben Gurion's leadership when his conflict with Kennedy over the secret nuclear weapon widened. The star of Rafi was Dayan, whom Eshkol's cabinet hoped to recruit to its ranks. With the cost of mobilization on the rise, the Israelis resolved to start the war sooner than later, rather than wait for a green light from their American allies. Thus, Helms was persuaded by his friend Amit, the Mossad chief, to inform Johnson of Israel's resolve to start the war alone, without seeking American assistance. General Odd Bull, the head of the UN Observer Team in Jerusalem, was then told that the war began due to an Egyptian plane violating Israeli air space. He was asked to convey a message to King Hussein, warning him against joining any Arab onslaught against Israel or he would suffer a full attack by his secret ally. The threat did not appear to be a warning that a full scale war was imminent, or that it would entail capturing the West Bank and Jerusalem as a first priority. Indeed, some Israelis, especially Rabin, felt that the destruction of the small Jordanian air force would be a sufficient retaliation. If this were to happen, Israel could speedily satisfy its deferred desire to adjust the borders by pursuing two limited objectives: taking swift control of the Latroun salient and its road in order to improve West Jerusalem's land access to Tel Aviv, and seizing Mt. Scopus to improve the city's defenses. This view of a limited response to the Jordanians failed to meet the generals' approval. Neither did hawks such as Allon and Menachem Begin, acting on strictly nationalist, rather than strategic, grounds, approve bypassing this opportunity to satisfy long-suppressed desires to take the Old City. Some cabinet members raised the issue of international retaliation since seizing the holy sites was fraught with legal implications.[4]

Eshkol's assessment of the best policy to avoid being forced by international pressure to relinquish the Old City and the West Bank was to come up with a simple argument. He explained to his cabinet: "In light of the situation that has evolved in Jerusalem, because of the Jordanians' bombing and after the warnings that were sent, we may have an opportunity to enter the Old City."[5] Therefore, the decision to take the city was presented as not incompatible with the overall needs of the state although based on purely political considerations. Eshkol's rationalization won the day.

In response to Jordanian shelling of West Jerusalem, Israel finally authorized Dayan to attack the Old City, but he allowed his troops to encircle it instead, in order to give pause before launching a full attack which he feared would destroy the holy sites. His motive seemed to be the avoidance of heavy casualties in the city's narrow streets, knowing full well that Israel may have to surrender it under international pressure. When hearing of a UN call for a cease-fire, he changed his mind and ordered the takeover of the city before receiving cabinet approval and before outside diplomatic intervention obligated Israel to change course. The rest of the West Bank was speedily captured once intelligence reports indicated that a mass flight of Jordanian troops across the Jordan had taken place. But once the Old City was captured, the multi-party cabinet reached the unanimous decision that it should be retained.[6] This unanimity was not present before the city's capture, but other differences persisted. Some, like Ben Gurion, were for seizing the Old City, but not taking the West Bank. But when ideas began to gel as to what should be retained and what their future uses would be, more diversity of opinions emerged. Allon recommended negotiating with Hussein after accepting his call for a cease-fire. If this failed, the West Bank should be made autonomous but kept economically dependent on Israel. However, Allon felt that even if Jerusalem was conquered, it should not be annexed. Begin expressed the view that the Christian world would go along with annexing the Old City, but he suggested allowing for a humane transfer of the Arab population of the rest of the West Bank.

What should be noted here was that the unanimous cabinet position on retaining East Jerusalem emerged as soon as Rusk began to seek a cease-fire to forestall the annexation of the Old City. At that time, he was in direct consultation with Barbour in Tel Aviv, hoping to gauge Israel's intentions concerning its newly won territories. In the meantime, the UN demand for a cease-fire calmed Israel's hawks since it did not call for withdrawal to the June 4 lines, to Eban's great satisfaction. Dayan, who was the man in the line of fire, managed to resist an attempt by Eshkol to visit the Western Wall claiming that the situation was still too dangerous to ensure his safety. Instead, he raced to the city himself in a helicopter with an IDF photographer to take pictures as he entered the city, a triumphant conqueror with Chief of the General Staff, Rabin, and Brigadier General Uzi Narkis in tow. The scene evoked memories of a similarly staged photo by that other conqueror of Jerusalem, Allenby.[7]

AMERICAN ALARM, EARLY REACTIONS

The fall of the Old City was either expected, or considered insignificant to warrant awakening the American President from his sleep. But Israel's supporters in the government were fully awake to all the possibilities that lay ahead. Fortas telephoned the President soon enough, recommending that no action be taken following the cease-fire in order to allow the Israelis and the Arabs full freedom to negotiate by themselves. Clearly, what Fortas was suggesting was that the United States should refrain from calling for withdrawal to the June 4 lines. Mathilde Krim, the pro-Israel friend of Johnson who frequently stayed at the White House, sent a long letter urging that this country should openly demonstrate its solidarity with Israel. She implied that opting for a permanent peace would be the best choice, meaning no withdrawal. But the one person whose opinion mattered the most was Ambassador Barbour. In his early reports following the Arab defeat he insisted that the intoxication with victory would not push the Israelis towards expansionism and that they would remain within their borders. He was deliberately ignoring loud calls for the annexation of the West Bank and never surrendering the Old City from within the cabinet. He also reported Israel's reference to the "liberation" of the Old City unquestioningly, appearing to endorse this idea. He even insisted that Israel made clear its intention to safeguard its rights in the Jewish holy sites only, ignoring other statements in the press by officials who openly referred to retaining the entire city.[8]

Yet, there was some lingering admiration for the tenacity of Jordanian soldiers who attempted to defend the Old City even when lacking air cover. When Rabin was honored by Hebrew University at the end of the war, he declared in his remarks while feted on the Mt. Scopus campus:

> The men in the front lines saw with their own eyes not only the glory of victory, but also the price of victory—their comrades fallen beside them soaked in blood. I know too that the price paid by our enemies who also touched the hearts of our men.[9]

These were brave words and an admission of the horrendous casualties sustained by the enemy, although he stopped short of recognizing the atrocities committed by the Israeli military during that war. There were already accounts of Egyptian soldiers killed in Sinai after surrendering their arms and a large number of Palestinians who were executed in cold blood due to their service with the Egyptians. According to reporter Gabi Brunn of *Yediot Ahronot*, eyewitness accounts told of POWs suspected of being Palestinian terrorists at al-Arish airport in the Gaza Strip who were ordered to dig their own graves before being shot. Some of these accounts were confirmed a few years later by historian of the Israeli military, Dr. Aryeh Yitzhaki.[10] The

swiftness with which Israel accomplished the task of defeating the Jordanians
in Jerusalem, however, gave rise to many unsubstantiated accounts in the
Arabic press of minimal Jordanian casualties. The influential Egyptian writer, Heikal, an insider with special access to Nasser, later confirmed these
accounts by contending that the Jordanians knew of the impending Israeli
attack and put up a symbolic fight, netting only sixteen casualties. He concluded that Jordan's attack against Israel was only a maneuver.[11]

Ambassador Barbour persisted in relaying information on Israeli views
regarding the surrendering of the recently occupied territories by tracking the
rise of palpable national sentiment favoring maintaining the new lines of
1967. Yet, he reported that those who favored retaining East Jerusalem were
limited to supporters of the Rafi Party. As an example, he cited the following
piece by the political editor of the liberal *Ha'aretz*, Shlomo Gross, calling for
the disposition of the West Bank to Hussein, but not Jerusalem and its surroundings:

> The decision regarding Jerusalem has already been taken. The Old City will
> again be part of the Capital . . . . We are reliable trustees to the world for
> safeguarding free access to the holy places and religious institutions, certainly
> no less than King Hussein, and there is no need for any international supervi-
> sion or guardianship . . . . The fate of the former Jordanian part of Jerusalem
> and the surrounding villages has been sealed.[12]

By June 29, continued Barbour, the Israeli Government was still focusing
its attention mainly on the holy places. He wrote that the government would
soon act on Eshkol's assurances to heads of various religious communities of
unlimited access to the holy places, in consultation with external religious
centers such as the Vatican. But Barbour defended the Government of Israel
on several grounds, including against allegations of having pushed the West
Bank population to the East Bank. He reported that the cabinet had taken
recent measures to restrict undocumented travel to Jordan. More importantly,
the briefing by the Director General of the Foreign Office Levari on the latest
Knesset acts to reunify the two Jerusalems by extending Israeli law to the
Jordanian side on June 28, he explained, was intended to steal a step on the
press. The media were already determined to publicize this as a maneuver to
block the call of the General Assembly for the return of all of the conquered
territory, including Jerusalem. Although Israel had agreed to postpone taking
any action upon US insistence, it did not agree to maintain this position
forever. "I argued that step had certainly complicated situation for us at GA,"
wrote Barbour, "and . . . that we took a dim view of being faced with *fait
accompli* however inevitable Israelis might deem it. Although it [is] now
academic, I understand there are many who deplore precipitate action and
attribute it in part at least to fact Eban not here to plead international repercussions [to] cabinet's haste."[13] Barbour, thus, acquiesced in a decision

which he fully understood to be one of Israel's most frequent faits accomplis. The adoption of Israel's Protection of the Holy Places Law was also reported with no argument or comment. The law which assured members of the various religious communities of unimpeded access to the holy places of the Old City superseded the Status Quo Law, thus, opening the door for the government's legal management of the religious places. The law was passed soon after by the Knesset following the destruction of the Mughrabi Quarter, located next to the Wailing Wall, which annulled the Status Quo Law, as well as weakened the recently signed Protection of the Holy Places Law. [14]

As soon as McClosky, spokesperson for the State Department who had a reputation for honesty, said "We are neutral in thought, word and deed," and issued a neutrality statement on the war, Jewish American leaders reacted strongly. Appointed by Rusk as Deputy Assistant Secretary of State, McClosky quickly assumed the role of Israel's critic. David Brody of the ADL of B'nai B'rith sent a memo to Johnson expressing anger at the hostility of the State Department and absolving the President of any responsibility for the neutrality statement. Brody derided the State Department for treating Israel as if it were just any other state, with no concern for its people. The President was thanked for the administration's UN position during the crisis, in which a cease-fire was sought but without stipulating any need for withdrawal from seized territory. The American Jewish community was concerned that after Israel won this war it would be forced to give up its rewards, just as during the Suez War of 1956. The community was hopeful that the UN would not be allowed to betray Israel and that only the United States was capable of preventing this from happening. American Jews were looking to the President to prevent a forced Israeli withdrawal as had happened in 1956 by the Dulles-Eisenhower team. B'nai B'rith hinted that the Jewish community, which was slated to demonstrate at Lafayette Park the following day, should not be allowed to resort to making anti-Johnson statements. Subsequently, the President was requested to send a message to the gathering crowd without any reference to "territorial integrity," which would act as a red flag for the demonstrators. [15]

The American Jewish community was also alarmed at the appearance of some Arab demonstrators who picketed the White House. While Jewish demonstrators were estimated to be 30,000, chartering buses from major east coast cities, their leaders were anxiously monitoring an Arab gathering headed by Dr. Muhammad Mehdi. The Iraqi-American activist estimated that his group numbered between three hundred to five hundred protesters, which still managed to aggravate the Jewish gathering. [16] Some pressure was applied by American oil interests in the Middle East, though it was not known at the time that this would be the last gasp of a lobby with an inflated influence. ARAMCO's representative in Washington, Robert I. Brougham, sent a memo to Bundy recapitulating a conversation he recently had with

Saudi Oil Minister Ahmad Zaki Yamani in Riyadh. The latter said that the Iraqi and Kuwaiti oil ministers, both of whose governments were close allies of Nasser, asked his country to take the lead in adopting strong measures, such as nationalization of Western oil interests in all of their countries. He said that this would be a protest against official Western support for Israel's aggression. Yamani also suggested that American, British, and French oil companies should help the Arab cause since they and the host countries shared a mutual interest in this crisis. The oil companies, he elaborated, should intercede with their own governments. The United States in particular should be dissuaded from acting as the policeman of the Gulf of Aqaba, leaving this role to the UN. Yamani reported that the Saudi monarch had asked him to convey the view that the American and British governments should remain neutral, something which Johnson was happy to accept. Yamani also asked that ARAMCO's shareholders should be encouraged to do their utmost to prevent Israeli gains from the latest attacks. He hinted that American oil companies in Libya should be made part of this effort. His appeal to the companies was made as an added enforcement of private letters exchanged between the Saudi King and the American President.[17] Efforts of Faysal and his oil minister to corral the oil companies and push them to intercede with their own governments appeared to have been rewarded when McClosky issued a statement claiming that the United States maintained a neutral position in this crisis. Jewish pressure, however, was taken much more seriously and its impact on the development of America's policy lines was taken for granted.

The CIA then forwarded to the NSC a summary of Eban's speech at the General Assembly on June 19, as well as a clarification of his government's position on the outcome of the war. The Israeli Foreign Minister revealed his government's intent to reject the Soviet call for a return to the former borders as they existed before the outbreak of the war. Emphasizing that the new Israeli policy was to insist on direct negotiations with the Arabs leading to their recognition of Israel's existence, he also eschewed any reference to possible withdrawal from newly seized Arab territory. But he singled out Jerusalem for special mention as the one case in which a return to the previous status quo was categorically ruled out. He implied that King Hussein must learn that rejection of the Israeli peace offer on the eve of the war was doomed to result in serious repercussions. Eban also asserted his government's wish to gain access to the holy places in Jerusalem, but without further elaboration. The speech was made a few days before Israel clarified its position on the optimal status of the Old City following the end of the hostilities.[18]

US assessment of the post-war situation was already complicated by Israel's attack on the USS Liberty, but that did not aggravate American-Israeli relations sufficiently to force the latter's retreat on the Jerusalem question.

As the United States turned a blind eye to the Israeli hardening of position on Jerusalem, a barrage of verbal attacks was directed at the Arab delegates who were meeting at the Khartoum summit, August 19–September 1, which netted the famous Three Nos. The summit, convened under Nasser's leadership, adopted the three rejections of recognizing Israel, negotiating with the enemy or accepting Israel's peace offer. Jordan, however, was allowed to seek its own resolution of the dire situation resulting from the war such as losing the entire West Bank and Jerusalem. The gist of this Arab hardened position at the summit was in reality enforcing a firm "No" on each member state of the ALS in attendance and cautioning against reaching separate deals with Israel. This was referred to sometimes as the "Fourth No." Later, Shuqeiry was blamed for leaking news of the Arab hardened and rejectionist position to the press, leading Israel to latch on to the Khartoum Declaration by amplifying its strident tone rather than its real limitations.[19] The ALS had actually tried to bar him and his pre-Fateh PLO delegation from attending the summit, but failed in its endeavor due to Syria's efforts. Shafiq al-Hout, Shuqeiry's aide, quickly grasped that what drove King Faysal to settle the Yemen dispute with Nasser was the loss of Jerusalem. Efforts were also made to coordinate steps by various Arab oil-producing countries to sharpen the so-called "oil weapon" in the battle for Jerusalem and Arab Palestine. The summit meeting and Shuqeiry's open denunciation of Arab intent on salvaging some strategic benefit from the debacle, as well as his explicit declaration that since the PLO was not a member of the UN, it was under no obligation to abide by its resolutions, finally stirred up Nasser's ire. The Egyptian leader terminated Shuqeiry's mandate as the head of the Arab-dependent PLO at meeting's end, forcing him to resign. He was succeeded as chairman of this organization by Yahya Hamoudah.[20]

In the meantime, the foreign aid package promised to Israel in the PL-480 Agreement, totaling $28 million, proceeded smoothly in the US House of Representatives. Israel was to receive notice by Assistant Secretary of State Battle that it would be the recipient of the first $10.5 million loan authorization, but must proceed slowly in order to avoid having this coincide with the Knesset's resolution extending Israeli law to East Jerusalem. Jordan was slated to receive a $2-million grant, subject to the President's approval, and a package consisting of $80,000 authorized for riot control equipment.[21] The White House Special Committee then drafted a telegram from the Secretary of State to Foreign Minister Eban on June 12, with a query regarding Israel's position on a number of issues such as refugees, the status of Sharm al-Sheikh, the Suez Canal and Jerusalem. This was occasioned by a storm of criticism in the Security Council seeking Israel's withdrawal to the former armistice boundaries. Apparently, the United States was questioning the seriousness of Eshkol's message to Johnson on June 5, in which he asserted in broad terms Israel's desire to live in peace "within our territory" and to enjoy the freedom of navigation in waters claimed by Egypt. But since the war had created a drastic transformation of the area, the United States felt that it was appropriate to inquire into the truthfulness of some claims made by Israeli officials. These uncertainties were caused by statements such as those by Israeli Ambassador to Washington, Avraham Harman, in which he claimed that his government had no "territorial ambitions," but also had no intent to pull back from newly acquired areas, except in the context of a final peace agreement.[22]

THE TELL-TALE SIGNS OF JERUSALEM'S ALTERED STATUS

Reports of Israel's unflagging attempts to change the status of several areas in the Old City in order to block the possibility of returning to the pre-June 1967 territorial status quo were widely disseminated. The demolition of the Mughrabi Quarter, located near the Wailing Wall, was the first instance of creating facts on the ground in order to steal a step ahead of any UN decision calling for a return to the old borders. The Mughrabi Quarter took its name from Moroccan pilgrims who began to flock to the city in the Eighth Century (Hegira), some of whom later deciding to form a Ribat and defend the city permanently. The Moroccans gained fame after a larger contingent joined the forces of al-Nasir, Saladin's son, in liberating the city from the Crusaders. Predominating in the navy, they were highly esteemed for their service and eventually given a *waqf* by Sultan al-Afdhal near the Buraq Wall which became their quarter. After the fall of Andalusia in the sixteenth century, visits by Moroccans and Andalusian Muslims accelerated. The quarter eventually boasted Islamic schools such as al-Madrassah al-Afdhaliyah, Sufi monasteries or *zawiya*, as well as small mosques dating back to the Mamluk period.[23]

Responsibility for the demolition order which flouted the norms of humanitarian law and the Status Quo regulations remained murky. A reconstruction of this fateful event later on demonstrated a clear case of deception in order to keep the prime minister in the dark, presumably so that there would be no opportunity to demand ending this operation. The officer charged with carrying out the demolition order designed to widen the plaza facing the Western Wall in time to accommodate large Jewish crowds flooding the Old City for the upcoming Pesach celebrations was Lt. Colonel Ya'kov Salman. Recently returned from Latin America, he was made Deputy Director-General at the Ministry of Finance and was ordered to clean up the quarter by Dayan, who took part in drafting this order along with three other co-conspirators: Shlomo Lahat, Military Governor of East Jerusalem; Teddy Kollek, the Mayor of West Jerusalem; and Uzi Narkis, Chief of the Central Command who had earlier rejected Chief Rabbi of the Armed Forces Shlomo

Goren's call for seizing the moment of conquest to demolish the storied Dome of the Rock shrine. According to Gershon Gorenberg's account in *The Accidental Empire*, Salman feared legal repercussions of his action once he was summoned by Eshkol. He arrived at the Prime Minister's office armed with documents found in the municipality of East Jerusalem providing evidence of the derelict state of the quarter and the resolve of the previous Jordanian administration to demolish it altogether. Eshkol's investigation of the incident which took place a few days after the fall of the Old City ran into a stone wall.[24]

Other accounts, such as that by the historian Tom Segev years later, revealed the bizarre circumstances under which this historic living space and its *waqf* buildings were erased. It all began when Ben Gurion was offended by the presence of ancient public toilets in the quarter within the vicinity of the Wall. These were quickly removed. But fearing delays if he consulted Dayan or waited for a legal opinion, he sought Kollek for advice. The mayor was able to summon an architect and an archeologist to assess the area's general condition and come up with a report. Narkis issued the order to start demolishing the entire quarter, justifying his decision in his later memoirs by claiming, without any supporting evidence that the original homes of the Moroccan pilgrims were purposefully built in that location in order to restrict Jewish pedestrians' access to the Wailing Wall. He also attached a running account of unsuccessful past attempts to purchase the entire area of the Wall. The Minister of Justice advised that the operation should commence quickly, admitting that there was no legal precedent for this action. The demolition was then started under the cover of darkness, as an army officer ordered the Arab residents to evacuate their homes, promising them new dwellings. This produced a lot of waiting and people asking for more time to carry out their belongings, while some refused to obey the order. Those who remained inside their homes saw their buildings razed by bulldozers, leaving one casualty under the rubble. The number of evicted families was 135, but no one seemed to care. Some journalists, like Uzi Benjamin, quickly claimed that this action was not warranted by security or urban-planning considerations but was simply motivated by the perpetrators' mystical belief that it was their special mission as representatives of the Jewish people to take possession of the sacred site. But responsibility for the decision remained muddled as the municipality and the military blamed the contractors' association for undertaking the work.[25]

Kollek and company were anxious to finalize the most famous fait accompli of the war before international law was called upon to restrain them. The Old City, which was captured on Wednesday, June 7, saw the beginning of the demolition on June 11, four days later. According to another account based on later information in the Israeli press, the quarter's population was over one thousand at the time. They lived mostly in small houses along narrow alleys, to which Kollek referred as "small slum houses." The man who led the demolition team was later identified as Eitan Ben Moshe, an engineer who was an officer with the IDF Central Command. Apparently, he had no regrets or remorse, even when he enthusiastically went about his work demolishing a small mosque near the Buraq Wall. The mosque was a *waqf* assumed to have been built on the spot where Muhammad tethered his horse, al-Buraq, when he ascended to Heaven. Ben Moshe was later quoted making the jovial remark, "Why shouldn't the mosque be sent to Heaven, just as the magic horse did?" The woman who died in the rubble was eventually identified as Rasmiyyah Ali Taba'ki, but Ben Moshe told journalists that he found three, not one, bodies in the rubble. These refused to leave their homes, he said. Kollek was particularly proud of this accomplishment, seeing the open plaza which now dominated the quarter as the best thing he and his group ever did. He said that the old quarter gave the entire place a feel of the *galut,* or diaspora, a place for loud lamentations. He also claimed that all the Arab residents were given decent housing, which the residents denied. According to their account, what they received were eviction notices dated 1968, offering each family the sum of 100 Jordanian Dinars. Half of the population accepted this compensation, but the other half declined, claiming that it would have legitimized the occupation. [26]

Years later, Major Ben Moshe disclosed the circumstances of his involvement in this episode. In an interview on November 26, 1999, with a small paper called *Yerushalayem* (Jerusalem), he told his story for the first time. He reported that members of the Israeli military toured the quarter, giving residents fifteen minutes' notice before the destruction began. He personally transported three corpses of people who elected to remain in their houses to Mikor Houleem Hospital in West Jerusalem. Other corpses were buried beneath the Wailing Wall. He explained that the demolition decision was made by Kollek, while admitting his own role in destroying al-Buraq Mosque. He acknowledged that the order came from one of his military superiors who told him that in the event of international protests, he should take full responsibility for the decision. If that happened, Ben Moshe was assured that in case of a trial, he would receive the maximum sentence of five years, which would be immediately suspended. However he admitted to the paper that he was a descendant of an Orthodox family and was a believer in Israel's right to impose its sovereignty over a place which belonged to Jews anyway. [27]

EVACUATING THE JEWISH QUARTER

Known to Jerusalemites as al-Sharaf neighborhood, the Jewish Quarter was another casualty of the June War and another illustration of Israeli disregard of international law. It was also another example of the Israeli authorities' faith in the effectiveness of confronting the world with a fait accompli. Designated as a Quarter by the British Mandate government, the area which was occupied mostly by the Old City's Jewish population consisted of rented *waqf* property belonging to the city's leading Muslim families. The intent here was to evacuate any remaining Arab families in order to enlarge the Jewish area and link it to the Moroccan Quarter, reserving it exclusively for Jewish residents. One of the first incidents resulting from this decision was the forcible evacuation of Ahmad Mahfouz Abu-Sneinah's family from its residence which was adjacent to the Khourba Synagogue and al-Umari Mosque. The family operated a *waqf*-owned bakery not far from its place of residence, recalling later that an Israeli military unit came to their home immediately after finishing the demolition of the Mughrabi Quarter, or a week after the fall of the city. The Israelis began to mark Arab homes with an X sign, followed by loudspeakers which announced a forty-eight-hour period before the homes were slated for destruction. Then, an armed military unit showed up, accompanied by a civilian evacuation team in variegated outfits which stormed Arab homes, forcibly removing residents, including women and children, while throwing furniture in the street. Doors were sealed to prevent the residents from returning. The Abu-Sneinah family took refuge in its bakery where they stayed for a period of four months. After witnessing the destruction of other homes in the area, they sought a residence outside the limits of their old neighborhood. Other evacuees who shared their recollections of the events of that particular month of June with reporters and authors provided more details. Some asserted that they bought or rented their homes from the Husseinis and other families who were the legal owners of these properties for centuries. The Israeli method here entailed either the forcible removal of families or confiscating or forcibly buying their properties by offering small monetary compensation. However, there was a semblance of legality here as the evacuated families were sometimes served with court orders sanctioning the rehabbing of their residences.[28]

Enlarging, or ethnically cleansing, the Jewish Quarter it turned out, was Ben Gurion's idea. It was his obsession with demographic challenges that inspired municipal and military authorities to take on the derelict buildings of this Quarter. Initially, he was quite perturbed by the prospect of adding one million West Bank Arabs to Israel's 1948 Arab residents. He also viewed the possibility of relocating 200,000 refugees from the Gaza Strip to the West Bank, as was proposed by some Israeli hawks, with great alarm. When informed by Kollek that Arabs were living in the Jewish Quarter, of which he was unaware, he responded that they should be thrown out, adding that, "There is no need for any law. Occupation is the most effective law."[29] This was a surprising statement by one of Israel's founders, but as things unfolded, turned out to be a true expression of how Israelis regarded the international community and its universal standards of behavior. It was also a reflection of the triumphalism sweeping Israel in the wake of the war, giving rise to Eshkol's unintentionally prescient statement to his party's political committee: "We've been given a good dowry—but it comes with a bride we don't like."[30]

THE UNITED STATES ABSORBS THE SHOCK OF ISRAEL'S INTRANSIGENCE

As soon as the United States began to comprehend the Hobbesian nature of the Middle East theater of war when hostilities ended, it felt the urgency to convey a nebulous message of reassurance and support to King Hussein. It was still uninformed regarding the extent of Israel's territorial designs and new strategic intentions, particularly following the Jordanian defeat. But the United States was still anxious to set its small Arab ally on a new course. Thus, King Hussein was advised on the eve of his visit to the White House in late June, that maintaining his strong American alliance was conditional upon his commitment to a peaceful resolution of the conflict. The Special Committee advising the President also emphasized in a memo to the chief executive that any delay in launching peace talks in the area, which the Israelis ostensibly were anxious to achieve, would only lead to solidifying their control over the West Bank and Jerusalem. This would also close any window for reversing these steps in the future and would harden choices in this theater of war. It was felt that the King's willingness to participate would make him an important cog in the wheel of the new Middle East. It was felt that the King should be pushed to the peace table, even if through third parties, confiding that he had a history of secret peace contacts with Israeli officials in recent years. At the same time, the Committee sided with the newly revealed Israeli position challenging the legality of Jordan's sovereignty over the West Bank which was tantamount to acceding to Israel's annexation plans. But the Committee clarified that it had cautioned Israel against confronting the international community with faits accomplis through unilateral action. The Israeli strategy, related the Committee, was to magnify the West Bankers' loud preference for autonomy and separation from Jordan, until they, the Israelis, came to a conclusion regarding the ultimate fate of this territory. But at the same time, the Americans understood that the only way Jordan would consent to signing a peace agreement with Israel would be after receiving pledges of support for regaining the West Bank with minor border adjustments and with an international regime over Jerusalem. The American view was that Jordan may be persuaded to reach a peaceful settlement if enticed with generous economic linkage to its former enemy. Such a deal, if it became a reality, would stabilize the Jerusalem situation, converting it into a center of economic activity. It may even lead to the creation of economic opportunities for the returned Palestinian refugees. Always placing its trust in the efficacy of economic solutions, the Committee did not differ from several past American efforts to wean the refugees away from the ideology of national liberation with promises of economic assistance. Thus, as early as June 26, the date of this memo, those around the President acceded to the Israeli position on the retention of Jerusalem.[31]

Additionally, the US mission to the UN was already forwarding reports of direct Israeli approaches to the Vatican to placate Catholic anxieties over the Christian holy places in advance of further Israeli steps to attach the Old City to West Jerusalem. Thus, on July 1, Israel sought to open talks with the Holy See, only to be told that the Vatican still held out for an international regime over the city. The Vatican then expressed its wish to dispatch a high-level emissary to Jerusalem to pursue talks for reaching a practical policy in place of the defunct twenty-year-old internationalization scheme. Vatican feathers were smoothed when it was assured that it was the first to be approached, rather than the Protestant churches, assuring the continuation of its primary role as the leading Western church in the city.[32]

Reports from the American Ambassador continued to defend Israel's commitment to upholding the sanctity of the holy places, with nary a reference to the manner in which it had already gutted the Status Quo regulations. Neither was there any criticism of demolishing Muslim cultural sites such as the Mughrabi Quarter and ethnically cleansing the Jewish Quarter. Ambassador Barbour wrote to the State Department lauding Israel's efforts to minimize any damage to the holy sites when capturing the Old City, risking the lives of its own troops in the process. He described this as additional proof of Israel's ability to manage these sites in the future. The capture of the city was simply motivated by defensive considerations, he asserted, which should soften US long-term commitment to maintaining the territorial status quo. Barbour's cable, commented Walt Rostow, sounded like a reflection of Tel Aviv's viewpoint rather than the expression of an independent assessment. The State Department's Under-Secretary for Political Affairs, Eugene Rostow, later added his own summation. He claimed that the municipal amalgamation of the two halves of the city did not translate into an act of annexation since Israel, just like other countries, lacked the jurisdiction to alter the laws of an international city.[33]

Israel was also engaged in a campaign to pass off the de facto annexation of East Jerusalem through the extension of its legal system as simply a matter of "municipal integration," avoiding the term "annexation." Israel instructed its own envoys overseas to present this move as a necessary step to assure the smooth functioning of services in both sections of the city, even while the city's boundaries were being expanded eastwards in order to augment its water supply. Some areas were spared in order to avoid aggravating Christian feelings abroad. For instance, the Israeli cabinet abandoned plans to annex areas around Rachel's tomb, near Bethlehem in the north. The site included a mosque built over the remnants of the Jewish tomb, both of which were revered by Muslims over the years, but also was too close to Christian sites in the city where Jesus was born. But even then, Israeli authorities had already annexed twenty-seven square miles to Israeli Jerusalem, which almost tripled its original size. By June 29, the Arab City Council of East Jerusalem was summarily dismissed by orders of Chief of the Army's Central Command, Uzi Narkis, who led the troops in taking the city. Apparently, what he feared the most was the survival of two city councils and two mayors which would lend legitimacy to the remaining Jordanian officials within the city. There-fore, his orders to Colonel Ya'kov Salman, recently named deputy-military governor and the man who played a role in the destruction of the Mughrabi Quarter, were to dispose of the Arab council quickly before its tenure as-sumed permanency. Salman was confused by this order for which there was no precedent. He was commanded to find a quick method of applying the *coup de grace* to this body which was hardly functioning anymore, and to do it in a legal manner. Salman eventually carried out the order by summoning the Arab mayor of East Jerusalem, Rouhi al-Khatib, along with four of the council's available eleven members. The short notice did not reach the others in time, so Salman read to the rump council a four-sentence dismissal notice in Hebrew, which was translated into Arabic on the only available piece of paper he could find, which turned out to be a paper napkin. This was upon Al-Khatib's demand who asked that the notice be made in writing. Goren-berg was able to document this momentous step in finalizing the annexation of East Jerusalem by interviewing Israeli journalist Uzi Benzamin, who ended his summation of the event by admitting that the whole episode lacked any shred of legality. But by the beginning of July, and before Israel admitted the annexation, Eshkol gave the order for the construction of the first settle-ment in the vicinity of East Jerusalem. This, he believed, would assure Is-rael's control over the eastern part of the city and prevent international pres-sure from forcing its return to the Arabs.[34]

THE HISTORICAL ACCOUNT OF THE CONSUL GENERAL

The real story of Israel's actions on the ground was provided not by the American Embassy in Tel Aviv with its filtered accounts, but by the American Consulate General in East Jerusalem. Ever since the division of the city in 1948 and the refusal of much of the international community to recognize West Jerusalem as Israel's capital, the consulate was made inde-pendent of the embassy in Tel Aviv. This set-up was unique in the experience of the State Department, making these lower-level diplomatic missions re-sponsible directly to the State Department, rather than the local embassy.

Only one other case similar to this one existed, namely Hong Kong. The consulate's role in East Jerusalem was transformed into a political, rather than an administrative one.[35] Ultimately, the consulate became adept at funneling significant political and economic information relating to events on the ground. This turned out to be particularly preternatural in the aftermath of the capture of East Jerusalem, but did not necessarily overturn the inflated and optimistic reports of the Tel Aviv Embassy.

Evan M. Wilson, the Consul-General at the time, held the rank of minister and was uniquely situated to assess Israel's actions in light of his long State Department experience and knowledge of the Palestine question. He had served in the past on the Palestine Desk of the Near East Division of the Department of State when the fate of this country was being debated at the UN. Wilson had also encountered intensified Zionist attempts to gain access to various US officials in the wake of the Biltmore Conference. He always bristled at the Zionist charge that all members of the Near East Division were fervently anti-Semitic. He often recounted that pro-Arab pressure had also targeted the same division, accusing it of being pro-Zionist, leading to the unofficial view that it was best to cease involvement with any side of this emotional dispute. Yet, Wilson and his State Department colleagues maintained the position that the creation of a Jewish state in Palestine was harmful to American interests in the region. Working alongside two recognized Middle East experts at the time, Philip W. Ireland and William Yale, he was detailed to devise a trusteeship agreement which the Truman administration sought to substitute for the General Assembly's Partition Resolution (181). He often recalled the stubborn opposition of the War Department during the 1940s to the creation of a Jewish state. This position was exemplified by Secretary of War Forrestal, who condemned Zionist plans based on his conviction that Arab oil resources were essential for the conduct of a major war, hence the need to avoid alienating the Arabs. Wilson's conclusion was that the role of the UN in this crisis did not fully gestate until January 1947, after he left the Department. It was only after Truman succeeded to the presidency in 1945 that US Palestine policy began to be drafted by the White House, shifting perceptibly away from the State Department. It was only then that the battle heated up at the UN, presumably with White House advisers working in unison with the US delegation and avoiding the State Department altogether.[36]

Supremely confident of his impartiality, Wilson became a competent monitor of events on the ground. The news of Israel's destruction of the three Arab villages in the Latroun area, which dominated the route to Tel Aviv, was the first to come to his attention. The first instance of Israeli mass scale removal or expulsion of the local Arab population in the newly conquered Jordanian territory took place quickly before the fate of the West Bank was settled. Apparently, UN Truce personnel became the first to discover the total

razing of the villages of Imwas, Bayt Nuba, and Yalo and the forced expulsion of the population eastwards. Wilson reported the inability of consular
officials to access the area once they reached Israeli military roadblocks. He
suggested that the American Embassy should try to reach the villages from
the west.[37] The three villages of mixed Christian-Muslim population, with
Biblical Imwas being the site of a Trappist monastery, were heavily populated but soon turned into a public park. This was given the name Canada Park
in honor of the Jewish Canadian volunteers and soldiers who died fighting on
Israel's side, as well as in gratitude for funding by the Jewish Canadian
community. The park was then turned over to the JNF, just like several
historical areas won since 1948, signifying that ownership was vested in the
"Jewish people," never to revert to Arab ownership again. The Arab inhabitants were eventually settled in Jerusalem and Ramallah. The park's 7,000
dunums (or dunam, Turk. a land unit measuring 1,000 square meters) were
later contested in the 1970s by the original Arab inhabitants who presented
signed petitions to Prime Minister Rabin. The authorities turned them down,
employing the same argument used to justify all acts of state seizure of land,
namely security considerations. Wilson also intervened with Israeli authorities to allow the villagers to return once he received news of their plight on
July 6 from the mayor of Beit Nuba. Wilson's appeal was joined by several
parties, presumably other diplomats.[38] He reported having personally interceded with the special representative of the Foreign Ministry at the military
governor's office in Jerusalem, who referred him to the military governor of
Ramallah. Wilson expressed his determination to continue his appeal on
behalf of the Arab mayor, asserting that Israel must realize that its actions
had fallen under a magnifying glass and are being observed by the entire
world.[39]

The participation of Canadian Jews in the 1967 War did not receive any
mention in this community's writings, leading one to believe that this topic
was considered politically sensitive at the time.[40] But foreign participation in
the war, particularly by American Jews, must have been widely rumored in
Washington. The American Consulate itself was called upon to verify this
allegation, considering that the United States always stressed its neutrality in
this conflict. Therefore, a consular officer had paid no less than ten visits to
the headquarters of the IDF within a period of three weeks, only to find out
that most of the officers in charge were not English speakers, but some were
fluent in Arabic. Yet he was unable to identify any Americans among them, a
fact attested to by the Arab mayors of towns in that area. One soldier, however, admitted to being a Canadian. Wilson also sought information on the
national background of several of Ramallah's military governors. His telegram to the State Department relayed rumors of participation by US citizens,
concluding that this may pan out, just as during the 1948 War.[41]

Wilson's report on the impact of the war on the Arab population of East Jerusalem and the city's political officers was decidedly grim. Less than a month after Israel's conquest of the Old City and its suburbs, a comprehensive plan to integrate these with the Israeli side was put in place and was followed by the erasure of the Arab structure of government. The local Palestinian population was subjected to an intense campaign of political intimidation and economic exploitation. Anwar al-Khatib, the outgoing governor of East Jerusalem, expressed disillusionment at the prospect of reaching a negotiated settlement between the Palestinians and their new occupiers. He explained to the Consul that he had already lost faith in any such development after witnessing official Israeli policies applied to his city. There were major high-handed Israeli attempts to promote the fiction of unification of the two sides of the city, but also unwillingness to safeguard the economic interests of the Arab merchant community. Israeli steps which belied their declared intention to treat the conquered population with deference, included the dismissal of the majority of the municipal workers who cared for the city during the Jordanian period. The Israelis also forced Arab banks to close and sealed the area from the West Bank which was highly dependent on financial and economic relations with the city. [42]

These were damaging developments for a city which subsisted on a combination of tourism revenue, government salaries, and remittances from workers in the Arab Gulf countries which were in jeopardy until the Israeli Government approved a new routing mechanism for them. The only source of income left was that generated by a revived tourism industry. The Consul stated that al-Khatib's pessimism was warranted unless alternate sources of income were provided by the Israeli Government. He also heard that the Arab business community in the city was very discouraged, leading some of its members to accept Israeli buy-outs, with the Arab tourist offices being the first to suffer such fate. All of this, he concluded, was leading to maximizing Israel's hold over the Old City. [43] But Wilson also reported that most of the Arabs who were contacted appeared to be pleased with the removal of barriers between East and West Jerusalem, hoping that this would lead to enhanced integration of the two sides. Yet, some Arabs were apprehensive about the likelihood of economic benefits reverting to Israeli commercial interests exclusively. Most Palestinians feared that the initial outcome of this integration would be beneficial to Israelis only and would bypass them. Some of these fears grew out of the separation of East Jerusalem from the West Bank, weakening the city's ties to the heart of the rest of the Jordanian-ruled territory, which used to be the normal state of affairs before the 1967 War. [44]

THE CONSUL AND THE PROPAGANDA WAR

Wilson reported that the streets of East Jerusalem were jammed with all kinds of vehicles and pedestrians, giving the city a semblance of normalcy. The government also planned a concert by the Israeli Philharmonic Orchestra at the outdoor amphitheater of Hebrew University on the Mt. Scopus campus. This was the former Palestine Symphony Orchestra which was now scheduled for this performance in order to highlight Israel's capture of an area considered until recently no-man's land.[45] All efforts were made to cast an aura of legitimacy and normalcy on Israel's rule over East Jerusalem. As a result, the propaganda war took off with Israel's Ministry of Religious Affairs accusing the Arab population of desecrating thirty-six synagogues during Jordan's nineteen years of rule. Wilson immediately doubted the veracity of this statement, declaring that the consulate's map of the holy places listed only four synagogues within the Old City. The Ministry and the Israeli press also repeated the familiar refrain of Arab violation of the old Jewish cemetery on the Mt. of Olives, facing the walls. Wilson clarified, however, that although the cemetery was always in a derelict state, the Jordanians could only be accused of neglecting it, rather than causing the damage in the first place. He pointed out that the State Department and other diplomatic posts were in possession of a copy of a photograph dating to 1921, which showed the dilapidated condition of the cemetery even as early as that date.[46]

If there was any destruction of property or demolition of historic sites, Wilson pointed out, it was the work of the city's new rulers. Most of the destruction was done as soon as the Arab side was captured, and mostly in the area immediately adjacent to the walls. The Convent of Soeurs Preparatrices near Allenby Square was completely demolished, and heavy damage was inflicted on Collège des Frères and the French Hospital. Using great amounts of dynamite explosives, the Israeli military were determined to change the historic features of the city if need be in order to widen and annex adjacent areas. The dynamite charge in this case was so powerful, it blew out the windows of the nearby office of the city's vice-mayor and led to the flight of thirty to forty individuals whose homes suffered serious tremors. The French Consul-General protested vigorously, prompting the firing of the army engineer for his lack of caution in carrying out his orders. What were these demolitions for? Wilson wrote that the government's intention was to open up Sulliman (sic) street and restore it to its British Mandate course when it extended from Allenby Square to Damascus Gate. The vacant houses belonging to a Syrian Catholic Monsignor and other religious officials in the same vicinity were also demolished without prior notification. Demolition work during the previous three or four weeks, Wilson added, exceeded the destruction which took place during the fighting itself. For instance, damage incurred by the Augusta Victoria Hospital during the war, which, according to the World Lutheran Federation ran as high as $400,000, was not compensated in full. Kollek offered to pay only a fraction of the cost. The consulate reacted by accelerating its efforts to coordinate relief activity for the fallen city. The agencies which enlisted immediately to offer their services to the city included religious and secular international organizations such as CARE, UNICEF, UNRWA, Lutherans, Mennonites, Caritas, Swedish, and Norwegian groups and American Friends Service Committee (AFSC).[47]

Another issue, however, affected American interests in the city directly. When the consulate attempted to take the usual diplomatic route by protesting the looting of properties of American citizens during the hostilities, the occasion was used to extort recognition of Israel's new status over the city. A similar pattern resulted from the consulate's efforts to obtain exit permits for Palestinian American citizens wishing to leave the city. In the past, the consulate would approach Rafael Levy, its chief government contact, but since the war Levy rejected the consulate's correspondence. He insisted that it be addressed to him as a representative of the Foreign Office in Jerusalem, hoping that this would lead to recognition of Jerusalem as part of Israel. The consulate yielded to this pressure in order to expedite the discharging of its duties, but had indicated each time that it was doing so under duress.[48]

As soon as the Israeli Government announced the extension of all its laws to East Jerusalem, calling it "unified administration," which amounted to de facto annexation, Wilson urged his government to deal with it as such, avoiding Israel's quest for *de jure* unification. He recommended that the city should still be considered internationalized for he feared that the latest Israeli move implied an intent to separate the city from the West Bank in the near future. Without necessarily favoring a return to the divisions of the pre-1967 city, he feared the impact of this unilateral act greatly. He had already witnessed Israel's arbitrary conversion of the Jordanian currency to Israeli currency in Jerusalem, and Israel's new strict set of travel rules between the West Bank and the city. Israel by that time had already indicated its lack of interest in any negotiations over the future of the newly annexed city, although the question of access for West Bankers remained vital for the conduct of any future talks. His own contacts had persuaded him that West Bank Arabs were free of any ties to Jordan, but were adamant in their belief that Jerusalem was vital for the economy of the West Bank. He offered the view that if Israel managed to reach a peaceful settlement with the Palestinians over Jerusalem and the West Bank, the Palestine issue would greatly lose its appeal as a rallying cry for Arab nationalists everywhere. Jerusalem remained the main issue which Israel must address through making meaningful concessions. This would be in the interest of both Israel and the United States, he concluded.[49]

The Consul also refuted a report by a West Bank Israeli military spokesperson which appeared in the *Jerusalem Post*, claiming that Christian and

Muslim leaders and citizens of Bethlehem endorsed a petition seeking the annexation of their town to Jerusalem. His staff investigated the matter by going directly to the deputy mayor of Bethlehem who assured them that the report was a deliberate distortion. The town's municipal council had apparently sent a letter to Israeli government officials reminding them of their town's historic and economic links to Jerusalem, cautioning against severing ties between Jerusalem and all the towns and cities of the West Bank. At the least, this would cause a serious disruption of the Christian pilgrimage economy affecting the holy town and city. Upon further investigation, Wilson wrote that the report was traced to recent Israeli plans to incorporate the shrine of Rachel's Tomb within the Jerusalem area. A site holy to Jews and Muslims, it held a historic mosque in addition to the tomb. The site was always within Bethlehem's municipal boundaries, and to include it within Jerusalem would have meant extending the city's perimeters north of the tomb. The intent was to coerce Bethlehem's residents into making such a request, forcing a return to the 1947 proposed boundaries which would have situated Bethlehem within the international boundaries of Jerusalem.[50]

THE PROSPECT OF INTERNATIONALIZATION

The American Consulate also investigated Arab reactions to Israeli plans for imposing an occupation regime on the West Bank while integrating Jerusalem within Israel. There were several assessments of this situation while the White House was faced with pressures of a different kind. The Consulate learnt of the disappointment of Arab officials in Jerusalem at the diminishing prospects of reaching a negotiated settlement. For instance, Hazem Khalidi, a high-ranking official during the Jordanian period, was very pessimistic about Israel's willingness to accommodate the needs of the Arab population. His recommendation was that the West Bank should be turned into a buffer state between Israel and its neighbors while remaining completely neutral and demilitarized like Austria. But for such a state to be economically viable, it should be allowed to participate in the administration of Jerusalem, as well as attach the predominantly Arab Galilee and Gaza regions to its area in order to provide access to the Mediterranean coast. He projected that the two capitals of Israel and the West Bank buffer state should be located in Jerusalem, calling for the creation of a mixed Israel-Palestine administrative council. Referring to a comment by an Israeli official that a return to the idea of appointing a UN administrator to run the city would confront a very determined Israeli agenda, Khalidi agreed that reviving the internationalization plan of 1947 was simply unworkable. The presence of a UN official would encourage both sides to present him with maximalist positions rather than deal with each other directly. His preference was for a bi-national Jerusalem, rather than an international one, even if the Arabs were outvoted due to increased Jewish numbers after the city was united. Khalidi's views, nevertheless, were not shared by the majority of young Arabs whose preference was to wait for better circumstances before pushing for the retrieval of their rights in the city.[51]

The Consul became a facilitator of meetings between visiting American officials and high level Palestinian figures who served during the Jordanian period. The meetings became urgent once it was made clear that the Israeli government was floating plans to eliminate any possibility of returning some territory to Jordan, specifically through the encouragement of West Bank calls for autonomy. Senator Birch Bayh, R–Indiana, was among the earliest officials to arrive in Jerusalem a few weeks after the hostilities stopped. He met with Anwar Nuseibeh, former governor of Jerusalem, who revealed that he was approached by Israel regarding the possibility of setting up a Palestinian entity independent of Jordan. His response was that for this to work, the consent of the Arab population must be secured, which would be based on reconciling the 4 June lines defined by the Partition Resolution of 1947 with the current borders. He added that Jerusalem must be declared Arab Palestine's capital under some type of power-sharing arrangement or condominium with Israel. He explained that this arrangement, furthermore, could only be adopted with the consent of the Arab states. Nuseibeh expressed the view that the victorious Israelis could afford to return some of the captured territory if they wished to make a permanent solution acceptable to the defeated side. He explained that the population of the West Bank would not be willing to negotiate separately without receiving prior approval from King Hussein. Wilson added his own understanding of this unrealistic position of the former Jordanian official as being a plea for third party intervention, meaning the United States, if the rigidity of both parties was to be overcome.[52]

NEW REFUGEES: EXPULSION OR VOLUNTARY DEPARTURE?

Both the American Consulate and the Embassy grew alarmed at rumors of the "departure" of Arabs from the West Bank. When told of such stories appearing in the *Jerusalem Post,* a representative of the Israeli Foreign Ministry at the Military Governor's office claimed that anyone could leave upon signing official papers to that effect, meaning that it was a completely voluntary process. But when a Consulate officer inquired if these same people could return to their original homes later, the Israeli official responded that it depended on the progress of Arab-Israeli peace negotiations. The same situation applied to retaining their property in the West Bank. American officers then inquired if the same applied to the property of Palestinians who were American citizens, only to be told "An Arab is an Arab," irrespective of their passports, which reminded him of Jewish property lost in Arab countries regardless of their nationality. Compensating the Arabs for lost properties, the Israeli officer concluded, was contingent upon the peaceful intentions of the Arab states.[53]

A follow-up undated memo for the attention of the US delegation at the UN and the Embassy at Tel Aviv expressed satisfaction at putting Eban on notice against pushing the new wave of Arab refugees across the Jordan River. The memo which was authored by the Acting Secretary of State, indicated that an official protest had been included in a telegram to the Tel Aviv Embassy. The tone of the memo was subdued, however, asking that Israel must be reminded that creating additional Palestinian refugees in the East Bank of Jordan would not be conducive to the creation of future conditions for a lasting political settlement. The memo asked that Israel be urged to offer the refugees immediate repatriation, which would satisfy the moderate Arab demand for recognition of Palestinian rights. Israel must understand that in the absence of direct contact with the Arab states, settling the refugees and taking them back offer great opportunities for cooperation on permanent matters, leading to a semblance of recognition. Eban should be advised to make such an offer before the General Assembly. Finally, the memo asked that if the Secretary of State approved of the message, he should call for further talks on this matter with Israeli Ambassador Harman, American Ambassador Barbour, as well as Prime Minister Eshkol. Apparently, the memo was inspired by what President Johnson strongly reiterated lately as "justice for the refugees."[54]

The CIA weighed in on this topic by July 14, expressing hope that this war could offer a final solution for the refugee issue, described as "a political cancer," preventing the normalization of Arab-Israeli relations. It reported that many Palestinians in the major urban areas of the West Bank, including East Jerusalem, held many grudges against the Hashemite regime and were willing to deal with the Israelis, provided that their gains would not dissipate or flounder on the rock of recurring Arab extremism as what happened following the Suez War. Neither King Hussein nor Nasser were likely to survive this defeat, with the former being held in low esteem and the Soviet Union remaining incapable of scaring the Israelis. The CIA resolved that what was needed now was a new generation of Arab governments open to making peace with Israel and aligning with the West. Despite this clear Cold War hype, the memo referred to the Israelis as too emotional (*meshuga*) even to consider surrendering the Old City. Waxing sentimental over the kindness and humanity of General Dayan, the CIA referred to him as the final arbiter of decisions affecting the newly conquered territories by virtue of his role as the Minister of Defense. He was also described as a man of courage and originality. The memo even sided with Israel in its dispute with UNRWA, accusing the refugee organization of padding its lists to inflate the number of refugees generated by the war. But the CIA also claimed that Israel was still unsure of how many refugees were planning to return after the cessation of hostilities since this required the signing of papers acknowledging the legitimacy of the Israeli administration. The memo concluded by claiming that Israel was capable of handling any security problem on its own.[55]

There were many indications, nevertheless, that Israeli officials were encouraging the flight of the refugees eastward to Jordan. Dayan alone was said to have pushed around 200,000 Palestinians to the border. He told his advisers that it was time to draw a new map of Israel. Rabin expanded on this idea by explaining to the ministerial security committee that the military simply provided the conditions enabling those wishing to leave to depart on their own. What he meant by that was that by refraining from blowing up the Allenby Bridge, which linked the two banks of the Jordan together, the military made sure that fleeing Palestinians faced no obstacle reaching Jordan. Dayan said that after the war ended, "Israel needed a better security map, a more spacious frontier, a lesser vulnerability."[56] It was Israel Galili, former Chief of Staff of the Hagana, Knesset member and close adviser to Golda Meir, serving at the time as a member of the Ministerial Committee on the Settlements, who propagated the idea of settling Jews in the Old City before the war ended. This was in response to Eshkol's hesitancy before the Old City fell as he voiced fears that even if the city was conquered, it would be forcibly taken back by any means possible.[57] Yet it was Eban in his capacity as foreign minister at the time who uttered the war's most supercilious summation of the Israeli expansionist impulse. He referred to Israel's pre-1967 borders as "Auschwitz borders," which could not be maintained.[58] Keeping the West Bank and Jerusalem populated by Palestinian Arabs, therefore, threatened the long-held vision of a purely Jewish and enlarged state. The seeds of the settlement policy were sown in this era.

The Israeli military protecting the eastern border with Jordan and who confronted the returning Palestinian refugees once hostilities stopped were doing so by following official orders. Palestinians in the hundreds who tried to return to their former homes, accompanied by women and children, were mostly pushed back or killed. This involved West Bank and Jerusalem residents, but the military governor of Gaza, Michael Gur, admitted that he too was encouraging the flight of refugees by lowering their standard of living. Returning from Jordan across the river was possible due to shallow waters during the summer months. But by August, some Israeli soldiers wrote to Eshkol protesting military orders forcing them to kill women and children. Rabin justified these acts to the cabinet, claiming that the laws of war allowed soldiers to shoot at people crossing the Jordan River at night, except if they identified themselves as protected persons, meaning women and children. Daytime rules required soldiers to warn the returnees loudly, followed by firing in the air as a warning. Reportedly, 146 people, including women and children, were killed in this manner upon crossing the river. Unpersuaded that the practice was inhumane, Eban recommended shooting and wounding the returned refugees in order to push them back, but to avoid killing them at any cost. Eventually, the Israeli authorities screened around 14,000 out of a total of 20,000, clearing them to re-enter. Unsure of what to call the new territories, Rabin and Dayan began referring to them as "the occupied territories," during their meetings. Displeased with the implications of this term, they switched to "the liberated territories," until the Military Advocate General, and later court judge, Meir Shamgar, coined the term "administered territories," which was met with favor by all cabinet members.[59]

CONTAINING JERUSALEM'S RELIGIOUS COMMUNITIES, LOCAL MERCHANTS AND UN OFFICIALS

Jerusalem's Arab population was subjected to special treatment designed to humiliate it and contain its threat. This began with acts of intimidation directed at the Arab merchants and resorting to theatrical steps of psychological pressure so as to eliminate any possibility of resistance. This went on for quite a while, despite Ambassador Barbour's quotation from a piece in *Ha'aretz* that a genuine "crusade" was undertaken to bring about harmonious relations between Arabs and Jews in the city. He also advised the State Department to drop the term "Arab Jerusalem" and start using "East Jerusalem" instead, a geographic term with no reference to Arabs. But by the end of July, it seemed that the Arab population was planning a civil revolt. There were demonstrations by women and students and the threat of store closure became real. In order to forestall such activities, Uzi Narkis, Commander of the Armed Forces in the Central Region, began to crack down on Palestinians by forcing some Arab shops to stay closed, while calling for a face-to-face meeting with the merchants. A meeting with representatives of the Arab Chamber of Commerce who sought to have their stores remain open was arranged. The general was advised by his assistants against open gestures of camaraderie such as the shaking of hands, and an inadequate number of chairs was provided in order to force the Arabs to remain standing. Not unlike similar meetings during British Mandate days, the idea of contriving to keep the Arabs from sitting down was proposed by Begin.[60]

The religious representatives of the various communities were deliberately subjected to a special treatment. When officers of the American Consulate called on prominent clerical leaders on July 14–15, such as the Latin Patriarch and Franciscan custodians of the Holy Land, they were given a grim report. They were particularly concerned over Israeli imposition of travel restrictions, inability to access funding due to closed banks and other regulations and disregard for the sanctity of holy sites by Israeli soldiers and civilians. Some clergy admitted thinking of closing holy places and churches, and even the cancellation of summer leave for their personnel, fearing being barred from re-entering Jerusalem. It was believed that Israeli visa restrictions were planned in order to reduce the number of Christian churches in the city. A Christian school belonging to the Monastery of St. Xavier was blown up without prior notification. The Latin Patriarch had taken his complaints directly to the Minister of Religious Affairs, citing confusion throughout the city even after the passage of six weeks since the war ended. The prelates also complained of lack of disclosure of contacts between Special Vatican Envoy, Monsignor Felici, and Israeli officials.[61]

Wilson also refuted general claims of IDF misconduct during and after the hostilities, insisting that there were no reports of rape or Israeli brutality, and any instances of abuse were justified by security considerations. He reported that IDF attacks on a refugee camp did take place and that reports of rampant looting were heard during the initial period of the occupation, though not always verifiable. IDF personnel were said to have engaged in extensive looting of stores and vacant homes during curfew hours. Hotels used for housing the troops reported extensive theft of furnishings. He concluded that IDF harassment of the civilian population was extensive, although difficult to document. He also reported on the expulsion of the population of border areas, such as the West Bank village of Qalqilya, and preventing its members from returning.[62]

When attempting to gauge the response of moderate Palestinians to treatment by the IDF, Wilson was very clear about widespread disillusionment in the area, particularly in the Old City. The unilateral act of merging the two sides of the city together alienated many people. Palestinian moderates were upset at Israeli treatment of the Arab city council, which was not put to any use. The only exception was Town Clerk Anton Safieh, whose services were retained. A meeting of Kollek and Rouhi al-Khatib was symbolic and did not lead to any meaningful integration of the two city councils.[63] Israel also seized control of Government House on Mt. Scopus, which served before 1948 as the headquarters of the British High Commissioner. During the Jordanian period, the building was a meeting place for the UN Truce Supervisory Commission (UNTSCO). Wilson reported that the Government of Israel justified this takeover by reference to the Israel 1950 Law which declared that all Mandate Government properties within Israel belonged to the state. The UN objected strongly, voicing fears of being considered as acquiescent in the forcible seizure of property. But the Israelis went ahead with the forcible fencing of the building and constructing a road connecting it to Bethlehem.[64]

JERUSALEM CONTESTED

At first, the State Department and White House advisers felt it would be sufficient to caution Israel against presenting the world with a series of faits accomplis. But putting the victorious militarized state on notice did not translate into automatic compliance. Israel was simply appraised of the limits of international tolerance of unilateral changes of the Jerusalem status quo but without making any threats of punitive action.[65] An initial study by several groups consisting of the Department of Near Eastern Affairs in the Department of State and White House advisers attempted to reconcile the US standing position on the internationalization of the city and Israel's latest "administrative" integration of the western and eastern sides. The US position had always been based on rejecting any exclusion of the international community from having an input in a final settlement. Barring such a declaration, however, Israel's latest action, it was feared, would soon become irreversible. The study referred to a realistic plan to reverse Israel's comprehensive measures to integrate united Jerusalem into Israel. A number of fears were expressed that if no effective measures were taken to change Israel's position, the Arab and Islamic countries would do so on their own. The study listed specific ideas which must amplify the American position, including US preference for a non-violent settlement between Israel and Jordan. It was noted that Jordan would not accept any settlement which was not centered on retrieving the West Bank, a position that was perfectly consistent with US commitment to safeguarding Jordan's territorial integrity. The problem, in the words of the study, was that Jordan was unlikely to go along with such a peaceful settlement unless Israel relinquished its hold over the Jordanian part of Jerusalem. This was due to the inevitable rejection of the Jewish state's sovereign control over the Islamic holy sites. In addition, Jordan was expected to insist on the return of the Arab part of Jerusalem due to its economic value as a source of foreign exchange from the tourism trade. The problem, it was made clear, was Israel's refusal to go back on its unification decree, especially after proclaiming the city as its capital.[66]

The study seemed to accept the notion that Jerusalem could only be restored to the June 5 *status quo ante* by military force, concluding that such a reversal of recent steps was undesirable. What the United States rejected, however, was a return to a divided city, the implication being that uniting the city, even by force, was preferable to what existed before. This was followed by a proposal for a new model of internationalization which entailed permitting Israel to retain its capital within the city while placing the holy places under an international domain. What this meant was depriving Jordan of the Old City but allowing it to benefit from the economic trade and from tourism and seemed to be a return to the idea of functional internationalization which Israel propagated before the war. But there were also proposals to link the

Old City to Jordan through a customs union and a special currency, thus depriving Israel of the foreign exchange revenue. Israel would still be able to enjoy the tourism revenue generated by those tourists who elect to stay in West Jerusalem. The Old City, or the internationalized sector, would be demilitarized and administered by an elected municipal council representing the various religious communities and headed by an interim representative. Additional information detailing the legal, police and economic powers of this council were specified. But as to citizenship, residents of the Old City living under the international regime would be allowed to opt for their current citizenship or elect to acquire the citizenship of the new regime. All of this, it was emphasized, hinged on the cooperation of Jordan, Israel and the UN, and on reaching a comprehensive settlement based on returning the West Bank to Jordan.[67]

Representatives of American oil companies, such as Mobil, continued to voice disgruntlement over US stand at the UN, particularly abstaining from voting on the Pakistani resolution at the General Assembly which called for Israeli withdrawal from Jerusalem. This was the only American sector to voice such strong objection to US maneuvers at the UN. Chris Herter, Jr., a Mobil representative, sent a message to Battle, Assistant Secretary of State for Near Eastern and South Asian Affairs, complaining that the United States should not have acceded to the Israeli justification of its action in Jerusalem as administrative, rather than an annexationist step since it immediately established a municipal council. This amounted to annexation, he wrote, though not through the adoption of laws.[68] Yet, the State Department stuck to its guns, claiming that it was still striving to bring about a peaceful settlement between Israel and Jordan, which would resolve the Jerusalem issue. Somehow, the State Department absorbed and accepted the Israeli argument that there can be no return to the situation as it existed under Jordan, with barbed wire and no-man's-land, hindering movement from one side to the other. Before too long, the United States accepted Israel's contention that its only objective was to prevent the repartitioning of the city. The United States was also told that Israel was willing to place the holy places under the jurisdiction of their own communities and grant them diplomatic status. The city of Jerusalem, emphasized the memo, should not be allowed to resemble a divided Berlin.[69]

In the meantime, Ambassador Barbour continued to press the Department of State to grant Israel credit for sacrificing a large number of its troops in order to protect Muslim and Christian holy site from damage. Israel, he proclaimed, would do a much better job than Jordan of keeping these sites open to everyone. His one advice to Israel was that it should remove the Christian and Muslim holy places from the jurisdiction of the Ministry of Religious Affairs since its portfolio was regularly assigned to the National Religious Party, an ultra-rightist party. But he also hammered at the idea that life under the Israelis would at least end the chaotic situation pitting the custodians of the various Christian churches against each other as in the past.[70] The Intelligence and Research Department of the State Department, however, sent a memo to the Secretary shortly after Israel's Ministry of the Interior released on 28 June the new municipal boundaries of the city based on the Knesset's integration decree. The memo noted that the Knesset also adopted new legislation for the protection of all the holy places and guaranteed access to all of them. It added that the General Assembly adopted a resolution expressing disapproval of recent Israeli laws which unilaterally altered the status of the city. The memo, however, left out any mention of the implications of these laws to the Status Quo regulations. Thus, no one noted that Israeli law, as administered by the Ministry of Religious Affairs, would be allowed to override the Status Quo regulations as they applied to the holy places.[71]

CONCLUSION

In his essay, "What Really Happened in the 1967 Arab-Israeli War?" British journalist Alan Hart wrote on the 2015 anniversary of the Six Day War that what Israel succeeded in pulling off was a "premeditated war." Israel trapped the Arabs, particularly Jordan, into a corner by simply launching an unstoppable and aggressive war against Syria over the waters of the Jordan River and Israel's right to plow in the no-man's-zone near the Golan Heights. Given the prevailing climate of pan-Arabism and the Arab public's impatience with Nasser's cautious approach to the inflamed Israeli-Arab theater on all fronts, such tactics were bound to result in a confrontation. Jordan turned out to be just as susceptible to public opinion pressure as Egypt, particularly after suffering the disproportionately violent attack on Samu'. This humiliating betrayal by his secret interlocutors and allies forced Hussein's hand and compelled him to fire the first shot and attempt a military attack, targeting West Jerusalem. His intention was to relieve pressure on his Egyptian and Syrian allies. Hart went back to the same terrain and questioned Israeli leaders about the events leading to the war, asserting that sometimes, though not often enough, they did spell out what really happened. He described the general state of fear gripping ordinary Israelis on the eve of the war, a fear nurtured by their leaders.[72]

The pre-emptive war against Egypt and Syria which followed and the disproportionate punishing blows directed at Jordan's impecunious air force and military forces in the West Bank proceeded according to a specific plan. Israel had long chafed at what it regarded as the unfavorable geographic and strategic map of 1948, particularly along Jordan's borders. Not surprisingly, an Israeli military and political consensus quickly emerged regarding the golden opportunity which presented itself in East Jerusalem. This was the moment to unite the two halves of the city and realize Israel's deferred dream of a unified capital. Not by chance did Israeli troops level punishing strikes at Jordan's military forces around East Jerusalem, followed by whipping up public frenzy of religious zealotry to reach the Wailing Wall. Yet, seizing the Old City turned out to be one of the major obstacles to a lasting peace with Jordan. Additionally, festering Palestinian grudges against Jordanian rule were stirred up as a supporting argument favoring separating the West Bank from the East Bank of Jordan.

The United States was hardly shocked by Israel's quick and lightning victory since American intelligence services had stressed the incomparable military strength and supreme preparedness of the small entity. They also predicted that it would be able defeat its combined enemies without any outside assistance. A wave of sympathy for Israel also swept the United States where it was presented as little David of biblical fame, or a country threatened with extinction. Public opinion restrained the United States from forcing the return of seized territories quickly, before Israel solidified land gains as adjustments to the old map. Avoiding any strong American criticism, Israel even managed to survive a serious rupture of relations after bombing the USS Liberty.

Watching from afar, the US Government worked to contain the damage through the State Department, the White House NSC and the Special Committee created to manage the Middle East crisis. But much depended on reports of American diplomats on the scene, where the information relayed by the Tel Aviv Embassy and the Jerusalem Consulate often conflicted. Ambassador Barbour's Israel-friendly analysis was repeatedly contradicted by Consul Wilson's investigative reports and detailed accounts of how Israel tightened its control over East Jerusalem and dismantled its institutions. Israel's disregard for international conventions as it speeded along with its project of unifying the two sides of the city under its control was described in detail. Wilson's reports were not publicly revealed although reports of Israel's excesses in the Old City were widely circulated. Wilson's eyewitness accounts which were eventually archived at the Lyndon Baines Johnson Library at Austin, Texas, offered valuable testimony to the reluctance of the Johnson administration to utilize this unmatched trove of information as a pressure tool against its errant ally. Wilson was the first to send alarming news of the expulsion of Palestinians from the Latroun villages before turning them into a park. He was the one who reported on extensive looting by the Israeli military, the destruction of the Mughrabi Quarter and the secret immunity from prosecution offered to the lieutenant who led the demolition operation. Wilson also reacted to Israel's propaganda war by clarifying the condition of the ancient Jewish cemetery near the city's walls before the Jordanians took over the eastern half of the city. His accounts of the disman-

tling of the Arab economic and political institutions of East Jerusalem provided evidence of Israel's determination to attach the city to the state regardless of any pre-existing Jordanian claims.

Meanwhile, White House advisers and State Department officials willingly absorbed the Israeli refrain of the undesirability of the three options of
returning to the June 4 borders, returning the Old City to Jordan, or surrendering control of the city to an international regime. Rather than stick to the
international norm of outlawing annexation by conquest, the strategy of the
United States turned out to be a piecemeal offensive, targeting one issue at a
time. This provided the Israelis with plenty of latitude to achieve their strategic objectives quickly while claiming to have created a superior and more
just administration than what existed under Jordan. Having faced only one
major Israeli fait accompli in the past, namely moving the capital to West
Jerusalem in defiance of the UN's internationalization decree, the United
States pretended not to comprehend the serious import of this final annexation step, which was an act of war, though taking place in time of peace.
Indeed while Nasser and fellow Arab heads of state were called extremists
for their proclamations during the Khartoum Conference, no one leveled
such charges at Israel when it refused to return East Jerusalem or the West
Bank to Jordan.

NOTES

1. Abba Eban, *An Autobiography* (New York: Random House, 1977), 197, 397, 410.
2. Jeff Gates, "Bibi's Back." http://www.weekly.ahram.eg/2010/1006/op12.html. Published in al-Ahram, July 8–14, 2010, issue 1006, Opinion. Accessed 17/8/2013.
3. Tom Segev, *1967: Israel, the War, and the Year that Transformed the Middle East* (New
York: Henry Holt, 2005): 253, 264.
4. Ibid., 327–50.
5. Ibid., 350.
6. Avi Shlaim, *The Iron Wall: Israel and the Arab World* (New York: W. W. Norton,
2000): 244–53.
7. Segev, *1967*, 350, 360, 364, 370.
8. Donald Neff, *Warriors for Jerusalem: Six Days that Changed the Middle East* (New
York: Simon and Schuster, 1984): 234–5, 243–4, 252.
9. Dan Kurzman, *Soldier of Peace: The Life of Yitzhak Rabin, 1922–1995* (New York:
Harper Collins, 1998): 230–1.
10. Segev, *1967*, 373–4.
11. Muhammad Hassanein Heikal, *Kalam fi al-siyaseh*/Political Talk (Cairo: al-Sharika al-
Misriyah lil-Nashr al-Arabi wa al-Duwali, 2000): 128–32.
12. Shlomo Gross, "What to Do with the West Bank?" June 30, 1967. Airogram from
Barbour to Department of State. NSF/Files of Special Committee of the NSC–Israel. Box 4,
Doc. 201, LBJL.
13. "Cabinet this Afternoon Considered Number of Matters," June 29, 1967. Telegram from
Tel Aviv Embassy to Department of State. NSF/Files of Special Committee of the NSC. Box 4,
Doc. 205, LBJL.
14. "Protection of Holy Places," 28 June 1967. Telegram from Tel Aviv Embassy to Depart-
ment of State. NSF Files/Files of Special Committee of the NSC—Israel. Box 4, Doc. 213,
LBJL.

15. From Larry Levinson and Beau Wattenberg to the President, "History of Middle East Crisis, May 12—June 19, 1967," June 7, 1967. NSF Files/NSC. Vol. 4, Box 18, Doc. 13, LBJL. See also: www.jewishvirtuallibrary.org/.../1967war6.html. Accessed 18/8/2013.

16. Memo for Marvin Watson, from Thomas L. Jones, SAIC-PPD, "History of Middle East Crisis, May 12–June 19, 1967," June 8, 1967. NSF Files/NSC. Vol. 4, Box 18, Doc. 15, LBJL.

17. Cable—"Extra Special Handling Category," from ARAMCO Washington Representative Brougham, June 10, 1967. McGeorge Bundy Memos and Saudi Arabia. Box 3, Doc. 68b. LBJL.

18. Memo, "CIA Special Assessment on the Middle East—Israeli Foreign Minister Eban's UN Speech," June 9, 1967. "History of the Middle East Crisis, May 12-June 19, 1967," NSF Files/NSC. Vol. 5, Box 18, Doc. 62b. LBJL.

19. Jack O'Connell, *King's Counsel: A Memoir of War, Espionage, and Diplomacy in the Middle East* (New York: W. W. Norton, 2011): 64–6.

20. Ghada Talhami, *Syria and the Palestinians: The Clash of Nationalisms* (Gainesville: University of Florida Press, 2001): 71–3.

21. 29th Control Group Meeting, "Immediate Issues in Israel," July 3, 1967. Minutes of Counsel Group Meeting. Box 1, Doc. 66. LBJL.

22. "Draft Telegram to Tel Aviv," NSF File/Files of the Special Committee of the NSC, June 12, 1967. Box 1, Doc. 93a. LBJL.

23. Adnan Abd al-Raziq, *Haret al-Yahoud fi al-Quds*/The Jewish Quarter in Jerusalem (Nicosia, Cyprus: Rimal, 2013): 99–100.

24. Gershom Gorenberg, *The Accidental Empire: Israel and the Birth of the Settlements, 1967–1977* (New York: Henry Holt, 2006): 44–8.

25. Segev, 1967, 400–2.

26. Jeremy Bowen, *Six Days: How the 1967 War Shaped the Middle East* (New York: St. Martin's, 2003): 300–3.

27. Abd al-Raziq, *Harat al-Yahoud*, 101–2.

28. Ibid., 104–6.

29. Segev, *1967*, 379–80.

30. Ibid., 369.

31. The Special Committee of NSC, Control Group, "Memorandum for the President," June 26, 1967. National Security Files, Box 2, Doc. 14, LBJL.

32. Telegram from US Mission in New York to Secretary of State, July 1, 1967. National Security Files/Files of Special Committee of the NSC, "Jerusalem," Box 10, Doc. 127, LBJL.

33. Gorenberg, *The Accidental Empire*, 63.

34. Ibid., 59–63.

35. www.The Consulate General of the United States—Jerusalem—Pdf. Accessed 7/17/2015.

36. Richard D. Mckinzie, "Oral History Interview with Evan M. Wilson," Harry S. Truman Library and Museum, July 18, 1975. www.trumanlibrary.o... Accessed 7/16/2015. See also Wilson's book, Decisions in Palestine: How the U.S. Came to Recognize Israel (Stanford, Calif.: Hoover Institution, 1979).

37. Wilson, "Destruction of Imwas," June 30, 1967. National Security Files/Files of Special Committee of the NSC, Box 10, Doc. 132, LBJL.

38. Jonathan Cook, "Canada Park and Israeli 'Memoricide,'" The Electronic Intifada, March 10, 2009. https://electronicintifada.net/.../canada...israeli.../8... Accessed 7/20/2015.

39. Wilson to Department of State, "Jerusalem," July 8, 1967. National Security Files/Files of Special Committee of the NSC, Box 10, Doc. 112, LBJL.

40. See: Shira Herzog, "Discovering a Homeland Abroad: How the Six Day War in Israel Galvanized Canada's Jews," Literary Review of Canada, May 2011. www.reviewcanada.ca/magazine/.../discovering-a-h...

41. From American Consul- Jerusalem, to Department of State, July 1, 1967. National Security Files/Files of Special Committee of the NSC, Box 10, Doc. 129, LBJL.

42. American Consul in Jerusalem to Department of State, "West Bank Views," July 3, 1967. NS Files/Files of Special Committee of the NSC, Box 10, Doc. 124, LBJL.

43. Ibid.

44. Wilson to Department of State, "Future of Jerusalem," July 12, 1967. NSF/Files of Special Committee of NSF, Box 10, Doc. 106, LBJL.

45. Wilson to Department of State, "Jerusalem," July 8, 1967. NSF/Files of Special Committee of the NSC, Box 10, Doc. 112, LBJL.

46. Ibid.

47. Ibid.

48. Wilson to Department of State, "Status of Jerusalem," July 7, 1967. NSFile/Files of Special Committee of the NSC, Box 10, Doc. 115, LBJL.

49. Wilson to Department of State, "Future of Jerusalem."

50. Wilson to Department of State, "Jerusalem," July 5, 1967. NSFile/Files of Special Committee of the NSC, Box 10, Doc. 121, LBJL.

51. American Consul to Jerusalem to Department of State, "West Bank Views."

52. Wilson to Department of State, "Jerusalem."

53. Wilson to Department of State, "Jerusalem," July 14, 1967. NSFile/Files of Special Committee of the NSC, Box 10, Doc. 92, LBJL.

54. Memo, "Action: New York USUN," n.d. NSFILE/Files of Special Committee of the NSC, Box 11, Doc. 10a, LBJL.

55. Central Intelligence Agency, Intelligence Information Cable, "Views on the Refugee Problem," July 14, 1967. NSFile/Files of Special Committee of the NSC—Refugees, Box 11, Doc. 31, LBJL.

56. Shlomo Ben Ami, *Scars of War, Wounds of Peace* (Oxford: Oxford University Press, 2006): 122–3.

57. Ibid., 123.

58. Ibid., 122.

59. Segev, *1967*, 540–3.

60. Ibid., 493–6.

61. Wilson to Department of State, "Holy Places," July 18, 1967. NSFile/Files of Special Committee of the NSC, Box 10, Doc. 82, LBJL.

62. Wilson to Department of State, "IDF Conduct on West Bank," July 18, 1967. NSFile/Files of Special Committee of the NSC, Box 10, Doc. 83, LBJL.

63. Wilson to Department of State, "West Bank Opinion," July 12, 1967. NSFile/Files of Special Committee of the NSC. Box 10, Doc. 103, LBJ10, Doc. 43, LBJL. Safieh was an uncle of PLO adviser and diplomat Afif Safieh.

64. Wilson to Department of State, "Government House," August 5, 1967. NSFile/Files of Special Committee of the NSC, Box 10, Doc. 43, LBJL.

65. Hal Saunders to McGeorge Bundy, "Jerusalem Memorandum," June 30, 1967. NSFile/Files of Special Committee of the NSC, Box 10, Doc. 12, LBJL.

66. Staff Study, "Jerusalem: A Proposal for Partial Internationalization," July 10, 1967, by a working group consisting of representatives of NEA, IO and L. Box 10, Jerusalem, Doc. 10, LBJL.

67. Ibid. See also: Leonard C. Meeker, State Department Legal Adviser to the Control Group, "Possible Plans for Jerusalem," July 12, 1967. NSFile/Files of the Special Committee of the NSC, minutes of Control Group Meetings. Box 1, Doc. 8 and 8a, Folder 5, LBJL.

68. Rodger P. Davies to Lucius Battle, NEA, "Mobil Oil Company's Concern at U.S. Position on Jerusalem Resolutions," July 12, 1967, Box 10, Doc. 8, LBJL.

69. From Rusk, Department of State, to various missions, "Jerusalem," July 26, 1967, Box 10, Doc. 68, LBJL.

70. Barbour to Department of State, no topic, July 1, 1967. Box 4, LBJL.

71. From Thomas L. Hughes, U.S. Department of State Director of Intelligence and Research, to Secretary of State, "Map of the Israeli Government's Municipal Boundaries for Jerusalem," July 20, 1967. NSFile/Files of Special Committee of the NSC, Box 4, Doc. 14, LBJL.

72. Alan Hart, "What Really Happened in the 1967 Arab-Israeli War?" www.redressline.com/.../what-really-happened-in-the-1967-arab-Israel . . . Accessed 7/20/2015.

Chapter Six

Israeli Faits Accomplis and Jordanian Weakness

Shlomo Ben Ami, former Israeli foreign minister and diplomatic negotiator, commented on the hardening Israeli position after the 1967 hostilities ended by tracing the evolution of a linguistic pattern, legitimizing the retention of the spoils of war. Western media quickly picked up emerging Israeli concepts which became the defining reality of what was transpiring on the ground. For instance, refusing to return to the territorial status quo of June 4 was now referred to as Israel's right to have "secure borders." He traced the phrase "land for peace" to the very first day of Israel's extension of its control beyond the armistice lines. The idea was favored by Under-Secretary of State Eugene Rostow, who began to advocate that the 1967 War was not such a disaster after all since it opened up doors for drawing a new map. The idea was that Israel would now be able to exchange land for Arab concessions, as his brother Walt Rostow put it as soon as the war began.[1]

Bundy sought to soften President Johnson's resistance to several Israeli requests, such as new weapons, despite Israel's human rights infractions, by reminding him that the power of the American Jewish community might come into play. Then, General Ezer Weizmann sought a meeting with the President to discuss Israel's military needs, especially expediting shipments of A–4F aircraft, but Johnson resisted, given the implications of this for relations with Arab allies. Bundy, however, asked that the President should keep in mind the alternative to accepting this visit which would amount to a meeting with American Jewish constituents on the grounds of the White House.[2]

US coordination with Israeli diplomats had actually started early. On July 5, Bundy called Eban for a conversation in order to coordinate maneuvers at the General Assembly, assuring him that the major lessons of the war should have been a reminder of US dedication to maintaining Israel's defensive posture against its neighbors. Even though the United States was reassured by Israel's military capability, which eliminated the need for American assistance, Israel should be reminded that the United States was its most reliable ally. Eban, however, hinted that this did not mean that Israel would not seek weapons in West European markets. Bundy then went to the heart of the issue, reminding Eban that if US support was to continue, other questions of grave concern to the United States must be taken into account. These included, first, the fate of Jerusalem, the situation of West Bank Arabs under Israeli control, preventing Jordan from acquiring Soviet weapons, and lastly, the nuclear issue, or Israel's bomb. All of these would impact Johnson's decision regarding the authorization of more arms. Eban understood from all of this that the United States would supply Jordan with weapons, which was a preferable option to relying on Soviet equipment. But regarding the Jerusalem issue, Eban favored limiting sovereignty over the holy sites to the religious communities, and making Jordan the only power entrusted with the custodianship of the Muslim holy places. But there was no discussion of returning East Jerusalem to Jordan and Bundy concluded the meeting by conveying his own personal congratulations to Israeli soldiers on the quality of their military performance.[3] The sensitivities of Israeli lawmakers, diplomats, and even fighters were, thus, always observed by American policymakers. If that was not an adequate gesture of reassurance, nothing else would have sent a stronger signal of approval to Israel when the map of Jerusalem and the West Bank was unilaterally redrawn. Bundy also recommended that Johnson draft a statement on Jerusalem, stating that while the United States should try to maintain the goodwill of both sides, it should also criticize certain Israeli actions, such as integrating the city with the rest of Israel. Bundy added that the United States should express understanding of the emotional reasons underlying this decision.[4]

But whenever peace plans were drafted by the State Department or the CIA, the Control Group felt that they were unworkable since they would require the surrender of too much Israeli-held territory. Others believed that not much would be accomplished until Israel and Jordan reached a comprehensive peace agreement.[5] By October, CIA reports injected a tone of realism into the discussion by noting that the situation on the ground favored Israel since Arab resistance in the West Bank and Jerusalem remained nonviolent. Israel had also received funding from abroad to assist in carrying out its multiple governing duties. The CIA confirmed that Israel encouraged, but not necessarily forced, the flight of West Bank Arabs to Jordan. The report contended that contrary to Israeli statements made at the UN regarding the assumption of temporary administrative duties in Jerusalem, the Old City had already been completely integrated with the Israeli state. The rest of the West Bank was placed under military control but was still governed according to

Jordanian regulations. Resistance to Israeli military rule was carried out by school teachers who went on strike, demanding non-interference in the selection of textbook material. The report emphasized that political resistance had been limited to urban areas and led mostly by figures of the former Jordanian regime. The Israelis retaliated harshly, such as by "exiling" former governor Anwar al-Khatib and others. The report, however, made no effort to debunk the Israeli abuse of this term, since citizens could not be exiled from their own country. By September, Shaykh Abdullah Ghosheh, head of the Shari'a Court in Jerusalem, was also expelled to Jordan under the guise of exiling him for inciting rebellion.[6]

The report admitted feeling increasingly uncomfortable at the pettiness and high-handed methods of control by the military occupation, but neither this agency nor the Israeli Government were willing to recognize that the PLO was beginning to have some impact on the occupied population. Israel reverted to its former method of demolishing the homes of those suspected of sabotage as in 1948, referring to all acts of resistance as "terrorism." It was emphasized that there was a variety of views among Israeli officials, but an unmistakable unanimity of opinion over keeping total control of Jerusalem. Surprisingly, the agency did not view the launching of settlements in occupied lands and around Jerusalem as a drastic and permanent policy, but merely as a warning to the Arabs to speed up their commitment to an early peace settlement with the victorious Israelis.[7]

LIVING WITH THE ISRAELI HARDENING OF POSITIONS

In preparation for aligning the US position on the Old City with that of Israel, a memo defining and classifying Muslim and Christian holy places in Jerusalem was readied for Lucius Battle. The most interesting and critical definition was that of the Wailing Wall. Prepared by the Near East Affairs Division of the State Department, it was based on an article by Dr. Paul Mohn, a one-time personal consultant to Count Bernadotte. It referred to the Western, or Wailing Wall, as partly Jewish, in as much as only its lower strata were considered part of Herod's Third Temple. But the article described part of the Wailing Wall as a Muslim site called al-Buraq esh-Sharif, where Muhammad tethered his horse before ascending to heaven during the nocturnal journey.[8] The study was in tune with the emerging US position favoring the revival of the policy of functional internationalization as was proposed by Israel in the early 1950s. Until then, recognizing Muslim claims to certain segments of the Wailing Wall was the prevailing view of the international archeological community. This view, nevertheless, came increasingly under attack by rival Jewish groups later on.

HUSSEIN'S PEACE INITIATIVE: CAN THE TWO ALLIES MEET?

By July 18, 1967, the United States was exploring various possibilities of reaching a peace settlement between Israel and Jordan. King Hussein was also signaling his interest in resuming secret contacts with his former ally. Hussein claimed that he received the green light from Nasser to reach such a settlement, but to avoid direct talks during the process of finalizing a peace treaty. Hussein asked the United States to send a message to Israel to that effect, and Eban responded that his government was ready to talk. Yet, no one was sure how far Israel would go in making the kind of concessions necessary for reaching such a deal. From the outset, the United States adopted a neutral stand, believing that the radical Arab states such as Egypt and Syria were setting up a trap for Hussein. Findley Burns urged stronger American involvement in order to save Jordan from total collapse. He expressed doubt as to the limits of the monarch's survival possibilities if post-war conditions in the West Bank and Jerusalem did not change. The issue for the United States, he underscored, was how to nudge Israel away from the idea of direct negotiations which they hoped would bolster their legitimacy in the region. The Jordanian monarch, as recognized by the United States, sought its mediation not only to deflect Arab criticism but also to pressure Israel into making more concessions. The belief in Jordan which was shared by most Arabs, he wrote, was that a settlement forced upon them by any power other than Israel, such as the United States or the UN, would be more palatable than by their victorious enemy. The United States began to bear down seriously on Eban through Rusk, in order to convey the view that Hussein's survival was in America's best interest, but recognized at the same time that the major Israeli concession to be made would have to center on Jerusalem. The United States knew that Hussein would not be able to sign anything which excluded Arab interest in retaining some connection to the holy city.[9]

Yet, Israeli officials began to issue their projections about the fate of the conquered territories as soon as the guns fell silent. Ben Gurion published a statement claiming that the country was ready to make peace with its defeated neighbors, but only through direct contact, without any third parties. He came out in favor of Allon's plan of keeping the Jordan Valley under Israeli military control and evacuating Gaza's refugee population to the West Bank. As to Jordan, Ben Gurion had his own ideas about the peace. These included demanding the repatriation of the pre-1948 Jewish residents of Hebron and providing Jordan with access to the Mediterranean, but there were no prospects for any negotiations over the fate of East Jerusalem. His words naturally resonated with the hawkish sitting cabinet which was in the process of debating various proposals for the West Bank, with Dayan combining the idea of autonomy with the imposition of martial law in order to prevent any military assault by the Arabs. He did consider restoring the West Bank to Jordan, but minus East Jerusalem. Despite the well-known hardening of the Israeli position regarding Jerusalem, King Hussein sent word that he was interested in direct, though secret, talks. His contacts in the run-up to the June War were with Ya'acov Herzog, Director General of the Israeli Ministry of Foreign Affairs, and mostly took place in London. The meetings resumed on July 2, at the offices of Dr. Emmanuel Herbert who doubled as his personal physician. According to the United States ambassador in Amman, Hussein expressed guilt and remorse over his involvement in the war, demonstrating an understanding for Israel's punitive response. Reportedly, Herzog described his own country's action as defensive in nature, while Hussein claimed that he did not receive Israel's warning by General Bull, until his airplanes were already leading the charge into Israel. [10]

The talks, it turned out, were merely intended to gauge Hussein's readiness to enter into direct negotiations, and Herzog made no mention of returning either the West Bank or East Jerusalem. Apparently, Israel had no intention of proceeding to more serious talks and was merely buying time. Herzog confessed to Allon that he saw the whole value of these talks as merely tactical in nature until there was some clarity over the future of the West Bank. Several Israeli leaders, including Dayan, Eshkol, Eban, and David Kimche of Mossad, were all holding talks with various West Bank Palestinians. [11] Yet, there was no reference to any talks with the Palestinians of Jerusalem. The talks with Hussein served also as a signal to an impatient Washington that Israel was willing to conclude a peace agreement.

Israel, clearly, lost faith in Hussein's reliability as a moderate Arab, but more importantly, was indifferent to his reduced status and inability to influence events after the war. What also became evident was that Israel was determined to keep the West Bank as a buffer between it and neighboring Jordan, with some like Dayan, showing no interest in peace talks. Once Israeli laws were extended to East Jerusalem on June 27, and building of settlements on the Golan Heights began, there was no turning back. Hussein continued with his patient diplomacy, announcing his readiness to make peace in exchange for the return of territory during a meeting of the General Assembly. [12] The idea of striking a compromise through the neat reductionism of "land for peace," was apparently the brainchild of presidential adviser Walt Rostow who wrote to Johnson as soon as the war ended that there was an opportunity then to use Israeli conquests as pressure leading the Arabs to make the hard concessions. [13]

But it was not clear how well was Hussein able to fathom the depth of the transformation overtaking his secret Israeli allies. Dr. Herzog, who claimed that his own vagueness was necessitated by lack of consensus within the cabinet, had already embraced the emerging geopolitical concept of Greater Israel. The concept opposed surrendering the fruits of victory to the enemy.

Neither did Hussein seem to mind being lectured on the reality of Jewish psychology based on the experience of the Holocaust. Supposedly, this explained the Israelis' military reaction to any threat to their survival, summed up by one author as "this grandiloquent lecture on the roots of Jewish nationalism."[14] Herzog sensed that the King acknowledged his diminished status among his Arab brethren, especially when he pleaded for more time in order to convene an Arab League summit and push for a clarification of a unified Arab position on the peace. Herzog also provided an impressionistic account of the King's mood, describing him as sad and not very hopeful. But not only was Herzog determined to extend the promise of a peaceful settlement into the future in order to give his cabinet more time to consolidate the occupation, other members of the Israeli political hierarchy hoped for more definitive gains. Meir Amit, director of Mossad, felt that Israeli contacts with the Jordanian monarch would be useful as a divisive tool to split the Arab stand on the issue of peace.[15]

After the London meeting with Herzog, Hussein returned to Amman where he was remembered as confiding to CIA station chief O'Connell, "I'll make peace, and I'll do it alone, but I have to get everything back to do it."[16] The big summit where Hussein hoped to emerge with a unified Arab willingness to seek peace turned out to be the Khartoum Conference which met at the end of August and which saw Nasser calling on each member state to seek the return of its lost territories on its own. O'Connell confessed that the CIA technical staff secretly taped the meeting and passed its report of the transactions to Jordan, while James Angleton, Chief of CIA's Counterintelligence Staff, passed a copy to Mossad and British intelligence. The famous meeting became a byword for Arab intransigence and determination to avenge the losses and humiliation of the war, whereas the extremist language of its participants, not necessarily Nasser's, were more hyperbolic than substantive. Israel's intransigence and nationalist zealotry regarding Jerusalem, however, was not highlighted by the Western media.[17]

THE DELIBERATE AMBIGUITY OF RESOLUTION 242

The United States developed a cunning policy which shielded Israel from meaningful international pressure to relinquish East Jerusalem. This was an adaptation of Israel's claim that it did not annex Jerusalem, it merely extended to it the laws and regulations of the rest of the state. Thus, the United States was able to assert that no formal changes affecting the status of the city were made, thereby justifying its decision to abstain from voting on the General Assembly resolution which condemned the annexation of the city. Israel was afforded the advantage of extended latitude to finish its job until a more serious and far-reaching resolution settled the issue of the occupied territories.[18]

A month prior to formulating the final resolution pertaining to settling the Arab-Israeli conflict, Security Council Res. 242, US chief representative to the UN, Arthur Goldberg, elaborated on his country's main position. He said in a statement during the Plenary Debate that the United States believed that the status of Jerusalem should not be decided by one state alone. It must be determined by all those concerned and with special consideration for the interests of the great religions represented in its holy places.[19] The United States, however, continued to uphold the idea that no occupied territory could be returned without a comprehensive peace settlement. Nevertheless, King Hussein's prime minister, Abdul Mon'em Rifa'i, emphasized that any UN resolution must demand the total withdrawal of Israeli troops and the safeguarding of the territorial integrity of Jordan. But Goldberg opposed this idea by reminding the Jordanian official that withdrawal from territory seized by war was not specified under the UN charter.[20] Yet, Goldberg told Hussein later that the United States rejected Israel's contention that Jerusalem was not negotiable, and that his country hoped to push for granting Jordan a special role in the city.[21] Jordan's expectation that the United States was committed to supporting a full Israeli withdrawal from all occupied territories was fading out.

As things developed, some members of the Jordanian delegation to the UN became more hostile than others towards the US expressed position on Israel and its territorial gains. One of these was UN Representative Muhammad al-Farra, who repeatedly disparaged the United States and its chief representative in the Security Council and the General Assembly. This led Goldberg to lodge a complaint with the Jordanian Foreign Minister Muhammad Adib al-Amri. Al-Farra had publicly attacked US policy for being based purely on domestic politics.[22] Indeed, a memo from Saunders to Walt Rostow on the latter's upcoming meeting with Eban made it clear that American elections were very much on the administration's mind. Since the President's policy towards Israel was expected to be determined largely by Rostow, Saunders wondered how tough could the United States be on Israel at that particular point in time? The tactical issue here, Saunders wrote, was to decide what would be the appropriate moment to crack down on that state. He recognized that it may not have been advantageous to alienate the Israelis at that point, which could lead them to stir up the American Jewish community. He wondered whether the United States was prepared to bear down on Israel to force it to accept a peace settlement during the American election cycle. He was aware, he wrote, that the American President might not be judged kindly by history if he failed to stand up to Israel's tactics. Nevertheless, Saunders recommended that the President challenge Israel's stubborn resistance when considering their demands for US military assistance.[23]

TACTICAL MANEUVERS AND VARIED PRESSURES

There were various versions of the kind of pressure applied to King Hussein to make him agree to a comprehensive UN resolution on a peace settlement without necessarily spelling out a definitive demand for Israeli withdrawal from Jerusalem. It should be remembered that he and Mahmoud Riadh, Egypt's Foreign Minister, represented the unified Arab position which anticipated that the cessation of hostilities would automatically lead to international pressure on Israel to withdraw from all of the seized territories. The two were present at the UN for the negotiations leading up to November 22, when Security Council Res. 242 was adopted. Although the final version of the resolution was drafted by Britain's Lord Caradon [Sir Hugh Foot], the actual mediation among various positions was handled by Goldberg and his staff. This included Sisco, Assistant Secretary of State for International Organization Affairs, William Buffum, and Richard F. Pedersen. Goldberg, a former Supreme Court judge, had one handicap according to some views, namely, that he was well-known for his pro-Israel politics which diminished Arab faith in his neutrality. O'Connell was temporarily added to his staff in order to repair some of this damage. Richard Helms, O'Connell's CIA boss, had told him that the State Department wanted to borrow him for that mission, based on Sisco's advice, who was well aware of O'Connell's close relationship to Hussein.[24] O'Connell admitted in his memoir that his role was to soften the Arabs into accepting American language prior to their face-to-face meeting with Goldberg. "It was a clever idea," wrote O'Connell, adding, "I knew I was being used, but it worked—for the time being. It unraveled later."[25]

At their first meeting, Goldberg inquired bluntly if there was any indication that the King was trustworthy. Goldberg then proceeded to place a direct telephone call to the President, in which he inquired whether he had a "blank check" to formulate an agreement between the two combatants, or a free hand never to be checked by other members of the chief executive's team. Goldberg then added that he also had a "blank check" to negotiate an acceptable deal from the American Jewish community. Apparently, before O'Connell was to sell Goldberg's language to the King, the American official had already cleared it with the Israelis. Sometimes, the King, rather than Riadh, suggested minor modifications and Goldberg eventually met with him to agree on a specific language. The only objection raised by Hussein was to the Israeli forces' withdrawal plan from the recently occupied territories, although he accepted the necessity of adjusting the previous borders which bisected some West Bank villages. The United States relayed to him that its interpretation of this provision would be to support minor and mutually agreed upon changes of the border. There was even preliminary agreement that if Jordan surrendered claims to the Latroun villages, it would be rewarded with access to a Mediterranean port such as Haifa. But then some chicanery was involved as the US negotiators made promises to Hussein which were never mentioned by Rusk in a subsequent luncheon meeting with the King. During a follow-up meeting with the President, Hussein was told that chances of retrieving all lost territory were nil, but he made no protest. Apparently, he figured that this statement did not override commitments made to him orally by Goldberg's team, which O'Connell reduced to writing. Believing that the President had not received the final, definitive word from Goldberg, the King remained optimistic. But in 1972, Goldberg denied in an interview with the *Washington Post* that he had ever made promises to the King regarding keeping any border rectifications modest. When Saunders was asked by O'Connell to correct this story, the former claimed that the relevant files were missing, preventing him from issuing such a denial. Later President Jimmy Carter received the same answer about the missing files when he requested such information from the State Department.[26]

King Hussein gave Avi Shlaim his own version of the events relating to negotiating the Security Council resolution. The Jordanians, he said, were hoping for a strong resolution, while the Israelis looked forward to a weak statement. As it turned out, what the Security Council adopted was the British version of the resolution, which was promoted internally in Jordan as a Jordanian victory promising the return of all lost territory to the Arabs. Hussein recalled that he received assurances from Rusk of US commitment to make Israel return all the conquered area but with minor border changes. The King also was told that the President was informed by Rusk of these commitments. But on November 8, Johnson pressured Hussein to support the American version of the resolution which was about to be submitted to a vote, and which deliberately lacked precise language on Israeli military withdrawal. Hussein felt after leaving Washington that if he did not raise any objection to the American resolution, the United States itself would see to it that Israeli withdrawal from the West Bank would be completed within a six-month period.[27] However, the United States strengthened Israel's position by calling for negotiations prior to withdrawal, with Saunders admitting in a memo to Walt Rostow that this kind of pressure would not be applied to Israel. But the United States was well aware that the Arabs would not negotiate while foreign troops were on their land, meaning having to make substantial territorial concessions. By August, Israel lost interest in applying the principle of this resolution towards reaching a final settlement with Jordan. Instead, the Israeli cabinet decided secretly to pursue separate talks with Egypt, and hopefully reach a settlement with its mightiest Arab enemy.[28]

THE ARTFUL VAGUENESS OF RESOLUTION 242

Much has been written on the studied ambiguity of Res. 242, but what must be conceded here is its leap over the boundaries of diplomatic instruments. Subsequent controversies generated by it revolved mainly around the language or phraseology of sub-title (i) of Article (1), which read "Withdrawal of Israeli armed forces from territories occupied in the recent conflict."[29] The Israelis took this to mean negotiating first, resulting, as was always the case, in some withdrawal but not in total withdrawal. The Arabs continued to insist on withdrawal from all "the" territories occupied through war, despite the absence of the definite article in the English version of the resolution.[30]

But English was not the only official language of the UN, leading many to uphold other versions such as the Arabic and the French, quoting the following statement from the latter: "Retrait des forces armées Israéliennes des territoires occupés lors du recent conflit."[31] The "des" meant "from the territories," supporting a different but unmistakable meaning of the resolution. Caradon, who continued to claim credit for the language of the resolution, affirming the version which Israel latched upon, was frequently pressed to explain some of the contradictions of said resolution. When he came up with a clarification, it was to remind the skeptics that the intent was to secure passage of the resolution by diverse members of the Security Council, who would not have voted for it without the second sentence in the preamble. This was the famous phrase, "Emphasizing the inadmissibility of the acquisition of territory by war. . . ." For him, this balanced, or perhaps nullified, the loose meaning of the withdrawal article. The preamble was probably what gave the Arabs, particularly Hussein, some hope, keeping them wedded to the idea that East Jerusalem could be regained through diplomacy. The Israelis gave a hint of why they feared precisely what seemed like an ambiguity to some and a fine balance to others. A year later after the passage of the resolution, Dayan told a closed meeting of the Israeli Labor Party that the resolution should not be endorsed since it meant a demand for withdrawing to the 4 June lines. This placed Israel on a collision course with the Security Council, he concluded.[32]

RETURNING TO THE SECURITY COUNCIL

The Jordanians continued to believe in the efficacy of diplomacy, particularly where Jerusalem was concerned. In typical fashion, two months after the adoption of the resolution, Rusk warned Eban that the Arabs were planning to raise the issue of Jerusalem again at the Security Council. Rusk requested that Israel exercise restraint while administering the city, believing that his own country had extracted promises from Jordan not to cause any trouble. He warned that any drastic measures which may be viewed as ending all prospects of reaching a peaceful accommodation should be avoided.[33] In order to persuade Israel to refrain from entrenchment in the city, the United States began echoing Britain's concern for Hussein's political survivability if there was no Israeli movement on the Palestine refugee issue or on East Jerusalem. Eban's response was to repeat his country's conviction that this was an Arab maneuver designed to impact the Jarring mission, and that Israel was still open to unilateral negotiations with Jordan. Eban's excuse for Israel's undertaking of new municipal projects in the city was to remind the United States of the neglect and desecration visited by the Jordanians on Jerusalem in the recent past.[34]

As Jordan pressed on with a renewed effort to restart the debate on Jerusalem at the Security Council, Israel sharpened its propaganda tools. Goldberg, on his part, defended its activities in the occupied city, justifying them as symptomatic of its lack of faith in the fairness and neutrality of the UN. He also escalated his attack on al-Farra, calling him a Palestinian at heart, with minimal loyalty to the Jordanian monarch. The Jordanian representative, Goldberg complained, was not following Amman's instructions to coordinate with the United States and follow its advice, which al-Farra viewed as an enemy state. To illustrate this, Goldberg referred to the recent scheduling of an address to the council by former mayor El-Khatib without prior US clearance. The American representative also advised the State Department not to succumb to the Arab demand for raising the Jerusalem issue separately, but instead to endorse Israel's call for a general political settlement. Any effort to reopen the Jerusalem question by seeking a new and separate resolution, he emphasized, would harm the Jarring mission and its quest for a comprehensive solution.[35]

Gunnar Jarring was appraised of the US, Israeli, and Jordanian positions as soon as he embarked on his mission. His diplomatic assignment entailed basically garnering support for the Security Council resolution while leaving the intractable Jerusalem issue until the end. But the Jerusalem question became the focal point of Arab attention, particularly Egypt, which persisted in calling for the return of Jordanian Jerusalem to its former authority.[36] By May 1968, Goldberg began to express the US shift to a preference for keeping Jerusalem a united city. He complained to the British delegation that the Security Council heaped undeserved criticism on Israel all the time while sparing the Arabs any blame. He echoed the views of US Congress which lambasted the Council's reluctance to castigate Egypt for its failure to apply its resolutions on the Suez Canal.[37]

THE JARRING MISSION AND THE ELUSIVE PEACE

By June 1968, the United States was directly confronted with Israel's resolve against returning East Jerusalem. In a meeting between Israeli officials and American presidential advisers Rostow and Saunders, the presence of Begin, Israel's Minister without Portfolio, added fuel to the fire of American agitation and impatience. He directly assailed the American effort to caution Israel on Jerusalem by stating without any subtlety his government's obdurate stand on the future of the city. When Rostow reminded him that the city remained the most complex segment of a future political settlement, Begin burst out that Jerusalem should not even be brought up in any negotiations since it was already the capital of Israel. He added that the United States need not fear preventing the religious communities from accessing the holy places. Neither did he see any need for proclaiming Hussein the guardian of the Muslim sites and interests. Begin could not foresee a better plan for the city than acceding to full Israeli sovereignty. But what really riled him up was Rostow's suggestion that Jordan should be accorded a part in directing the security, educational and legal services of the city. [38]

Another campaign to reverse the results of the 1967 War was launched in the UN following the stalemated peace process resulting from the adoption of Resolution 242. The man who headed this latest effort was former Swedish Ambassador to the Soviet Union Gunnar Jarring. He was assigned to this mission by the UN Secretary General for the expressed purpose of seeking the implementation of the principles of the famous resolution by all the affected parties. All the Arab states, with the exception of Syria which voted against the resolution, supported his mission. Israel, however, had neither faith in reaching a satisfactory diplomatic solution nor confidence in the effectiveness of Jarring's personal approach to these negotiations. Israel also did not believe in the UN's ability to broker what might be considered an equitable settlement. Israel's tactics involved providing Jarring with a constant stream of proposals for the benefit of the other side in order to gauge the Arab reaction, while extending the duration of the mission in order to obstruct returning the issue back to the UN. [39] The usefulness of this approach was later explained by Eban in an interview with Avi Shlaim:

> Some of my colleagues did not understand that even a tactical exercise fills a vacuum. Even diplomatic activity that is not leading anywhere is better than no diplomatic activity at all. Activity itself gives Arab moderates an alibi for avoiding the military option. [40]

These delaying tactics which did not appear to have perturbed the United States at all, suited the broad outline of the Israeli Government's total Middle East policy perfectly.

During Jarring's Middle East negotiations, Hussein pursued another round of direct secret contacts with the Israeli Government in September 1968. It was during these talks that Allon offered his notorious eponymous plan, seeking Jordan's approval of the annexation of one-third of the area of the Jordan Valley and around Jerusalem as the price of peace. The plan also called for converting the remaining West Bank territory into an autonomous entity under Israeli sovereignty. Hussein balked at this proposal, and the United States was made aware of the nature of the talks. Israel, meanwhile, was hoping that the talks with Jordan would ease UN and US pressure to accept Res. 242. But in the absence of peace, Palestinian guerrillas intensified their attacks on Israel from the Jordanian side. This led to greater Israeli aerial bombardment of several Jordanian towns which became totally exposed to the new Israeli military positions in the occupied Syrian Golan Heights.[41]

Secret negotiations between Jordan and Israel in 1968, thus, were notable for being the only time in which the latter offered to cede some territory. The Allon Plan, which encapsulated this offer and was supposedly based on the Security Council Resolution, would have split the Jordanian Kingdom in two, while surrendering Jerusalem completely. Allon rationalized his proposed map by claiming that there was a need to bring the Jordan Valley under his country's military control due to security considerations. This maximalist logic did not convince Hussein, who argued that peace did not require such militant security guarantees. According to Israel's maximalist views, however, there would always be the possibility of attack not necessarily by the Jordanians but by other Arab forces using Jordan as a staging area from which to attack Israel. Writing years later, O'Connell added that the King repeatedly sought President Johnson's intervention to prevent the breakdown of Israeli-Jordanian talks, to no avail. Neither did President Nixon, who came to office in 1969, respond to these requests.[42]

THE AFTERMATH OF ISRAEL'S UNIFICATION DECREE

The UN kept up the pressure on Israel since 1967 by adopting resolutions in the General Assembly invalidating any unilateral changes which it made in Jerusalem. First, UNESCO began to send observers to document Israeli archeological activities in the city which changed its historical character. Then, after the adoption of "Basic Law: Jerusalem the Capital of Israel" decree on 20 August 1980, the Security Council adopted Res. 478, calling for the removal of the diplomatic missions of UN member states from the city. Only Costa Rica and El Salvador did not comply, refusing to move to Tel Aviv. Several Arab states came out openly for the internationalization of the city

soon after the war ended, but some continued to insist on the return of East
Jerusalem to Jordan.[43]

The Vatican also maintained its policy on internationalization, despite
some dissident views on the part of some of its officials. For instance, Rev.
Pierre de Contenson, Secretary of the Vatican's Commission on Religious
Relations with the Jews, claimed in an interview on Israel Radio that the
Vatican no longer adhered to its demand for internationalization as expressed
in the General Assembly Partition Resolution (181) of November 1947. He
claimed that the Holy See was willing to accept international guarantees for
maintaining the status of the holy sites, a claim quickly denied by Rome.[44]
Israel continued to tighten its grip on East Jerusalem, while the international
community persisted in fostering the illusion of being on the brink of reaching a settlement. But Jerusalem's last Arab mayor, El Khatib, who was
replaced by the Hungarian-born Kollek, persisted in his efforts to jolt UN
agencies out of their somnolence by enumerating and recording Israel's
infractions of international law. He became a record keeper of these events,
beginning with the summary dismissal of the Arab city council, followed by
the seizure of its furniture and records. Since his expulsion from the country
on March 7, 1968, the Israeli Government accelerated its arbitrary and draco-
nian measures to bring the Arab part of the city under its control. He noted
Israel's rejection of all Shari'a Court rulings, which aimed at compelling the
Muslim population to refer their judicial cases to Israel's highest Islamic
court at Jaffa. This court which served the needs of Israel's own Arab citizens, applied the country's civil laws to personal stats cases since applying
the Shari'a had been severely limited, particularly in the areas of marriage
and divorce. Now, Israeli law was also applied to Muslim cases of East
Jerusalem's population. He also released reports of the confiscation of the
funds of Arab banks of the Old City which forced residents to file their
transactions with Israeli banks, an activity described earlier by US diplomatic
personnel in Jerusalem and Tel Aviv. Neither did the Arab educational system escape Israel's blunt measures to impose a unified Israeli curriculum on
all of its schools. Some Arab school administrators were imprisoned and
many school teachers dismissed in the process. The worst instance of denying international rules and regulations, he wrote, were practiced openly by
imposing Israeli taxes and commercial and municipal laws on the captive
population in violation of Security Council resolutions and the edicts of the
Geneva Convention. Israel, he complained, treated the city as though it was
subject to its total sovereignty. No human rights considerations were followed, exemplified by the most egregious case of obstructing the return of
some 20,000 Arabs who were caught outside the country when hostilities
began.[45]

Kollek, however, never tired of advertising and promoting the humaniz-
ing impact of Israel's seizure of Arab Jerusalem. The main fiction which

anchored his story was that all Israeli measures were intended to improve the daily lives of the city's inhabitants. A follower of Ben Gurion, Kollek's early career was as a successful procurer of illicit weapons abroad. Kollek relished his role as head of the two Jerusalems following his years as mayor of the Western part during its uneventful days. Always boastful of his dedication to this experiment in Arab-Jewish co-existence, he also worked tirelessly to ensure that the city would always have a Jewish majority and a quiescent Arab minority. His dedication to these myths was tested on several occasions, beginning with an unsuccessful legal suit by one hundred Arab residents who tried to reclaim their properties and assets in West Jerusalem with the help of Israeli lawyers. When the Israeli Minister of Justice who exercised a degree of authority over the city recommended the appointment of some Arabs to the city council, Kollek resisted, claiming that he feared their public objection to the occupation regime. Even when the city during his tenure signaled its readiness to compensate the evicted Arab residents of the Jewish Quarter, it was going to be at the expense of other Absentee Arabs. These were defined as such by the absentee laws, which gave the evicted families vacant Arab homes in the nearby neighborhood of Silwan. [46]

As to Eban, his justification of Israel's takeover of East Jerusalem shifted within a few months to a more measured language. Thus, on October 8, 1968, he elaborated on the future of the city before the UN:

> Israel does not seek to exercise unilateral jurisdiction in the Holy Places of Christianity and Islam. We are willing in each case to work out a status to give effect to their universal character. . . . Our policy is that the Christian and Muslim holy places should come under the responsibility of those who hold them in reverence. [47]

Less than a year later, he addressed the Knesset on May 13, 1969, describing a more pronounced policy to keep the city under Israeli rule:

> Three demands which Israel will not waive are a permanent presence at Sharm al-Sheikh, a unified Jerusalem despite concessions to Jordan over the holy places, and a Golan Heights forever out of Syrian hands. [48]

By that time, he had already claimed on July 10, 1967, in a letter to the UN Secretary-General U Thant that the legislation passed by the Knesset did not amount to annexation. After reviewing the neglect and division which the city suffered under Jordanian rule and the denial of Jewish access to their holy sites, he painted a rosy picture of life under Israeli rule. He claimed that peace and unity had reigned over the city in its two halves since June 27, 1967, the date of the extension of Israeli law to Jerusalem. It was an act of "integration," not "annexation," he confirmed. He boasted that a general state of amity prevailed between Arabs and Jews who were free to re-establish their former contacts as neighbors. Municipal services in the Old City have been improved, with water now supplied on a regular basis, health services functioning better than before, and the school population being well served. The Arab inhabitants, he affirmed, were connected to Israel's general welfare system, receiving benefits for the first time.[49] The contrast with El Khatib's report could not have been more stark. The Israeli diplomat ignored the clear characteristics of a system of political and military occupation, invoking, as often in the past, the logic of development and progress to trump that of national and human rights.

THE ROGERS PLAN—THE FAILURE OF GOOD INTENTIONS

By 1969, Johnson's presidency gave way to that of Richard Nixon, who, along with his National Security Adviser, Henry Kissinger, was focused more on Vietnam than on the Middle East. Nixon's Secretary of State, William Rogers, became easily distracted by the thorny Arab-Israeli conflict, while the President and his adviser set their sights on the East Asian region. But in Israel, Eshkol's tenure ended as head of state as he was succeeded by the more hawkish Golda Meir. All of this did not bide well for Jordan which also ranked very low on Kissinger's global scheme of things. Yet, since none of the UN resolutions have been successfully adopted by the major parties in this conflict, the fiction of searching for a permanent solution had to be maintained. Because Kissinger did not view the Jordanian monarch as a valuable player in his perception of the primacy of the cold war among the titans, the King was simply sidelined.[50] In the words of Edward R. F. Sheehan:

> Kissinger, like Nixon and President Johnson before him, took King Hussein for granted. Jordan, after all, was nearly an American protectorate; but unlike Israel, it possessed no American constituency and thus had to be content with whatever scraps Washington might care to cast its way.[51]

The King lost all leverage when he agreed to promote Res. 242 among his Arab partners. He was simply stranded by the Johnson administration which reneged on all promises to get Israel to relinquish some of the territories seized by war. Jordanian-Israeli relations were overtaken by diplomatic paralysis, which cost the King dearly on the domestic front. Palestinian guerrillas then seized the military initiative along the new Israeli-Jordanian frontier with constant attacks aimed at forcing a return to military engagement.[52]

The Rogers Plan was developed primarily with input from Sisco. Once again, it called on Israel to withdraw from the areas seized in 1967, in return for a peace agreement with the Arab belligerent states under the auspices of the United States. It also called for the rejection of unilateral steps in Jerusalem and reaching out for a peaceful settlement between the parties concerned, meaning Israel and Jordan. However, the Rogers Plan, for the first time ever, officially called for maintaining Jerusalem as a united city which would facilitate the freedom of movement for people and goods, with special commitment to maintaining the interests of all the religious communities in the city.[53] "Jerusalem should be a unified city," it read, adding "There should be roles for both Israel and Jordan in the civil and religious life of the city."[54] The Israeli Government reacted quickly, rejecting the latest American initiative within one day. What aggravated it was the new emphasis on charting a role for a shared Israeli-Jordanian administration in the city. Nixon immediately recognized the negative fallout of Israel's rejection among members of the influential American-Jewish community and quietly informed Golda Meir that there would be no pressure to force Israel's acceptance of the plan.[55]

THE 1973 WAR LIMITS HUSSEIN'S ROLE

A new perception of the Arab-Israeli conflict emerged when Kissinger rose to prominence and took charge of the foreign policy of the United States. Essentially, he and Nixon were convinced that the key to maintaining peace in the Middle East was to keep Israel strong. This would dampen Arab interest in challenging the post-1967 territorial status quo, and perhaps weaken their ties to the Soviet Union. When the Arabs finally realize the value of seeking an alliance with the United States, Kissinger made it clear he would be ready to launch another diplomatic initiative in order to secure a peace agreement. This view contrasted with that of Nixon who was amenable to superpower cooperation in the interest of ending quarrels among smaller states. But as of 1973, his preoccupation with the Watergate scandal sapped his energies, leaving the foreign policy arena to Kissinger, who rose to the position of Secretary of State in September of that year. Kissinger's management of US-Middle East relations, it became clear later on, was always conducted in secret collaboration with Israel.[56]

Based on his research in the official Israeli archives, historian Yigal Kipnis documented the existence of political favoritism and dependency between a super power's foreign policy chief and the policy makers of one of its dependent client states. For instance, Simha Dinitz, Israel's ambassador to the United States, wrote on June 2, 1973, to Prime Minister Meir:

> He [Kissinger] told me that this would be the first time in American history that the Secretary of State would be Jewish and that this would help us, as he would be able to delay initiatives of the State Department even before they found their way to the White House. . . There is a possibility that he will

request my assistance on the Hill [i.e. Congress] to have his appointment approved.[57]

Meir responded three days later that she was willing to move her friends in Congress to support Kissinger's nomination.[58]

The Secretary of State, who was often referred to by the code name "Shaul" (sometimes Shaulson), before he assumed his cabinet post, was advising Israeli diplomats on how not to succumb to pressure by the State Department or accept Sisco's plans. In a move which surprised Dinitz, Kissinger at one time shared messages from Egyptian National Security Adviser, Hafiz Ismail, in 1972, then followed this by seeking the ambassador's advice on who should be his choice to succeed Sisco as assistant secretary of state. Yet, Kissinger turned down Dinitz's suggestion that Alfred Atherton should fill this post.[59]

By 1972, however, King Hussein's secret contacts with Israeli officials had run dry. His United Arab Kingdom plan, uniting the West Bank and Jordan, which he tried out on his secret interlocutors after making it public, found no favor with the Israelis. This turned out to be a losing battle for Hussein since Israel had already drastically altered the territorial and demographic characteristics of the West Bank and Jerusalem through settlement building. What he proposed was still the "liberation," of all the occupied territories, including Gaza and East Jerusalem, which he would declare to be the capital of Palestine. The entire demilitarized area would be part of his kingdom. The only border changes which the King said he would accept entailed merely an adjustment to the 1949 armistice line in order to reunite some villages with their agricultural lands. But Hussein balked at the Israeli insistence on a peace agreement before his demands were met. The Israelis also demanded the right to build bases on Jordanian territory. They declined to accept Jordan's demand for a ban on Israeli flights over its skies as they completing their surveillance of Syrian positions. But Meir was very specific when explaining her views on March 16, 1972, before the Knesset. She claimed that it was never her intention to meddle in internal Arab issues. She added that Hussein's plan for a federated kingdom was unacceptable simply because it touched on Israel's security and borders without promising to pursue unilateral talks with her government.[60] Egypt and the PLO also rejected the Arab Kingdom plan. Yet, the King travelled to Tel Aviv on September 25, 1973, two weeks before the outbreak of the October War, specifically to warn Israel against a possible Egyptian-Syrian attack. Rumors of the meeting, which were leaked by the Israeli press, soon found their way to the Arabic press, angering the King. He claimed in his own defense that all he wanted was to avoid a ruinous war which would negatively impact his country.[61]

The Israelis did not take Hussein's warning seriously since all he conveyed to them was that his intelligence sources detected Syrian military preparations close to the Golan Heights. The Agranat Commission, which investigated Israel's failure to anticipate an Egyptian-Syrian attack on October 6, concluded later that this was the result of a prevailing view that Egypt would not start a war until it repaired its devastated airforce. The Israelis were confident that the damage inflicted as a result of the 1967 June War caused the Egyptian air force to lag behind Israel's air-force. They believed that only by bridging this serious gap would Egypt be able to penetrate Israeli territory. This was later referred to as "the conception," leading the Israelis to ignore all signs of an imminent war. The King was fearful of joining such a war and had clarified his position to President Sadat. He was also wary of a possible Arab demand for granting safe passage for PLO fighters to cross into Israeli territory.[62]

Jordan received no compensation for abstaining from the 1973 War, certainly not from Kissinger. It was left with waving the banner of the PLO threat as the next contender for ruling Jordan in order to attract Kissinger's attention. Rather than facilitate the return of its occupied territories, however, the Secretary of State stood by as Israel continued to turn down these demands.[63] Kissinger had actually given his solemn promise to Hussein that his request for the return of the West Bank would be honored once the war was over. Hussein was feeling empowered since he managed to stay out of this war, even towards the end when the besieged Egyptians and Syrians sought his military assistance. The Jordanians expected that their demands would receive priority in the peace talks once the war ended. They were also encouraged to promote the Geneva Conference, which aimed at bringing together the major warring sides, thereby strengthening Jordan's credentials as the representative of the Palestinian people. The conference was held under the co-sponsorship of the Soviet Union and hoped to secure the adoption of Security Council Res. 338, which affirmed Res. 242, its more famous predecessor. While only Syria abstained, the United States focused its efforts on bringing peace between the Egyptians and the Israelis. But the conference had a short duration, its sole accomplishment being the creation of an Egyptian-Israeli committee to work out the details of Israeli withdrawal from Egyptian territory. Both Kissinger and Sadat were seemingly disinterested in any other negotiations. But once Kissinger became involved in Jordanian-Israeli talks, all he came up with was a modified version of the Allon Plan and keeping all of Jerusalem under Israeli jurisdiction. He explained that this was not the first stop in a more comprehensive plan, but was indeed the whole Israeli offer.[64]

Hussein's failure to produce some tangible results from reliance on his American allies weakened his position at the Rabat Summit Conference a year after the October War ended. Arab heads of state adopted the Rabat

Resolution of 1974, which recognized the PLO as the legitimate representative of the Palestinian people, and Kissinger moved on to try and restore occupied Sinai to the Egyptians and part of the Golan Heights to Syria. He admitted to the Jordanians after Rabat that he had miscalculated, adding later that actually it were the Jordanians who miscalculated his ability to influence the outcome of events in this region.[65]

Never one to mask his Israeli loyalties, Kissinger executed several bold political maneuvers during the 1973 War on behalf of the Israeli state. Apparently, his ability to influence the outcome of events in this case was not an exaggeration. During a closed-door meeting with American-Jewish intellectuals and editors on December 6, 1973, he reportedly was apologetic over failure to deliver military assistance to Israel once the war broke out. He said that the United States warned the Israelis from the beginning that they would be facing a UN cease-fire once their advances on the battlefield became known. He said that he then advised them to race against time in order to maximize their territorial gains before the cease-fire took effect. But then he revealed that as soon as pressure for a cease-fire started, he resorted to all kinds of delaying tactics in order to allow them more time. Thus, he absented himself from UN discussions by flying to the Soviet Union, gaining a total of ninety-six hours of continued Israeli military activity. Yet, he complained that Israel was not forthcoming about the precise nature of its military maneuvers, leaving him in the dark. He also predicted that a global oil crisis was about to take effect, referring to King Faysal as a "religious fanatic," whose main desire was to retrieve Jerusalem. Faysal, Kissinger insisted, was not interested in the Palestinians or the return of the Sinai, but found himself at last in a position to lead the Arab World.[66] Kissinger explained that the Palestinian problem was not ready for a solution yet, emphasizing that "They [the Palestinians] would have to be a lot hungrier than they are now," before showing willingness to accept a peace settlement and recognize Israel. The issue of Jerusalem, he insisted, must be reserved for the last phase of any peace talks.[67] His blind spot where Israel was concerned centered on ignoring Jewish fanaticism regarding Jerusalem and reserving the fanaticism label for King Faysal. Kissinger demonstrated this again and again when he ignored Israel's stubborn resistance to early American demand for a return to the 4 June armistice lines in the West Bank. Instead, he pushed for maintaining Israel's new boundaries at the 6 October lines following the end of the 1973 war, knowing full well that these territorial concessions would have to come from the Egyptian side.[68] But while the Palestinian issue receded to the end of the line, Jerusalem remained the focal point of Arab and Muslim states, especially, the new player in this arena, namely Saudi Arabia.

THE OIL LOBBY AND ITS ILLUSIONS

No understanding of America's pronounced tilt in Israel's direction in the aftermath of the 1967 War would be possible without an examination of the role of the Arab oil lobby. Moreover, whether it was an oil lobby or a general effort by the moderate Arab Gulf states, this was increasingly on Israel's mind and that of its sympathizers ever since the Eisenhower era. The oil lobby was also linked to the influence of the State Department Arabists whose impact on American policy-making towards the end of the 1967 War was visibly in decline. The Arabists monopolized the Bureau of Near Eastern Affairs but were losing influence to the Bureau of International Affairs by June of 1967 when Sisco assumed the leading role in managing the crisis. His title was the Assistant Secretary of State for International Organization Affairs. This placed him on Goldberg's team as the international battle to settle the Jordanian-Israeli dispute shifted to the UN. Samuel Lewis, former US Ambassador to Israel, explained later that the view in Washington from the Eisenhower to the Johnson years was that US interests demanded maintaining close relations with the Arab World, and that Israel was merely a "nuisance." American presidents began to involve themselves directly with the Middle East beginning with John F. Kennedy, as they carved for themselves a niche in this area of foreign policy which previously belonged within the State Department. However, the perception of the Israeli state changed drastically during the Johnson administration when its victory over the Arabs enhanced its value as a military and strategic ally in the region. [69]

The influence of the Arab states, nevertheless, was exerted through the oil lobby, although Israel's friends continued to point a finger at the influence of the Arab embassies. AIPAC was still a limited organization administered by Isaiah Kenen, who directed its activities in Congress. When the 1973 War broke out, Israel was the recipient of a large American subsidy, but the development of the oil weapon as an element in Arab foreign policy posed new challenges for the Jewish-American community. Although the first instance of direct pressure on the State Department by a representative of the Arab oil lobby was that of ARAMCO's Vice-President James Terry Duce who approached the State Department on November 4, 1946, to agitate against Truman's pro-Zionist tilt, the Israeli lobby always claimed that this was the result of pressure by the Saudi Government. During that meeting, Duce warned that ARAMCO might have to register as a British company if its oil concession was to be saved. Complaints by the Saudi Government to American oil interests in the kingdom figured prominently during the run-up to the Saudi oil embargo of 1973. But whether these were gentle reprimands or direct pressure on some of the industry's giants operating in the Saudi fields such as Standard Oil of California, Texaco, Exxon, and Mobil, the State Department was made aware of them. For instance, in a meeting with these companies in May 1973, in Geneva, the Saudi monarch attempted to activate them to lobby on his government's behalf or face the loss of America's economic interests in the region. When the Arab oil embargo was imposed, the companies voluntarily curbed their oil production by ten per cent. The US defense industry which depended on Arab weapons' markets was also considered part of this lobby. The close coordination between some members of the State Department, such as Ambassador James Aikens, and this lobby during the embargo resulted in his firing by an unsympathetic Kissinger. During that time, Saudi dependence on American weapons was simply due to their willingness to recycle the petro-dollars by easing the burden of American trade deficit resulting from the high price of oil. Saudi Arabia's detractors in the United States, nevertheless, continued to claim that its oil policy was not necessarily a reflection of its commitment to the Palestinian cause.[70]

What explains the apparent ineffectiveness of the Arab oil lobby in stopping the United States from drifting further towards the Israeli camp? One obvious reason was the lobby's reluctance or inability to influence members of Congress. An exception to this was the sale of Airborne Warning and Command System (AWACS) to Saudi Arabia in 1981 which directly impacted the country's interests. But even when this commercial deal stood to benefit the American economy, pro-Israel members of Congress attempted to block it. This case became a test case of Congressional commitment to maintaining Israel's qualitative military edge in the region. But, pressuring US presidents depended on several variables, including presidential perception of the priority of a certain issue and limiting this to times of extreme crisis in the Middle East.[71] Even during such intense involvement of the executive branch in Middle East affairs such as the Arab oil embargo of 1973, the right of the oil lobby to shape US foreign policy was often blunted by the enormous influence of some secretaries of state such as Kissinger. The secretary of state in this case monopolized decision-making in this arena and managed to sideline the professional Arabists in the State Department. Thus, erasing the after-effects of the 1967 War hinged on several factors, not the least of which was the alignment of several conditions which would impact the final decision of the Chief Executive, his secretary of state, or even, as happened under Johnson, some of his advisers.

CONCLUSION

The 1967 Arab-Israeli War turned out to be the major and defining military confrontation between these two sides since the founding of the Israeli state. Whenever the Sykes-Picot Agreement is usually sited as having resulted in a new Middle East map, it should always be coupled with the 1967 War as another conflict which changed borders and radically altered the maps of Jordan, Egypt, Syria and Israel alike. The fact that neither the United States nor the international community succeeded in reversing its outcome which hardened into an entrenched Israeli occupation regime was also indicative of the war's unanticipated and surprising results. It should also be noted that in 1964, when Israel sought to receive offensive weapons from the United States for the first time it was asked to comply with certain conditions. Among these were consenting to a similar arms deal for Jordan, refraining from attacking Syria's Jordan River project, declining to acquire nuclear weapons, and more significantly, pledging against launching a pre-emptive strike against any Arab state. These demands were not accepted quietly, as Rabin fumed at what he perceived to be an infringement on his country's right of self-defense. He later indicated in his memoirs that by 1967, Israel was involved in a massive restructuring of the IDF in preparation for an inevitable outbreak of hostilities.[72]

All of these restrictions on the occasion of Israel's first request for offensive weapons from the United States were forgotten as soon as the war began. The US President and his advisers who were repeatedly assured that Israel held a military edge over all of the Arab armies, never considered restricting its attacks or preventing the occupation of the Jordanian West Bank and East Jerusalem. Instead, there was elation over Israel's victory which was not tempered by the enormity of Jordan's losses. Neither was the Jordanian monarch forgiven for reacting to Israel's attack on one of the frontline villages of his territory by staging a military offensive against West Jerusalem. The Samu' attack, which severely narrowed the King's margin of political survival was actually intended to discourage guerrilla attacks from the Syrian border. The United States hardly noted the damage done by this operation, even though the UN reacted to it quickly. The Johnson administration was not only preoccupied with the Vietnam War, the President himself was surrounded by an unusual array of pro-Israel advisers, friends, and political allies, a situation making any severe response to Israeli attacks nearly impossible to execute.

The 1967 War resulted not only in the loss of Palestinian territory to Israel, it also heralded a radical transformation of US policy on Jerusalem. The shift from upholding the UN's position on the internationalization of the holy city to that of supporting a unified Jerusalem, irrespective of who its rulers might be, ended up facilitating Israel's plan of converting the conquered city into its capital. This became a muted endorsement of Israel's position, even though the United States continued to criticize Israel's actions. The idea of restoring Jordanian sovereignty over East Jerusalem was quickly abandoned in favor of offering the Arabs, particularly Hussein, merely custodianship over the Muslim holy sites. Separating the fate of these places from that of the rest of the city was a throwback to the Israeli preference for functional internationalization when Jordan was in charge of East Jerusalem and its Old City. This idea which would often be revived in meetings such as the Camp David II conference, allowed the United States to maintain the sanctimonious posture of an even-handed peace broker.

As soon as the 1967 War ended and diplomacy took over, Hussein pursued his two-track diplomatic offensive, seeking to salvage something from the wreckage of the war through his American allies, while at the same time reopening his secret channel to Israel's leaders. But whether he understood this or not, Israel was using its hallmark tactical diplomacy of delayed action not in the interest of arriving at a solution, but rather to buy time and extract acquiescence in its faits accomplis. As long as it perpetuated the fiction of seeking a diplomatic solution, including meeting UN envoy Gunnar Jarring but not necessarily yielding to his demands, Israel managed to persuade the United States of its peaceful intentions. Israel's offers to King Hussein, on the other hand, were based on the expansionist Allon Plan, which would have forced Jordan to yield one-third of the West Bank in the Jordan Valley and around East Jerusalem. Neither did Israel retreat from its legislation on administering a united Jerusalem. This hardening of positions became a de facto annexation of all of East Jerusalem.

The United States and Britain contrived to co-sponsor the only operative resolution on the Arab-Israeli conflict in the history of the Security Council. Res. 242, with its duplicitous and glaringly contradictory language combined a reminder of the illegality of acquiring territory by war with a call for withdrawal from occupied territories without necessarily defining what was meant by this statement. Israel's position hardened into a call for negotiations first and surrendering some territory later, but with no relinquishing of sovereignty over Jerusalem. Hussein was duped by Johnson into accepting the resolution, with the promise of getting his lost territory back. This helped to ease the way for other Arab states to follow suit. But he continued to struggle against Israeli pressure to sign a unilateral peace agreement first.

What could the United States have done? One of the most puzzling aspects of this chapter in US Middle East diplomacy was the Johnson administration's palpable disinterest in using Israel's human rights infractions as a lever to force the return of the occupied territories. The evidence was supplied by its diplomats on the ground, as well as by international agencies and Arab reports documenting Israel's abuses, especially in the Old City. Thus, while Israel was finalizing its famed faits accomplis in a race against anticipated UN censorship, the American Consul in the city was documenting every violation of international law for the benefit of his State Department superiors. His cables exposed Israeli secret activities bordering on war crimes, such as the destruction of the Mughrabi Quarter, the ethnic cleansing of the Jewish Quarter and the erasure of the Latroun villages, as well as massive looting by members of the IDF and initiating Jewish settlements in and around the occupied city and on the Syrian Golan Heights. He also detailed the flagrant and illegal extension of Israeli laws to East Jerusalem, the dismissal of the city's Arab council, followed by the expulsion of its mayor and the head of the Islamic Shari'a Court.

The rise of Kissinger to the apex of the foreign policy decision-making apparatus within the executive branch further skewed United States policy in the direction of Israel. But one could even claim that if the Johnson administration bore any historical responsibility for enabling Israel to keep its ill-gotten fruits of war, which was always defined as defensive action, Kissinger and the Nixon government could also be charged with excessive favoritism to Israel which aided and encouraged its extralegal policies. Never one to conceal his disdain for minor foreign policy issues, such as the Jordanian-Israeli dispute or Palestinian rights under an abusive system of occupation, Kissinger's approach to these questions was always to buy Israel time in order to gain more territory. Such was the case along the Egyptian frontier in 1973 when the secretary of state was willing to coordinate with the Israelis every step of the way. Kissinger was also the first high-level US official to face the wrath of an Arab monarch during the events leading up to the 1973 War, in which Arab Jerusalem emerged as the central issue. The Jewish official who always chafed at King Faysal's open reference to the twin scourges of Communists and Jews, lived to experience the durability of the Jerusalem issue, particularly the holy sites, as the thorniest aspect of the Arab-Israeli dispute.

NOTES

1. Shlomo Ben Ami, *Scars of War, Wounds of Peace* (Oxford: Oxford University Press, 2006): 128–9.

2. McGeorge Bundy to Walt Rostow, Memo, August 11, 1967. NSFile/Files of Special Committee of the NSC, Box 4, Doc. 3a, LBJL.

3. Foreign Minister Eban, Ambassador Harman and McGeorge Bundy, "Memo of Conversation," 5 July 1967. NSFiles/Files of the Special Committee of the NSC—Chrono, Folder 2. Box 1, Doc. 7a, LBJL.

4. Bundy to the President, "Draft Statement on Jerusalem," July 14, 1967. NSFiles/Files of the Special Committee of the NSC, Box 1, Doc. 9a, Folder 3, LBJL.

5. Howard Wriggins, to Hal Saunders," Control Committee Meeting—Jerusalem," minutes, July 10, 1957. NSFiles/Files of Special Committee of the NSC. Box 1, Doc. 12, LBJL.

6. CIA, "Arab Territories under Israeli Occupation," Special Report, Weekly Review, October 6, 1967. NSFiles/Files of Special Committee of the NSC, Folder 5, Box 3, Doc.1, LBJL.

7. Ibid.

8. Alfred Atherton to Lucius Battle, "The Holy Places," July 13, 1967.

9. Bundy, "Memo for the President through Walt Rostow: Our Response to King Hussein," July 18, 1967. NSFILES/Files of Special Committee of the NSC, Folder 1, Box 3, Doc. 41a, LBJL.

10. Tom Segev, *1967: Israel, the War, and the Year that Transformed the Middle East* (New York: Henry Holt, 2005): 503–9.

11. Ibid., 511.

12. Avi Shlaim, *Lion of Jordan: The Life of King Hussein in War and Peace* (New York: Alfred A. Knopf, 2008): 260–2.

13. Ben Ami, *Scars of War*, 129.

14. Shlaim, *Lion of Jordan*, 263–4.

15. Ibid., 266–7.

16. Jack O'Connell, *King's Counsel: A Memoir of War, Espionage, and Diplomacy in the Middle East* (New York: W. W. Norton, 2011): 63.

17. Ibid., 64–5.

18. Circular Telegram from Department of State to all Posts, July 5, 1967. Subject: Jerusalem. Resolution in the U.N. General Assembly. FRUS, Vol. XIX, 164–1968, 616–8.

19. Statement by Ambassador Arthur J. Goldberg in the Plenary Session in the General Debate, September 21, 1967. NSFile/Agency File, Box 69, Doc. 7i, LBJL.

20. Department of State Telegram, From US Mission at UN, November 4, 1967. NSFile/ Agency File, UN, Vol. 8, 7/67–11, Box 69, Doc. 48, LBJL.

21. Relevant Portions of Ambassador Goldberg's Conversations with Hussein, For the Press, November 8, 1967. NSFile/Agency File, UN, Vol. 8, 7/67–11, Box 69, Doc. 19, LBJL.

22. From US Mission to the UN, A. Goldberg to Department of State, September 30, 1967. NSFile/Agency File, Vol. 8, Box 69, Doc. 81, LBJL.

23. Hal Saunders to Walt Rostow, "Your Preparatory Meeting on the Eban Talks …," October 20, 1967. NSFile/Country File/Israel. Box 140, Doc. 70a, LBJL.

24. O'Connell, *King's Counsel*, 68–70.

25. Ibid., 70.

26. Ibid., 70–6. See also, Donald Neff, *Warriors for Jerusalem: Six Days that Changed the Middle East* (New York: Simon and Schuster, 1984): 337.

27. Shlaim, *Lion of Jordan* 273–5.

28. Neff, *Warriors for Jerusalem*, 338–9.

29. Ibid., 345.

30. Ibid., 344–5.

31. UNISPAL.un.org/…/7D35… Accessed 7/30/2015.

32. http://www.cjpme.org… "Factsheet: Resolution 242, Interpretation and Implications." Accessed 7/30/2015.

33. From Department of State to American Embassy in Tel Aviv, "Message from Secretary of State to Israeli Foreign Minister Eban," February 13, 1968. NSFile/Country File—Israel, Box 141, Doc. 49, LBJL.

34. Department of State to Embassy in Tel Aviv, "UK Officers," March 1, 1968. NSFile/ Country File—Israel, Box 141, Doc. 104, LBJL.

35. Goldberg to Department of State, "Jerusalem in Security Council," April 30, 1968. NSFile/Agency File/UN, Box 70, Doc. 55, LBJL.

36. US Mission in UN to Department of State, "Jarring—Riad Meeting in Stockholm on 25 June," July 6, 1968. NSFile/Agency File/UN, Box 70, Doc. 29, LBJL. See also: US Mission at UN to Department of State, August 6, 1968. NSFile/Agency File/UN, Box 7, Doc. 8, LBJL.

37. Goldberg to Department of State, "US-UK Exchange Re Middle East," May 14, 1968. NSFile/Agency File/UN, Box 70, Doc. 45, LBJL.

38. Memo of Conversation, Participants: Menachem Begin, Ambassador Rabin, Ephraim Evron, W. W. Rostow, Harold H. Saunders. FRUS, Vol. XX, 380.

39. Shlaim, *Lion of Jordan*, 277.

40. Ibid., 277.

41. Ibid., 290–8, 313–4.

42. O'Connell, *King's Counsel*, 88–9.

43. Avraham Sela, *Political Encyclopedia of the Middle East* (New York: Continuum Publishing Co., 1999): 421–2.

44. Rev. Joseph L. Ryan, "The Catholic Faith and the Problem of Jerusalem," in Islamic Council of Europe, *Jerusalem, the Key to World Peace* (London: Islamic Council of Europe, 1980): 41–2.

45. Rouhi El Khatib, "The Judaization of Jerusalem and its Demographic Transformation," *Jerusalem, the Key to World Peace*, 114–8.

46. Segev, *1967*, 482–8.

47. Priscilla Roberts, ed., "Jerusalem," *The Encyclopedia of the Arab-Israeli Conflict, Vol. IV* (Santa Barbara, Calif.: ABC CLIO, 2008): 1295.

48. Ibid., 1295–6.

49. Electronic Documents: Israel Ministry of Foreign Affairs. IV. Jerusalem and the Holy Places: 16. Letter from Foreign Minister Eban to UN Secretary General U Thant on Jerusalem, July 10, 1967.

50. Shlaim, *Lion of Jordan*, 303.

51. Edward R. F. Sheehan, *The Arabs, Israelis, and Kissinger* (New York: Reader's Digest Press, 1976): 136.

52. Shlaim, *Lion of Jordan*, 303–4.

53. William P. Rogers, "A Lasting Peace in the Middle East," December 9, 1969, in: Roberts, ed., *The Encyclopedia*, 1298.

54. Center for Public Affairs, "Perspectives–Jerusalem."jcpa.org/wp-content/uploads/2023/02/Strategy_Baker_Jerus.pdf. Accessed 8/26/2013.

55. "Statement by the Israeli Government Embodying a Reaction to the Rogers Plan, December 11, 1967," in: Roberts, ed., *The Encyclopedia*, 1299.

56. William B. Quandt, "Forward," in Yigal Kipnis, *1973: The Road to War* (Charlottesville, Virginia: Just World Books, 2013): 15.

57. Kipnis, *1973*, 159–60.

58. Ibid.

59. Ibid., 174, 177–8.

60. Avi Shlaim, *The Iron Wall: Israel and the Arab World* (New York: W. W. Norton, 2000): 313.

61. Shlaim, *Lion of Jordan*, 354–5,365–6.

62. Kipnis, *1973*, 193–4, 206.

63. Sheehan, *The Arabs*, 147–8.

64. O'Connell, King's Counsel, 125–9.

65. Sheehan, *The Arabs*, 148–50.

66. Ibid., Appendix Four, from Yediot Aharonot, February 15, 1974, 230–4.

67. Ibid., 234.

68. Ibid., 55.

69. Mitchell Bard, "The Arab Lobby: The American Component," *The Middle East Quarterly*, Vol. XVII, No. 4 (Fall 2010): 3–15. www.meforum.org/2773/arab-lobby. Accessed 1/15/2015.

70. Ibid.

71. Lucia W. Rawls, "Saudi Arabia, Aramco and The American Political Process: Cause for Concern," *Arab-American Affairs*, No. 18 (Fall 1986): 95–100.

72. Dan Kurzman, *Soldier of Peace: The Life of Yitzhak Rabin, 1922–1995* (New York: Harper Collins, 1998): 199–200.

Chapter Seven

Oslo: The Chimera of a Just Peace

President Sadat's 1973 war initiative was not intended to result in a radical redrawing of the boundaries. It was merely a limited offensive to force Israel to come to the negotiating table. Sadat's rhetoric regarding liberating the West Bank and restoring Arab Jerusalem to the Palestinians was intended for Arab consumption. After recognizing the wide gap separating the two sides on Jerusalem, both Sadat and Prime Minister Menachem Begin decided to drop the issue altogether.[1]

King Hussein then attempted to conclude a secret agreement with Israel after all hopes of reasserting his kingdom's rights to Jerusalem through the Camp David agreement faded. He launched the secret London talks in 1987, only to see Prime Minister Yitzhak Shamir torpedo them fearing that the proposed international conference, even by sidelining the PLO, would bring about undue pressure to cede occupied territories. Hussein was later persuaded by his Palestinian adviser, Adnan Abu-Odeh, to disengage from the West Bank when the first intifada erupted in 1987, but without surrendering his claims over the Muslim holy sites.[2] By 1980, Jerusalem was fully annexed when the Knesset adopted the Jerusalem Basic Law. Hussein's declared abandonment of his claim to the West Bank brought the PLO centerstage to the conflict. As more and more Palestinians appeared to carry on with their uprising in pursuit of Palestinian statehood, little was left of Jordan's historic leadership of that side of the Jordan River.[3]

THE SHULTZ INITIATIVE

US Secretary of State George P. Shultz stepped into this emerging situation by traveling twice to the region in 1988, hoping to replicate the Camp David Agreement's call for "Palestinian self-rule." Moderate Arab leaders such as

Hussein and Egypt's Husni Mubarak welcomed the initiative and urged the Arabs not to reject this new effort off hand. The Israeli reaction, by contrast, was that of anger and suspicion. Shamir, always fearful of an international conference which would force Israel to grant concessions, feared that the end result would be American backing for Palestinian self-rule or some expression of self-determination. Shamir told Shultz of his openness to the idea of negotiating with Hussein and any Palestinians he would include in his team, as long as the process did not entail surrendering control over any territory. Shultz, who felt that he was operating within the perimeters of Res. 242 and its underlying premise of "land for peace," was shocked to discover that he was facing the most intransigent of Israeli leaders who had never actually accepted this resolution. Neither was Shamir, with his long history of terrorism and leadership of the Irgun and Stern gangs, open to the idea of including Palestinians in the Arab negotiating team. When Shultz suggested that Faysal Husseini was a moderate Palestinian worthy of an invitation to the negotiations, Shamir responded that Israel had been keeping taps on his suspicious activities for a long time.[4]

But when Hussein declared his separation from the West Bank on 31 July 1988, thereby effectively taking himself out of any negotiations on behalf of the Palestinians, he sent a message to Peres through the State Department. He wrote that his intent was to prod the PLO to assume full responsibility for its actions and negotiate in good faith for a final settlement. Thus, the so-called "Jordanian option," on which the Israelis had long fastened their hopes, seemed to dissipate before their very eyes. Hussein, who never appreciated this description of his role which implied a conspiracy to reach an agreement behind the Palestinians' back, announced publicly the demise of this idea. Finally, the Israelis realized that any Israeli-Jordanian negotiations would only deal with their common borders. The PLO responded to these transformative developments by quickly adopting resolutions to enable it to enter into a dialogue with Shultz. By November 1988, delegates to the meeting of the Palestine National Council (PNC) in Algiers defeated the rejectionist wing of the organization by adopting a resolution which recognized Israel. The moderate majority also accepted all previous UN resolutions on the Arab-Israeli issue, beginning with the Partition Resolution (181) of November 29, 1947, which effectively endorsed the two-state solution. This historic shift in the PLO's ideology seemed to bypass the historic claim to all of Palestine as enshrined in the PLO Covenant. The declaration, however, defined the future state as a small entity encompassing the West Bank and Gaza, with East Jerusalem as its capital. This resolution which was adopted on November 15, 1988, elicited hostile reactions from Shamir and his government who described it as sheer PLO propaganda which intended to cloak itself with the mantle of moderation in order to deceive world opinion. Neither was the United States receptive of the PLO's official renunciation of terrorism which followed the declaration. Arafat yielded to American pressure and read the Department of State's approved text which renounced terrorism during the opening meeting of the Geneva Conference. He also stated his unconditional endorsement of Res. 242 and Res. 338, both of which offered a clear recognition of the Israeli state. This step nullified Kissinger's past condition for recognizing the PLO. The Reagan Administration finally recognized the Palestinian organization, and followed this with the establishment of formal contact through its ambassador in Tunis. But Shamir was not pacified, labeling this step a great mistake. Peres, the rotation cabinet's vice-premier, also described launching the PLO-US dialogue as a "sad day for all of us."[5]

In order not to be excluded from defining this inevitable normalization of relations, Peres advised the government to come up with its own peace plan. Shamir responded by suggesting that elections be held in the West Bank and Gaza in order to come up with independent Palestinian representatives who were unaffiliated with the PLO. These would be permitted to negotiate a blueprint for transitional accords leading to self-rule. The perimeters which were set for the negotiations were inspired by the Camp David Agreement, which would exclude all PLO representatives and would decline to call for the establishment of an independent Palestinian state. The Shamir government, thus, followed the example set by the Begin government before it in signaling tolerance only for an autonomous Palestinian entity. General Sharon was among the most vocal opponents of this plan, however, claiming that it would be disastrous for Israel and would unleash another wave of terror against it. But the cabinet remained unmoved by this argument and voted for the Shamir plan. US Secretary of State James Baker came down hard against this Israeli strategy, calling in an address before the annual meeting of AIPAC on May 22, 1989, for the state to bring its Greater Israel project to an end. He reminded the Israelis that Res. 242 specifically called for withdrawal from the occupied lands if Israel and the Palestinians were successful in negotiating a peace settlement. Baker also strongly urged the Israelis to stop building settlements in the occupied territories. Yet, this drastic change in American foreign policy failed to receive the full endorsement of the Palestinians. The United National Command (UNC), the shadowy leadership of the intifada, dismissed Baker's plan primarily because it called for Palestinian elections under the conditions of the occupation. Instead, the UNC called for an international peace conference, a demand which placed it at odds with the PLO. The Palestinian organization was actually willing to go along with Baker's election plan, provided the Israelis agreed to withdraw partially before the elections and the United States committed to demanding full withdrawal shortly after that. Sharon and two other rightist members of the cabinet, David Levy and Yitzhak Moda'i, called for putting a violent stop to the intifada and for barring all Arab residents of Jerusalem from participating in the elections. They also declared that no negotiations with the PLO were acceptable. Shamir agreed to this plan rather than crushing it outright, and sabotaged the American call for a dialogue with the PLO.[6]

Thus, all peace strategies deadlocked, despite the strong intervention of the United States Government. A coherent Israeli position opposed to PLO participation in any peace negotiations and favoring keeping Jerusalem's Arabs out of any elections began to solidify. Many Israelis on the right and center were determined not to tolerate any threat to the status quo in Jerusalem, keeping it under Israeli rule.[7]

A DECADE OF SETTLEMENTS AND RESISTANCE BY THE ARAB INSTITUTIONS

During the decade leading up to the momentous opening of an internationally sponsored Arab-Israeli peace conference, Jewish settlements continued to grow. At the same time, the appearance of parallel Palestinian institutions in Jerusalem, though asymmetrical in power when compared to the outsized settlement communities, signaled a quiet determination to maintain an Arab presence in the city. The decade of the 1980s also witnessed a visible fluctuation in the traditional official American attitude towards the building of Israeli settlements in the West Bank, without making an exception for the Jerusalem area with its great significance to the international community. Reagan was particularly guilty of refusing to stick to the official American position on these settlements, or simply being unable to comprehend the seriousness of this position.[8] But in an address to the nation on August 27, 1983, he corrected his earlier stance, declaring that the continued building of settlements in the occupied territories was "an obstacle to peace." He interpreted this to be an impediment to Israel's returning of land in the hope of being assured of security. Rather than threatening Israel with dire consequences if the settlement activity continued, he quickly reiterated the commitment of every previous American president to guarantee Israel's security.[9] Only when George H. W. Bush assumed the presidency in 1990 was there any direct castigation of Israel for its settlement building in the Jerusalem area.[10]

FAYSAL HUSSEINI AT THE HELM

Even though the star of Yasir Arafat was in the ascendant ever since he rose to the helm of the PLO in 1969, the Israelis never permitted him to take up residence in Jerusalem. The man whose presence in East Jerusalem made a huge difference in the lives of its Arab residents was Faysal Husseini. Though constantly under the watchful eyes of the Israelis, the son of Abd al-

Qadir Husseini, the hero of the battle of al-Qastal, represented the PLO in the city. He spent much of his youth in Iraq and other Arab countries but was seen as the most qualified to assume the informal role of the leader of Arab Jerusalem. He also received an officer's training in Egypt, returning to Jerusalem in 1964 when East Jerusalem was still part of Jordan. He served as head of one of the departments of the earlier PLO under Ahmad Shuqeiry and later joined that organization's army in Syria. After Israel captured the West Bank and Jerusalem, he secretly made his way back to Jerusalem, along with many who infiltrated into the occupied land from various Arab countries. Though a member of the Arab Nationalist Party (al-Qawmiyoun al-Arab), he was recruited by Arafat to join Fateh, which was beginning to spread its control over all of the Palestinian guerrilla factions in the region. Husseini's political activism and availability for military action did not escape the Israelis' notice, who began to shadow him. He served time in prison until he pledged to forsake such activities and then spent ten years pursuing ordinary civilian occupations, such as managing his family's farmland in the Jordan Valley. By 1979, he turned to a peaceful form of activism, such as creating the Association for Palestinian Studies, a research institute operating out of a historic Husseini building known as Orient House. When he turned to secret political work on behalf of the PLO, he was placed under town arrest from 1982 until 1987. This did not prevent him from engaging in human rights' work by setting up an organization for the protection of the Palestinians rumored to have been affiliated with the PLO. He also took to the pages of the most prominent paper in East Jerusalem, *al-Fajr,* to advocate for the peaceful activities of the city's Arab residents. Husseini's political and civic activism succeeded in creating an institutional network influenced by the PLO to fill the void resulting from the Palestinians' boycott of the Israeli-dominated municipality.[11]

The boycott left an Arab leadership deficit in its wake, threatening to further marginalize the city's inhabitants. Caught between political participation, which risked legitimizing Israel's occupation of the city, and total abstention from politics, resulting in severe isolation or in increased underground resistance, Jerusalem's Arabs had few difficult choices left. Throughout the post-1967 years, only a handful of the city's Arabs participated in municipal elections and none ran, or were permitted to run, for seats on the municipal council. The only exception was the editor of *al-Fajr,* Hanna Siniora, a pharmacist by profession, who almost ran in the 1998 municipal elections.[12]

Husseini proved to be an able unifier and conciliator, recruiting members of various PLO factions beside Fateh to work in Orient House. In addition to providing a forum for all voices regarding the political, economic and social issues pertaining to daily life under the occupation, he reached out to Israeli moderates, especially those representing anti-Zionist and leftist groups. Neither the PLO's Fateh-centered leadership in Tunis, nor the leadership of the newly emergent Hamas which established a presence in Jerusalem during the first intifada, recognized Husseini's near-successful bid to represent Jerusalem's diverse Arab community. The PLO experienced an understandable state of unease at the sight of an independent operative, fearing the consequences of its diminished status in the city. But Husseini was also able to include the twelve-member UNC which directed the intifada in his Orient House base of operations. Neither was the Tunis leadership able to claim credit for the restoration of Jerusalem as the hub of all political activities of the West Bank which was Husseini's singular achievement. His leadership status was eventually recognized when the PLO appointed him head of Fateh in the West Bank. By 1989, he was elevated to the membership of Fateh's Central Committee, the core group which numbered nineteen representatives from the West Bank and Gaza. Thus, the leadership of the first intifada was integrated with the central leadership of the PLO. Even though Hamas succeeded in building its own institutions in the West Bank, the Fateh-led PLO faction remained in command. When the Israelis eventually shuttered Orient House, its activities were moved to various buildings.

Husseini's leadership group did not succeed in achieving all of its goals. Its call for the resignation of Arabs from the police and taxation departments in 1989 was unheeded. Its long-standing boycott of municipal elections was challenged by Hanna Siniora who called for the formation of an Arab list in order to compete with other Zionist municipal lists. Yet, Husseini bypassed the PLO by calling for keeping Jerusalem an open city on the ground, to be shared by all, even as the Israelis pushed to make their sovereignty over the city the cornerstone of any future peace settlement. This coincided with the PLO's decision to recognize Israel in 1988, which not only snuffed the remaining embers of the intifada, it also opened a track to pursuing direct peace negotiations with Israel. When Secretary Baker began his contacts with Arab representatives in Jerusalem in preparation for assembling a joint Jordanian-Palestinian negotiating team for the Madrid Peace conference, he held most of his meetings at Orient House. Eventually, he selected Husseini and Hanan Ashrawi from Jerusalem and Zakaria al-Agha from Gaza to represent the Palestinians in the talks.[13]

ARAB JERUSALEM'S TRIUMPHS AND TRAGEDIES

Writing on the eve of the second intifada in 2000, Husseini painted a pessimistic picture of the narrowing options of the city's Arabs. He was particularly despairing of the lack of Palestinian agreement as to which Jerusalem should be the focal point of their struggle. If the historical Jerusalem, then this should include all of the city as it was administered under the Mandate. It would include the Western and Eastern halves of the city, as well as all the Arab suburbs outside the walls, such as Shaykh Jarrah in East Jerusalem and Talbiya in West Jerusalem. Or was it the Jerusalem being demanded by the Palestinian peace negotiators as the capital of their future state? If that was the case, then it would entail adhering to UN resolutions such as 242, which accepted the 1967 borders. The resolution, which limited Palestinian demands to the pre-1967 Jordanian Jerusalem and Israeli demands to West Jerusalem, he reflected, disappointed both sides. His own assessment was that the best choice, in line with this latter international position, was the most suited to the current stage of the conflict. This would not allow the Palestinians to look to West Jerusalem, nor the Israelis to covet East Jerusalem. This pragmatism, however, was reinforced by his insistence on regaining East Jerusalem as it existed in 1967, including the entire Old City, reaching all the way to Shaykh Jarrah and the suburb of Silwan. In other words, he took a stand in favor of rational pragmatism, but with limits, not to be challenged by Israeli expansionists. If Israel sought to impress the need for pragmatism on its Palestinian interlocutors, then, he wrote, it must be willing to live with the consequences of the Palestinian definition of that pragmatism. The Palestinians would accept nothing less than all of pre-1967 East Jerusalem, since it was the capital of the Palestinian people, irrespective of what was left of Arab Palestine at the time. He emphasized that this was the city which served throughout history as the Palestinian people's social and economic capital, not to mention its spiritual center.[14] Thus, he was able to articulate a rational Palestinian definition of their sovereignty, hoping that the Israelis would come to grips with this visceral Arab attachment to the city.

Husseini, at the same time, was mindful of the contraction of Arab Jerusalem under recent alien regimes due to the priorities of different states and the consequences of military defeat. Perhaps, he averred, the Palestinians were buoyed by the decision of the Mandate Government to treat Jerusalem as the administrative, economic and political capital of the Palestinian state. Neither did pre-statehood Jews object to that reality. But in 1948, the city suffered under the impact of three devastating blows: The capture of most of Jerusalem in 1948 by Zionist militias; the loss of most of the city's hinterland and satellite villages and towns as a result of the Israeli-Jordanian Armistice Agreement of 1949; the loss of status as a capital when the Jordanian regime downgraded it to a position secondary to Amman as the first capital. The diminishing of its status by the Jordanians, he asserted, resulted in the transfer of most of the city's institutions to the Jordanian capital, while converting what remained of Arab Jerusalem into a large village, or at best, a small provincial town. This shrunken town was rendered incapable of providing its children with employment opportunities, forcing them to migrate to other capitals in search of the kind of employment to which they were accustomed in their own city. He added that Arab Jerusalemites working in various Arab capitals constituted the highest percentage of Palestinians working abroad. But in time, the city gradually reprised its role as the capital of religious tourism for both Muslims and Christians, as well as the unchallenged second capital of Jordan.[15]

Husseini then outlined the perimeters of three additional blows directed at what remained of Arab Jerusalem when the Jordanian regime suffered its greatest military defeat at the hands of Israel. Dwelling on the calamitous consequences of the 1967 War, he pointed to the gravity of the total capture of East Jerusalem by the Israelis who placed it under their direct rule and then severed its ties to the West Bank although both were occupied by the same power. He emphasized that the third painful blow was the timing of the Israeli invasion, being in June. Had this occurred in August, then the Israelis would have found themselves facing a city teeming with returning family members at home for the summer holiday. Israel would have confronted a city of one hundred thousand, not fifty thousand, since each family had as much as five members working abroad in other Arab countries. But Israel quickly took fateful steps to alter the reality of this city, first by annexing it and then by converting its Palestinian citizens into captives of the Israeli state. According to a law adopted in 1954 which was applied to the city, the Palestinians became aliens living in Israel, not citizens existing on their own historic land. They were allowed to claim permanent residency rights in their own country, but were denied nationality rights as though they were part of a massive invasion of Israel. Then Israel launched a huge project to expand the city's boundaries by annexing maximum Arab territory but with minimal Arab inhabitants. Thus, Jordanian East Jerusalem which measured six square kilometers in total became a city of seventy-two square kilometers, all of which were annexed to Israel.[16]

In a masterful analysis of the Arab residents' struggle to wrest control of their institutions from the occupation forces, Husseini outlined the response of Palestinians, moving along parallel Arab, Palestinian, Islamic, and Christian tracks in order to save their city. The first of these entailed the creation of the Higher Islamic Council (HIC), acting on a statement by the thirteenth-century theologian, Ibn Taymiyyah, which said that when Muslim lands were invaded by non-Muslims, then Muslims must run their own affairs by themselves. Thus, the newly constituted HIC took it upon itself to manage the Islamic holy places and administer Shari'a schools and courts, thereby successfully barring the Israeli military from intruding on al-Aqsa Mosque and the Islamic foundations in its vicinity. Husseini noted that this was achieved by returning these foundations to the Jordanian Islamic *awqaf*, where they had previously belonged, while leaving them to be managed by the HIC. Education turned out to be the second significant battle, which was waged in order to block Israeli efforts to impose a Zionist regimen over Arab schools and their curricula. Believing that in order to Judaize Jerusalem it would be necessary to Judaize culture and education as well, the municipality began to extend its direct control over the Jordanian school system. This action was the product of a mentality which believed that it was the rightful heir to the Jordanian government and all of its institutions and schools. When the municipality annexed Arab public schools, the residents quickly organized by establishing an alternative school plan, with some being placed under the Muslim Orphange School System, named after Husni al-Ashhab, its director at the time. The battle between these schools and the municipality's system raged for two years, culminating in the Israeli seizure of the Rashidiyah high school, the flagship of the Arab public school system dating back to the Ottoman period. But by the time this school was annexed, its enrollment totaled seven students in all. This obliged the Israeli authorities to abandon their plan by reinstating the Jordanian curriculum, satisfying themselves with adding only the study of the Hebrew language.[17]

Husseini then depicted a similar battle to maintain the Palestinian integrity of the healthcare system within the city, focusing an al-Maqasid Charitable Islamic Health Network. Having built a new hospital just before the occupation, The Islamic Foundation was still in the process of providing it with new machines and equipment. But the Israelis tried to seize the hospital and place it under their supervision, an effort which was thwarted within forty-eight hours by hastily filling it with patients and medical personnel. This was achieved in cooperation with smaller hospitals in the city willing to lend al-Maqasid Hospital their patients, equipment, and staff. Husseini added that he was able to reveal for the first time that not all of the patients and doctors were real, but impersonators willing to defend the Arab Islamic character of this institution. Indeed, all of Jerusalem's institutions fought hard in order to maintain the Arab character of the city. Even those who stood to benefit materially from affiliating with Israeli institutions, such as the Palestinian Chamber of Commerce, resisted all efforts to join hands with the Israeli Chamber of Commerce at a personal loss to themselves. Finally, Husseini confirmed that the struggle to maintain the independence of Palestinian institutions in the 1990s achieved its goal when Orient House was proclaimed the main address for the city's Arabs.[18]

Yet, some battles were not totally won, but neither were the Israelis able to realize all of their objectives. This was true of the struggle to control land and establish settlements in the vicinity of the holy city, which went to the core of the historic Zionist project in Palestine. Husseini explained this process by referencing relevant facts and figures. He noted that after succeeding in expanding the city's boundaries to a maximum area of seventy-two square kilometers, 43 percent of this territory was earmarked for the building of settlements. Additionally, 52 percent of the total area of the city was declared green lands in order to deny Palestinians the right to build there. Only 14 percent of the land was set aside for Palestinian construction and natural population growth. The city's Arab population quickly sensed that Israel's intent was to import Jewish settlers to East Jerusalem as a rival block to its Arab inhabitants. This was Israel's most determined effort, which it pursued for several years when thousands of Jewish settlers were permitted to live in the city and its surroundings. The first target of this settlement project was the Old City, which suffered well-documented attacks on its Arab neighborhoods, especially immediately following the war. Thus, the Mughrabi Quarter, known to Israelis as the Jewish Quarter, was demolished in secrecy and under the rubric of urban rehabilitation of derelict structures. The demolition work eventually spread beyond the quarter, and by 1986, Jewish Yeshiva schools began to emerge within the Old City through the purchasing of Arab homes. Efforts to seize a section of the Old City known as Uqbat al-Khalidiyyah, involved pressuring the residents to leave by staging massive demonstrations with the help of outside settlers. This stiffened the Arabs' determination to resist, driving them to organize what came to be known as the Committee of the Old City, or simply the Jerusalem Committee. This group undertook the planning of defense activities, such as recruiting young men to place iron bars on people's windows. Attempts were also made to seek judicial redress. Husseini declared that between 1986 and 1987, Arab residents succeeded in blunting the edge of the settlement plan inside the Old City. He asserted that this was the achievement of the Palestinian institutions which the leadership was able to preserve. [19]

ARAFAT AND THE MARCH TO OSLO

Ultimately, the man who made all the decisions pertaining to the future of the city was not Husseini but Arafat. While their restrained and understated rivalry was well-known, both shared a visceral and instinctive attachment to the city. For Husseini, this was the place which his ancestors dominated through recent centuries, but for Arafat, it was the arena of some of his clerical forbears who were anchored in the Old City. Although the Husseinis were sidelined and exiled during the Jordanian period, they retained a strong grip on the emotions and loyalties of the city's Arab population. Both, however, maintained powerful links to the people of Jerusalem. The third knight in this perpetual drama was Hussein of Jordan, who constantly invoked his family's political claims to the city and historic custodianship over the Muslim holy places. Not being part of the Arab community of Jerusalem denied him the credentials of family ties to its residents, shared memories of their anti-British struggle, and later, shared activism against the Israeli occupation. Though deeply affected by the loss of the city in 1967, leading him to lament the denial of control over his grandfather's burial place, Jerusalem for him was mostly a political symbol and the only reminder of his ancestors' Greater Syria historical map.

Arafat, a.k.a. Yasir al-Qudwah, was either born in Cairo or Jerusalem, depending on which version of the truth, or which biographical account, was accepted. One thing for sure, it was he who denied a Cairo birthplace based on a dubiously authenticated birth-certificate, contending that he was born in Jerusalem where he spent his early childhood years. He always claimed that he was born next to the Wailing Wall, or the Buraq Wall as Muslims knew it, in the house belonging to the Abu-Sa'ud Zawiyya, a thirteen-house complex belonging to the family from which his mother descended. His guardian during his early years there was a clerical figure, Shaykh Hasan Abu-Su'ud, an official of the Islamic Courts' system and an associate of the Grand Mufti of Jerusalem. Abu Sa'ud was deeply involved in anti-British and anti-Zionist activities by mainly safeguarding the Buraq Wall from attempts by Jewish extremists to hold prayers in its vicinity.

After the 1967 War, Arafat infiltrated back to Jerusalem, crossing from Jordan when still a young Fateh guerrilla fighter. He also managed at one time to come through across one of the land bridges from the Jordanian side. He visited relatives in the city while in disguise. This visit took place in July 1967, when he began to ponder the necessity of launching organized military activities and contacting potential allies in the occupied West Bank. During his stay of few months, while attempting to recruit and organize a Fateh network, he met Husseini in Ramallah. The latter's father, Abd al-Qadir, mentored Arafat as a young militia fighter while on his frequent visits to Cairo, when still the Palestinians' unrivaled hero of the 1948 War. When he met Arafat, Faysal headed the political department of Shuqeiry's earlier PLO, created in 1964 in Jordanian Jerusalem. Husseini tried to persuade Arafat to engage in political, as opposed to military, resistance against the occupation, but the future PLO leader committed only to providing secret military training to young recruits. Arafat's career continued to take him to far away destinations but he remained ever the devout Muslim even in the most unexpected places. As the true son of Islamic Jerusalem, he viewed his faith as a personal commitment which did not infringe on his relationship with political and social acquaintances and allies. While on many of his frequent trips to Moscow, he was known to take time out for the performance of the Muslim prayers and often abstained from official banquets due to observing the Muslim fast. [20]

When his faction within the PLO voted to accept the American and Russian invitation to participate in an international peace conference, Arafat met some opposition. His greatest fear, however, was unrelated to the uproar on his left flank, but to the looming competition by East Jerusalem's more conciliatory representatives on his right. Thus, the initial step on the road to the Madrid conference turned out to be to negotiate the role of the Palestinian delegation. By 1991, the internal, Jerusalem-based Palestinian leadership was approached directly by Secretary Baker about representing the Palestinians precisely because it was not recognized as formally affiliated with the PLO. Surprisingly, the PLO accepted this leadership not only because it represented Jerusalem's institutions but also because it always followed the directives of the PLO's Executive Committee. By that time, Orient House had emerged as the hub of all diplomatic activity, which reinforced the legitimacy of the Jerusalem representatives.[21]

Yet, as early as 1985, Assistant Secretary of State Richard Murphy was beginning to assemble a list of Palestinian representatives who would be acceptable both to the Israelis and the PLO. Peres was given seven names by the US diplomatic mission in Tel Aviv who were already endorsed by Arafat. These included: Khaled al-Hassan, co-founder of Fateh; Hatem Husseini, former director of the PLO's Washington office; Henry Cattan, a prominent international law expert; Fayez Abu-Rahmeh, a Gaza lawyer and PLO member; Nabil Sha'ath, an independent member of the PNC; Hanna Siniora, publisher of *al-Fajr*, and a Jerusalem pharmacist; Yousef Sayegh, an economist on the staff of American University of Beirut and an adviser to Arafat; Salah Ta'mari, one of the leaders of the battle of Karamah. A day after reviewing this list, Peres announced before the Knesset that only Abu-Rahmeh and Siniora were acceptable, presumably because they were officially unaffiliated with the PLO. The same list was forwarded to the United States by Jordan, which protested Israel's rejections loudly. Peres, however, announced his preference for Faysal Husseini, who was more acceptable to his Likud coalition partner. But then many things transpired, leading to the loss of US confidence in the PLO, such as the *Achile Lauro* hijacking incident which was blamed on this organization rather than on its real perpetrators, the Palestine Liberation Front (PLF).[22]

Peres' interest in establishing a back channel to Palestinian moderates came as a result of the Jordanian disengagement from the West Bank during the height of the intifada. According to Peres' biographer, Michael Bar Zohar, the Israeli Prime Minister, along with Deputy Foreign Minister Yossi Beilin, began to scout around for Palestinian interlocutors in the late 1980s as a sure way of proceeding to direct negotiations at Oslo. They began secret contacts with Husseini and Ashrawi, who was at the time a Birzeit University professor. The main emissary to the Palestinians was Professor Yair Hirschfeld of Haifa University. But, the Oslo secret track almost did not materialize, not due to bickering within the PLO ranks at Madrid, but due to Rabin's idea of seizing the moment to push for secret talks with Syria through the Israeli ambassador in Washington, Syria expert Itamar Rabinovich. Then, Hirschfeld received a secret message from Abu al-Alaa' (a.k.a. Ahmad Qurei'), the PLOs treasurer, that Arafat was ready for an alternate to Madrid. Norwegian diplomats such as Terje Larsen of the Norwegian Peace Research

Institute (FAFO), offered to host the meeting at Oslo. By this time, the Tunis leadership was at logger heads with other factions, leading to the triumph of trusted Arafat's men such as Mahmoud Abbas (Abu-Mazen), Qurei', Maher al-Kurd, and Hasan Asfour, who proceeded to the Oslo talks.[23]

But as the Madrid conference was about to commence, the internal Palestinian leadership meeting in Washington was instructed by Arafat not to compromise on the question of Jerusalem, later directing them to drop the issue altogether. This was considered a concession to Israel which always insisted that Jerusalem was non-negotiable, leading the Palestinians to resign their office as delegates. Thus, the door was left wide open for pursuing the secret Oslo track.[24] Israelis braced themselves for what the Oslo track might deliver, expressing derisive views from the right and the left. Netanyahu, for instance, absorbed the inevitability of achieving Palestinian statehood by referring to it as a future Puerto Rico or Andorra. Israelis expected such an entity to include most of the West Bank and Gaza, but without absorbing any of the settlement blocks or parts of Jerusalem. The logic was that no Israeli government would risk accepting such a deal. The Israelis still remembered the fall of the Labor Party when it lost the elections due to Netanyahu's charge that Peres was planning to divide Jerusalem.[25] But the Oslo talks moved forward with the secure knowledge that the United States approved the process. Uri Savir, one of the main Israeli delegates, reported that assurances of US involvement, though from a distance, were provided by the Norwegian foreign minister Johan Jorgen Holst. This was an indication of the seriousness of the PLO, adding that Secretary of State Warren Christopher was briefed on the progress of the talks and his Assistant Secretary of State on the Middle East, Dan Kurtzer, was constantly appraised of the state of the negotiations. But Savir clarified that the Americans never sought information from Holst, perhaps because of their preoccupation with setting up the Syrian track or because they were reassured by the intentions of both sides.[26]

ISRAELI INTRANSIGENCE SEALS JERUSALEM'S FATE

While still in charge of directing the Palestinian negotiating team at the Madrid Conference, Gaza statesman Dr. Haider Abd al-Shafi articulated a clear vision of most Palestinian pragmatists. He recognized that the Palestinian dream of statehood must be subject to two conditions: Gradualism and an eventual sharing of power with Jordan. What he seemed to be admitting was that negotiated settlements never yield the maximum demands of the weaker side. He, therefore, noted that a transitional phase could ultimately lead to a federation with Jordan, but that the embryonic institutions of the future Palestinian state created by the intifada were already in place. Thus, the core of

Palestinian demands were openly stated, while he seemingly refrained from seeking immediate and total statehood. [27]

The imagined Palestinian state, nevertheless, was always understood by the Palestinian side to revolve around East Jerusalem as its capital. But when the actual negotiations shifted to the Oslo track, the issue of Jerusalem threatened to be the deal breaker, not the ultimate deal-maker. Both sides, as it turned out, harbored fully formed ideas and expectations concerning the future of the holy city. Only the Israelis, however, demonstrated a relentless determination to maintain a tight grip over its future. The Oslo Conference, stretching over a period of eight months, began with setting out the priorities of each side. The Israelis quickly displayed a strong desire to control the agenda and relegate the Jerusalem question to its rightful place in the plan of discussions. As soon as both sides seemed to be in agreement over Palestinian autonomy, Savir informed the delegates that this would not include Jerusalem. He defined the city by echoing repeated Israeli statements that it was the center of Israel's life, based on instructions by Peres and Rabin. Without recognizing this reality, he emphasized, no progress would be made. He challenged the Palestinians to proceed as partners of the Israelis, rather than return to the Security Council and end up with a number of useless paper resolutions. But one day after meeting with Arafat in Tunis, Terje, and Mona Larsen, the facilitators of the conference, met at a private luncheon with Foreign Minister Peres. That was during the middle of the talks when Peres told them that Arafat must understand that if the Oslo track was to succeed and usher a new era for the entire region, the Israelis' threshold for peace which cannot be crossed would have to include keeping Jerusalem out of any Palestinian autonomy plan. He described some Israeli concessions which he felt would be advantageous to the Palestinians, such as enlarging the Jericho area destined to be the first stage of the territory surrendered to the PLO, and creating a land passage to Gaza linking the two areas together. [28]

The Palestinians, however, continued to demand the return of East Jerusalem to Arab control and allowing its residents the right to participate in the elections of the proposed Palestinian Legislative Council (PLC). Arafat also scaled back from the original demand for the inclusion of Jerusalem into the autonomous area of Palestine by seeking guarantees and protection for its Arab institutions instead. The Israelis agreed, on condition that none of these would be PLO-affiliated or in any way linked to the future Palestinian autonomous government. The Israelis, largely at Peres' behest, expressed willingness to tolerate only institutions of a religious or cultural character. [29] To reassure the Palestinians, Peres sent a letter to Holst dated 9 September 1993, expressing his government's clear intentions to address their concerns in East Jerusalem. He wrote:

The Palestinian institutions in East Jerusalem and the interests and well-being of the palestinians [sic] of East Jerusalem are of great importance and will be preserved. Therefore, the palestinian [sic] institutions of East Jerusalem, including the economic, social, educational, cultural, and the holy city and Moslem places, are performing an essential task for the palestinian [sic] population.[30]

In August 1993, Peres travelled to California to appraise Christopher of the final contours of the Oslo Accords, and then began preparing to face his government and the Knesset. Avi Shlaim explained the nature of the Israeli breakthrough at Oslo as an essential and unprecedented departure from the idea of seeking approval for partitioning Palestine, as in the Peel Commission of 1937. Whereas the Palestinians had always rejected any interim agreement that was not accompanied by the agreed-upon features of a final settlement, at Oslo, they buckled under the pressure of Israeli intransigence. There, they accepted the idea of an interim settlement that was already separate from the final settlement. Israel persuaded the Palestinians to accept a five-year transition period, but without any agreement or commitment to a specified final or permanent arrangement.[31] Once the Accords were signed, there was no incentive left for Israel to grant any concessions, nor for the rest of the Arab governments and former PLO allies to withhold recognition or economic and strategic cooperation from Israel.

THE AMBIGUITIES OF OSLO

Israeli officials made no secret of their intent never to accede to Palestinian demands on Jerusalem. This became apparent whenever they addressed their own political constituency in the immediate aftermath of the Oslo talks. Prime Minister Rabin took on this task with the utmost zeal. In an address to the Knesset on 21 September 1993, he was explicit in assuring his listeners that the Oslo peace did not result in yielding to Palestinian demands. This was a prelude to submitting the agreement for ratification by the Israeli legislature, and the chief architect of Oslo had nothing but reassuring words:

On the question of Jerusalem, we said that this government, just like its predecessors, believes there are no differences of opinion in this House over the eternalness of Jerusalem as Israel's capital. United and unified Jerusalem is not negotiable and will be the capital of the Israeli people under Israel's sovereignty and the subject of every Jew's yearnings and dreams for ever and ever. . . . In Washington, Foreign Minister Shimon Peres signed on Israel's behalf the declaration of principles agreement for the interim period only. This agreement, which permits the Palestinians to run their affairs, safeguards the following issues for Israel: Unified Jerusalem remains under Israel's rule, and the body that will run the lives of the Palestinians in the territories will have no authority over it.[32]

He explained further in an interview with *Davar,* Labor-leaning paper, a week later:

> I personally oppose the creation of a Palestinian state situated between us and Jordan. I also reject the "right of return." . . . As to the unity of Jerusalem, this was determined in conjunction with talks with an Arab partner, when we agreed on a transitional arrangement during which Jerusalem will remain under Israeli control. During this phase, the Palestinian side which will run the affairs of the territories, will have no influence over Jerusalem.[33]

But when reminded that Arafat proclaimed the imminence of the establishment of the Palestinian state in the territories within three years, with Jerusalem as its capital, Rabin replied:

> We say that Jerusalem will remain united under Israeli sovereignty and we continue to oppose the creation of a Palestinian state between us and Jordan. We have arrived at an agreement regarding the interim arrangement only, and it was well known from the beginning that there were some differences of views between us regarding the shape of the final settlement.[34]

He then refused to be described as favoring a Jordanian-Palestinian confederation, explaining that confederations can only join sovereign nations. He was asked where did he think the capital of the Palestinian entity would be located, and he answered: "Jericho, if that was their wish, or Nablus, but that was their own problem."[35]

In another interview with *Davar* on September 24, this time with Peres, the message to the Palestinians was even more blunt. The interview was timed to deflect criticism from the Labor Party by the opposing Likud group, which announced that the Oslo Accords were articles of surrender. When asked if he feared the rise of a Palestinian state, he replied:

> . . . the Palestinian state is no more than a piece of paper. . . . What we are proposing creates other opportunities—an Israeli—Palestinian confederation, a Jordanian—Palestinian confederation . . . these proposals will not solve all the problems, but will create opportunities which did not exist before.[36]

When asked if the Accords endangered Jerusalem's future as a unified city under full Israeli sovereignty, he offered the following explanation:

> We always feared for Jerusalem, but these Accords, if anything, have reduced our fears. Why? This is the first time that Jerusalem is dealt with in a single document, not three. Throughout our recent Israeli history, there were always three documents: Arab, American and Israeli.

This time, there is only one version stating that Jerusalem is outside the perimeters of the area of autonomy rule. Note that Arafat did not mention Jerusalem in his speech on the White House lawn. Compare this to Sadat's address before the Knesset, when Menachem Begin headed the government. Sadat spoke at length about Jerusalem, but Arafat did not mention it at the White House.[37]

By contrast, Rabin said during the White House signing ceremony: "We came from Jerusalem, the ancient and eternal capital of the Jewish people,"[38] a triple defiance of the United States, international opinion and the PLO since all three never acceded to this claim. Yet, Palestinian negotiator Asfour continued to insist that East Jerusalem would revert back to the Palestinians once the Accords went into effect. He wrote after the Accords were signed responding to Arab criticism of the secret talks by asserting that the negotiations have accomplished one of the Palestinians' long-cherished objectives, namely the application of Res. 242 and Res. 338, beginning with Israel's evacuation form Palestinian territories. This would be followed by evacuating the West Bank, the Gaza Strip, and Jerusalem, he added. He claimed that Israel's willingness to negotiate these issues was in itself a recognition of the Palestinian people's existence and the illegality of the annexation of Jerusalem. Israel also acknowledged the right of the Palestinians of Jerusalem to participate in West Bank elections, an admission that they were an inseparable part of the Arab Palestinian people. Thus, the Accords have accomplished a political first, namely protecting the status of Jerusalem, contrary to all claims that they have dropped this issue from the agenda. Indeed, the Accords did not delete any issue concerning the Palestinian people, even though definite answers have yet to emerge and be adopted.[39]

PLO personalities, like Sha'ath, a close adviser to Arafat, also joined the chorus of supporters by continuing to claim that a great breakthrough had been achieved. He attributed this to freeing the Palestinians from dealing with Israel exclusively through the United States, which monopolized all the cards. He insisted that Israel's acquiescence in the Palestinian demand for listing Jerusalem on the agenda of the final status talks was an admission of the illegality of the annexation of the city and that Jerusalem was still an open subject, waiting to be negotiated. He argued that by reaching an agreement with the PLO, an organization founded specifically to fight Israel, not Palestinian elements in the West Bank, the Israelis were dealing a severe blow to Zionist ideology.[40]

CONCLUSION

Contrary to conventional wisdom, the PLO's submission to Israeli demands was not the result of America's formula for peace which was unveiled during the Madrid Conference. The PLO, in reality and despite all the bluster, was reacting to the cumulative effect of the dwindling of all of its options. It was this desperation which drove it to the secret Oslo track. King Hussein's failure to convince the Shamir Government to participate in an international peace conference under the sponsorship of the Great Powers but sans the PLO, coupled with the latter's inability to reap major rewards from the first intifada, opened the door for Secretary Shultz's diplomacy. The Shultz time-line for moving towards an American-sponsored peace conference drove the PLO's leftist opposition to the margins where they remained fixated on the Oslo concessions. At the same time, the demise of what the Israelis always called "the Jordanian option," epitomized by Hussein's separation from the West Bank, contributed to their grudging willingness to extract a final settle-ment from the weakened PLO.

Secretary of State Baker eventually took charge of identifying a non-PLO affiliated representative slate from the occupied territories, Gaza and Jerusa-lem in order to render the Madrid peace conference palatable to the Israelis. But the PLO was not marginalized and continued to pressure the Palestinian team at Madrid to abide by its directives from its Tunisian exile. Thus, the battle of the external, versus the internal Palestinian leadership emerged, culminating in sidelining the open and public Madrid talks, in favor of the secret Israeli-PLO track at Oslo. The Norwegian capital quickly became Arafat's own diplomatic arena which he ran with the help of his men on the inside, just as Rabin and Peres became the puppeteers of their delegates to the conference. The main difference between the two sides was the degree of clarity of vision and determination which they displayed, with the Palestin-ians barely prepared to resist Israel's onslaught and vaguely cognizant of the enemy's agenda. Once the PLO yielded to America's prodding to deal with the issues across the negotiating table rather than on the battlefield of dis-puted and occupied lands, its options became narrower than ever.

Conflicting perceptions of Jerusalem's destiny emerged as the most seri-ous barrier to a final settlement. The Israelis stubbornly clung to the defini-tion of the city as their eternal capital, particularly when defending their diplomatic strategy at Oslo. This definition was purveyed before the Knesset and in friendly journals in order to win over wide sections of Israeli public opinion not yet ready to deal with the PLO. The Palestinians, by contrast, continued to nurse the illusion of maintaining the city's Arab links to the political institutions of the West Bank and to call for the return of East Jerusalem to its former role as the capital of any emerging Arab entity. Yet, the Israelis never conceded the possibility of the inevitable Palestinian state-hood, nor accepted the idea of Palestinian autonomy which they continued to resist since the Camp David Agreement. This wide and seemingly unbridge-able chasm was finally closed when Israel successfully floated the idea of "final status talks," to which they relegated the most intractable issues of the conflict, namely Jerusalem and the Palestinian refugees. The Palestinian negotiators inexplicably grasped at this ill-defined concept, leaping into the Oslo void without any guarantees of the final outcome of these deferred talks. Moreover, the Clinton administration continued to be appraised of the progress of the secret track, giving its blessings even when the Israeli position crossed the boundaries of reasonable accommodation and compromise. Uri Savir would admit later that whenever the peace talks stalled, particularly during the Taba phase of the negotiations, the United States would be called upon to apply pressure to the Palestinian side.

NOTES

1. Jimmy Carter, *Palestine: Peace, not Apartheid* (New York: Simon and Schuster, 2006): 478.

2. Avi Shlaim, *The Lion of Jordan: The Life of King Hussein in War and Peace* (New York: Alfred A. Knopf, 2008): 446–72.

3. _____ *The Iron Wall: Israel and the Arab World* (New York: W. W. Norton, 2000): 450–2; Tom Segev, *1967: The War and the Year that Transformed the Middle East* (New York: Henry Holt, 2005): 449.

4. Ibid.

5. Ibid., 457–8, 467.

6. Ibid., 467–70.

7. Ibid., 471.

8. Ronald Reagan, "Interview with Henry Brandon, The London Sunday Times and News Service," March 18, 1983. Ronald Reagan, FRUS, Vol. I, 418.

9. Ronald Reagan, 1983, FRUS, Vol. II, 1213.

10. George H. Bush News Conference, Palm Springs, California, March 3, 1990. George H. Bush 1990, FRUS, Vol. I, 313.

11. Hillel Cohen, *The Rise and Fall of Arab Jerusalem* (London: Routledge, 2011): 12–3.

12. Avraham Sela, *Political Encyclopedia of the Middle East* (New York: Continuum Publishing Co., 1999): 421.

13. Cohen, *The Rise and Fall*, 13–7.

14. Faysal Husseini, "Al-Quds munthu Huzairan 1967,"/Jerusalem since June 1967, in *Al-Quds wa al-hal al-Filastini wa qira'at fi al-amn al-qawmi al-Arabi*/Jerusalem and the Palestinian Condition, and a Reading in Arab National Security, ed. Tawfiq Abu-Baker (Amman, Jordan: Mu'assesat Abd al-Hamid Shouman, 1999): 148–9.

15. Ibid., 149–50.

16. Ibid., 150.

17. Ibid., 151.

18. Ibid., 151–2.

19. Ibid., 152–3.

20. Janet Wallach and John Wallach, *Arafat: In the Eyes of the Beholder* (New York: Carol Publishing Group, 1990): 48–9, 71–2, 135–7, 207–8.

21. Cohen, *The Rise and Fall*, 17.

22. Wallach and Wallach, *Arafat*, 320–5.

23. Michael Bar Zohar, *Shimon Peres: The Biography* (New York: Random House, 2007): 414, 427–8.

24. Cohen, *The Rise and Fall*, 17.

25. Shlomo Ben Ami, *Scars of War, Wounds of Peace* (Oxford: Oxford University Press, 2006): 247.

26. Uri Savir, *The Process*, (New York: Random House, 1998): 21–2.

27. Shlaim, *The Iron Wall*, 489–90.

28. Savir, *The Process*, 13–4, 43.

29. Ibid., 38–9, 72.

30. "Perspectives—Jerusalem," Center for Public Affairs. Jcpa/wp-content/uploads/2013/02/Strategy_Baker_Jerus. pdf. Accessed 26/8/2013.

31. Shlaim, *The Iron Wall*, 519–20.

32. "Yitzhak Rabin Statement to Knesset on the Declaration of Principles, Jerusalem 21 September 1993," in *The Palestinian-Israeli Peace Agreement: A Documentary Record* (Washington, D. C.: Institute for Palestine Studies, 1993): 149–55.

33. "Hadith li-ra'is al-hukumah al-Israiliyah fi ithri itifaq 'Gaza-Jericho First',"/An Interview with the Head of the Israeli Government Following the 'Gaza-Jericho First' Agreement, *Majallat al-Dirasat al-Filastiniyah*, No. 16 (Fall 1993): 92.

34. Ibid., 94.

35. Ibid., 95.

36. "Hadith li-wazir al-kharijiyah al-Israili bi-sha'an itifaq i'lan al-mabadi',"/An Interview with the Israeli Foreign Minister regarding the Declaration of Principles, *Majallat al-Dirasat al-Filastiniyah*, No. 16 (Fall 1993): 97–102.

37. Ibid., 100.

38. "Al-Kalimaat khilal al-ihtifal bi-tawqee' i'lan al-mabadi'"/Speeches During the Ceremonies of the Signing of the Declaration of Principles, *Majallat al-Dirasat al-Filastiniyah*. No. 16 (Fall 1993): 190.

39. Hasan Asfour, "Ru'yah li-itifaq I'lan al-mabadi'/ A Viewpoint Regarding the Declaration of Principles, *Majallat al-Dirasat al-Filastiniyah*, No. 16 (Fall 1993): 21–2.

40. "Itifaqiyat Oslo: Muqabalah ma' Nabil Sha'ath,"/An Interview with Nabil Sha'ath, *Majallat al-Dirasat al-Filastiniyah*, No. 16 (Fall 1993): 74–6.

Chapter Eight

Clinton's Quest for a Mideast Legacy

No American peace initiative involving the Israelis and the Palestinians was preceded by as many studies and preparation as the Camp David II conference. Several events were orchestrated by an American president in quest of a legacy, which necessitated the utmost degree of proficiency. Clinton appeared to be anxious not to risk his presidential prestige on an uncertain venture, unless he felt secure enough regarding its outcome.

THE BACKGROUND

American advisers and strategists were always probing for areas of Palestinian and Arab weakness, seeking conditions favorable for a peace settlement with Israel. They were also of the belief that the United States must take the lead in any of these negotiations. Martin Indyk, for instance, felt that 1990 was such an occasion. He was at the time a close adviser to Clinton on Middle East affairs and was soon to serve for two terms as the ambassador to Israel. He admitted later that he told the President that "those Arab states" which fought Israel largely with the Soviets' help had lost their benefactor. The leader of the Arab nationalist camp, Saddam Hussein, had just been pushed out of Kuwait, causing further weakening of the Arab military option. Therefore, an unusual strategic picture had just emerged, favoring reaching a peaceful settlement with Israel. Since the two were involved in direct talks and since Rabin was heading a new government, Clinton was told that he had an opportunity to preside over the signing of four peace agreements involving Israel, with the Palestinians, the Jordanians, the Syrians, and the Lebanese. Indyk stressed that the United States was denied an opportunity to claim a victory such as the Oslo Peace Agreement. Israelis, he said, had never told Clinton about their Palestinian negotiating partners or the bless-

177

ings Arafat gave to the proceedings. This situation was viewed as a conspiracy hatched behind the American President's back, though Warren Christopher was made aware of the secret contacts from the beginning. [1]

But the Syrian track was different. As soon as Peres, at that time the foreign minister, realized that the Israeli-Syrian talks were advancing but that the Oslo talks were about to be concluded, he sought US backing. He approached Christopher and Dennis Ross, chief of Middle East negotiators under the Clinton and George H. W. Bush administrations, seeking the US seal of approval in order for the Oslo deal to hold up. Clinton seized this opportunity to offer to host the signing ceremony at the White House and invited Rabin and Arafat to his official residence. That was when several advisers, basically Indyk and Anthony Lake, realized that an American president was prohibited legally from dealing openly with a leader classified as a terrorist. Rabin also raised the same issue, though it was later revealed that he was hoping never to have to meet Arafat in person. The issue was quickly resolved when the American President took the PLO off the terrorist list. With his first foray into Arab-Israeli diplomacy behind him, Clinton took another plunge in October 1998 by inviting Arafat and Netanyahu to the Wye River Conference in Maryland. After nine days of talks, a memorandum was signed, detailing steps to implement the Interim Agreement of September 1995, and specifically transferring land in the occupied territories to full or partial Palestinian control. These were known as Areas A, B, and C, and were protected by the necessary security arrangements to make this division workable. The 1995 Agreement also stipulated that the American President should be invited to a session of the PNC meeting in Gaza to call for the abrogation of the Palestine National Covenant. [2] The plenum took place on 14 December 1998, and was the occasion of the following remarkable presidential statement, which captured the US distinction between the national claims of the two sides to Palestine:

> Palestinians must recognize the right of Israel and its people to live safe and secure lives today, tomorrow, and forever. Israel must recognize the right of Palestinians to aspire to live free today, tomorrow and forever. [3]

Clinton felt that the time was right for bringing the two sides together when the hardliner Netanyahu lost the elections in May 1999 to Ehud Barak and the Labor Party. Barak had promised to pursue the Rabin peace agenda. One side of this optimum environment for peace was still being formulated, however, namely peace with Syria which Barak made his first priority. [4]

There was a domestic and an international dimension to Barak's Syria first determination. He implied to his American allies such as presidential adviser Ross that a deal with the Palestinians may weaken his political base and undermine receptivity for any final solution which he might reach with

Syria. Barak was hoping to pull Israeli troops out of Lebanon, a feat which could only be accomplished with the help of Syria, the only power capable of protecting Israel's interests during the operation. Linkage between Lebanese withdrawal and Syrian peace, an elusive objective despite Rabin's tentative commitment to withdrawal from the Golan Heights before his assassination, remained the first item on Barak's docket. Finalizing a peace agreement with Syria was the only achievement that would encourage the Israeli public to accept wrapping up Israel's misadventure in Lebanon.[5] But getting all the parties, particularly Arafat, to commit to another round of the peace process face-to-face with Israeli leaders proved to be a challenging task. The Americans subjected Arafat to a great deal of psychological intimidation to prod him to agree to a new round of American peace diplomacy. This included the reminder that only the United States was capable of bringing about such a settlement since the Israelis would trust neither the Europeans nor the Russians with their security. That this was a leaf straight out of Sadat's Camp David book which sought to persuade a skeptic public that greater benefits would result from switching to an American alliance remained unnoticed. Openly disparaging Arafat was also an important part of this psychological game. As he asserted in his memoirs, Clinton was always fond of heaping praise on Israeli leaders and mocking Arafat's unfamiliar ways. During the Oslo signing ceremonies, for instance, he wrote effusively regarding Rabin's logic and peace rationale. But as to Arafat, he was mocked for exchanging kisses with prominent members of the audience. During the Camp David II negotiations, Clinton praised Barak as "brilliant and brave, . . . the most decorated soldier in the history of Israel."[6] What Clinton overlooked, of course, was the Israeli premier's long history of assassination attempts targeting major PLO figures in exile. The final unkindest cut came as a result of the American president's frustration with Arafat's resistance to his cajoling, charming efforts, and promises of aid so that he could yield on the issue of Jerusalem:

> At times Arafat seemed confused, not wholly in command of the facts. I had felt for some time that he might not be at the top of his game any longer, after all the years of spending the night in different places to dodge assassins' bullets, all the countless hours on airplanes, all the endless hours of tension-filled talks. Perhaps he couldn't make the final jump from revolutionary to statesman. He had grown used to flying from place to place, giving mother-of-pearl gifts made by Palestinian craftsmen to world leaders and appearing on television with them.[7]

THE THREE VILLAGES WHICH OVERSHADOWED THE TALKS

Efforts were made to settle some issues in the Permanent Status Agreement just before January 2000. This period proved to be the crucial background to the diplomacy of Camp David II and it revolved around the fate of three villages or suburbs in the vicinity of East Jerusalem. Arafat had asked Barak to add the three suburbs of Abu Dis, Ezariya, and al-Ram to territory which he promised to shift from Area B to Area A. This would have enlarged the area earmarked to fall under Palestinian control during the negotiations. Barak assumed that this was Arafat's maximum bargaining position and that he held no hope of receiving all three, so Barak denied this request altogether. Once again Israeli domestic politics trumped any international pressure for moderation, leaving Arafat feeling betrayed and publicly humiliated. Barak's coalition partners like Shas, the religious party, were dead-set against giving up areas so close to the municipal boundaries of East Jerusalem. Abu Dis was under discussion in Palestinian circles as an alternative Arab capital instead of the former Jordanian Jerusalem. The idea behind this humiliating substitution was the result of secret contacts between Abbas and Yossi Beilin of the Labor Party and Meretz, which Arafat secretly instigated in order to test the waters. When Palestinians angrily dismissed the idea, Arafat pretended that he never authorized such talks. Eventually, all three villages were transferred to the PA Government, except that Abu Dis never replaced Jerusalem as the designated Palestinian capital.[8]

The Americans activated several back channels in the process, linking Palestinians and Israelis who were anxious to discuss final status issues together. Arafat supported the idea, but Barak did not, keeping his eyes on the Lebanese withdrawal instead. Two leading figures from the Oslo generation, Qurei' and Asfour, entered into such contacts with Gilad Sher, Barak's Chief of Staff, and Israeli Minister of Internal Security, Shlomo Ben Ami. Veteran Palestinian negotiator, Saeb Erekat, and a leader of the DFLP, Yasir Abed-Rabbo, dialogued with Barak's special envoy and lead negotiator, Oded Eran. Barak, however, remained unreceptive to the idea of beginning any discussions with the Jerusalem question, while Eran continued to push the idea of leaving this sensitive issue to the peace summit. Ross, a close observer of these initial contacts, noticed a state of confusion among the Palestinian negotiators. He felt that this was a deliberate Arafat maneuver to prevent the rise of any rivals to his leadership. Ross concluded that little was accomplished since each of the Palestinians was constantly checking back with the PA to guard against accusations of making unauthorized concessions. The early negotiations went nowhere, with considerable haggling over the Israeli team's definition of Israel's security needs and how much land was it willing to concede to the Palestinians. Land swaps were discussed to ensure the survival of Israeli settlements by folding them within Israeli territory. The

Palestinians, however, were willing to accept a state with provisional borders, which could be defined in the future.[9] The idea of provisional borders was the brainchild of Peres, who persuaded Qurei' to sell it to the Palestinians during the Oslo talks, pending the resolution of the final status issues. But most Palestinians never trusted this concept, fearing that provisional borders inevitably turn into permanent borders.[10]

While the Israelis fretted over starting the negotiations with concessions on Jerusalem, the Palestinians made their rejection of any territorial deal prior to settling the Jerusalem issue very clear. Any early gains on the Jerusalem front were viewed as necessary if for nothing else than to demonstrate the value of making territorial concessions within the occupied West Bank. But efforts to soften Palestinian resistance to making concessions continued with direct pressure by Ross and even a visit by Secretary of State Madeleine Albright to Arafat in Ramallah. Thus, when summoned by Clinton, Arafat arrived in Washington feeling angry and defeated, particularly as Barak declined to transfer the three villages to the Palestinians even when the Knesset authorized the move. More intimidation followed, with Albright and Ross putting the burden of risking damage to the American president's prestige on Arafat unless the Palestinians were serious about wanting to reach an agreement. Arafat, however, expressed great fears, admitting that he lost sleep over the prospect of conceding control over Jerusalem, a theme to which he returned several times during the Camp David II talks.[11]

CLINTON'S SUMMIT:
PRESSURE, PAIN, AND THE PERCEPTION OF BETRAYAL

There were several versions of what transpired at the summit meeting, but Ross' account, through projecting all blame on Arafat, remained anchored in the long-held American belief in the unreliability and obdurate personality of the Palestinian leader. As to Clinton, he was ill-disposed to trust Arafat from the beginning, developing a personal animus and disdain for his tactics which reinforced the American president's prior belief in Arafat's inferior mental capability and the superior intelligence of his Israeli counterpart.

Clinton began the summit fully prepared, having been coached by his advisers about the likely tactics of each side, the possibility of deadlock and what trade-offs could be proposed in order to streamline the process. Ross reported that the president was not anticipating a comprehensive peace, but an accommodation that would grant the Palestinians a state over 75 percent of the West Bank. Clinton was said to have acquainted himself with the neighborhoods of East Jerusalem thoroughly. He also accepted his advisers' suggestion of presenting a detailed paper early on, covering all of the final status issues. He was coached on how to flatter Arafat and how to move him from dwelling on historic Palestinian grievances to a realistic posture of negotiations. Clinton was to lead the parties to accepting his own parameters for peace, or the definitive ideas on each issue which his advisers prepared, touching on borders, the refugees and Jerusalem. On the latter, Clinton's parameters were to propose viewing Jerusalem as three cities in one: A municipal entity, a holy city and a political capital.[12]

Contention arose quickly over political control of the city. Barak was open to negotiating over the other issues of borders and surrendering territory, but was unwilling to reveal the limits of his proposed concessions. The Palestinians, however, were fixated on Jerusalem and complained of lack of details in the first original American draft agreement. Clinton proposed the creation of two capitals within the existing Israeli-controlled municipality by incorporating Abu Dis within its boundaries in order to designate it as the Palestinian capital. This pleased Arafat and appeared to be a return to the idea of Abu Dis as the capital in the Belin-Abu-Mazen plan. Ross then added the idea of granting the Palestinians sovereign control over the new ring of Arab neighborhoods, but only Palestinian control, which he defined as anything but sovereignty, over the holy places. They would be allowed to raise their own flag over the Noble Sanctuary and even place their own police there, but political sovereignty would ultimately reside with the Israelis. Yet, Barak resisted the idea of compensating the Palestinians for lack of sovereignty over the Noble Sanctuary with political control over the outlaying Arab suburbs. As Ross reminded him, how could Abu Dis be the capital if it remained outside the municipal boundaries of East Jerusalem? When the Palestinians disagreed over a map presented by Clinton in which his team proposed border modifications of the proposed Palestinian state, Clinton was angered. Ross chided the Palestinians in the following words: "You guys are taking advantage of the President of the United States and he has had it.'[13]

The Palestinians did not respond to the matter of the map, but only regarding the Jerusalem issue. When Erekat suggested that East Jerusalem be divided according to the ethnic composition of its neighborhoods so Israel might rule the Jewish areas and the Palestinians the Arab areas, the Israelis balked at the idea. But the Americans still insisted on keeping the inner Arab neighborhoods such as Shaykh Jarrah and Wadi al-Joz autonomous, remaining under Israeli sovereignty within the Old City, while being provided with municipal services by the Palestinian capital, to be referred to as al-Quds. In other words, the Old City was to remain Jewish. The Israelis contributed to the president's ire by rejecting his ideas, but were given a pass since the Palestinians did not accept any of his recommendations either. Arafat continued to argue with Clinton, claiming that Rabin had offered him more than that, a claim disputed by Ross who dwelt on Arafat's ongoing betrayal of the president.[14]

Barak, in the meantime, sent an emotional message to Clinton which the president did not read until after the meeting with Arafat concluded. If the PA chairman was always accused of being a muddling, overly emotional individual who constantly cited the travails of the Palestinian, Barak proved to be just as capable of calling on Clinton's sympathies. The Israeli prime minister accused the Palestinians of being manipulative, and the American team of lacking objectivity. He reminded the president of the political risks he was taking by submitting to this process. He declared that he had no intention of presiding over the collapse of the Israeli state which was the embodiment of the historic yearnings of the Jewish people. He called on the president to bear down hard on Arafat in order to give the process a chance. One reason for Barak's gloomy message, explained Ross, was the realization that the price of peace was higher than originally estimated. Barak, it turned out, was not a supporter of the Oslo Agreement, did not vote for the Interim Agreement, nor belonged to the handful of official Israelis willing to engage in secret peace contacts. Arafat's counter-offer turned out to be prioritizing Palestinian sovereignty over East Jerusalem, which included Jewish neighborhoods. These had become settlements which were acceptable to Arafat in principle. He was also willing to allow land swaps involving minor land blocks.[15]

This time, however, Ross felt that Arafat was capable of submitting a real offer. Yet, the Israeli delegation quickly shot down the idea of surrendering sovereignty over the Muslim Quarter in the Old City, insisting that the Palestinians simply did not appreciate how significant Jerusalem was to Jews. That is when Ross and Indyk came up with bizarre ideas to gain Arafat's acceptance, such as building the American Embassy in Palestinian-controlled Abu Dis, consisting of few hundred meters of territory slated to fall within the boundaries of East Jerusalem. Another idea that Ross proposed to Arafat in order to enhance his prestige was to plan for the American President to head an international delegation on a visit to the Palestinian-controlled Noble Sanctuary as confirmation of the significant role entrusted to the Palestinian leader. This, in addition to granting the Palestinians sovereignty over some neighborhoods in the Old City, entailed providing an office for Arafat within the walls, functional autonomy within Jerusalem's inner neighborhoods, and official jurisdiction, though not sovereignty, over the Noble Sanctuary. All of these were expected to bolster Arafat's prestige in Arab eyes. But the Palestinian leader misunderstood all that, thinking that the Americans were willing to transform the holy sites into a diplomatic mission under Palestinian jurisdiction, which, in Ross' view, was tantamount to bestowing political sovereignty and barring Jews from entering it without the Palestinians' permission. But how was this to be achieved? The one suggestion approximating an understanding of the international mechanisms which could be expected to achieve this was submitted by Clinton's Egyptian adviser, translator, and

State Department official, Gemal Helal. His idea was that Israel, the real sovereign over the Old City, could grant the status of diplomatic overseers of the holy sites to the five permanent members of the Security Council, who then would grant custodial status to the Palestinians. Ross believed that this would resemble Saudi authority over the Islamic holy sites in Mecca and Medina, ignoring the fact that political sovereignty undergirded the Saudi position. Ross, nevertheless, recognized that Israel itself would have to authorize the transfer of these rights to the Security Council members, plus the Vatican, and particularly Morocco, which held the chairmanship of the Jerusalem Committee within the Organization of Islamic Cooperation (OIC). The international body would then act to declare Palestine the permanent custodian of the holy sites. Israeli negotiators were thinking along similar lines by offering Palestinian quasi-sovereign status over the Muslim Quarter. Not unsurprisingly, all of these concessions never departed from the notion of reserving genuine political sovereignty to the Israelis. Ross continued to refer to all of these international models as functional autonomy, custodianship, quasi-sovereignty, and shared responsibilities interchangeably, but not once by their real name, limited autonomy. [16]

Arafat's response to the idea of transferring sovereign custodianship to the Security Council, and eventually its devolution to the Palestinian state, revealed his deep concern over the religious impact of such a decision on his and the Palestinians' legitimacy as the natural and historic custodians of the holy sites. He felt that this was tantamount to surrendering Jerusalem to the Crusaders all over again. He also balked at the idea of maintaining Israel's sovereignty over the ruins of the Jewish Temple believed to be below the Noble Sanctuary. Instead, Arafat's idea was to grant sovereignty not to the Security Council but to the OIC itself, which already had a Jerusalem Committee. He also reminded the delegates that he had been serving as the vice-president of the Jerusalem Committee for a long time. Clinton countered by proposing that the membership of the committee should be enlarged in order to include others willing to safeguard Israel's interests. But Arafat remained skeptical regarding the committee's willingness to go along with that idea since by definition, the OIC was an Islamic body. Ross then floated the concept of a special regime for the Holy Basin and a different one for the Palestinians. The Holy Basin was a novel Jewish idea which extended holiness not only to the territory which they believed held the ruins of the Temple, but also to the entire Old City, Mount Zion, Mount of Olives and the Garden of Gesthsemane, all of which, minus the first one, lay outside the walls. Arafat would be given rights over the Muslim and Christian holy places, including two-thirds of the territory of the Armenian Quarter. Fearing the tarnishing of his legitimacy in the Arab World, he turned the idea down. [17]

THE DENIGRATION OF ARAFAT

Before too long, the summit participants, especially Clinton, as well as Arab and international leaders subjected Arafat to ridicule, threats, and unexpected pressure. The entire blame for the failure of the conference was placed on Arafat's shoulders, resulting in the dispatching of American envoys to various world capitals to destroy his legitimacy as a leader. Clinton and Barak used the threat of concluding a peace agreement with Syria as a lever against any procrastination by the Palestinians. Arafat was always treated as a novice and Clinton and advisers refused to believe that he was capable of making any sound suggestions. Clinton said that, "Arafat did not come with a set of negotiating points, this was all strange territory to him."[18] Despairing of making the Palestinians take his offer, Clinton kept repeating Eban's often-quoted statement that Palestinians "never miss an opportunity to miss an opportunity."[19] Arab leaders were called by Clinton who asked that they pressure Arafat into accepting the American and Israeli deal. Ross met with Qurei' to make him pressure Arafat into understanding the consequences if no settlement was adopted, emphasizing that it was Clinton's summit, not one of Arafat's inconsequential games.[20] More importantly, Clinton was enraged by Arafat's assertion that Solomon's Temple was not in Jerusalem, but in Nablus, where the ancient Samaritan community claimed to live in the vicinity of the ancient temple. Clinton held on to this idea even when his advisers reminded him that the American Government refrained from taking sides in the raging archeological debates about the location of the Jewish Temple. The American president, however, was never perturbed at the Israeli adoption of the Holy Basin concept, which was popularized by extremists and which cast the net of holiness much wider than before. Clinton believed that Arafat lied to him when the latter reneged on an earlier promise to accept the final deal before Clinton's term of office expired. But when the Palestinian leader found out that he could not fulfil his promise, Clinton considered this a deliberate and personal affront by someone he never valued in the first place. Clinton unleashed his fury by warning George W. Bush, his successor in office, not to trust Arafat, supposedly telling the latter, "You made me a failure."[21]

As was well-known, American presidents were never bashful when it came to acknowledging their indebtedness to Jewish-American votes and campaign contributions. With only a few days left for him in the White House, Clinton declared his gratitude to his Jewish-American backers even at the risk of damaging the integrity of his Middle East summit. In an address to the Israel Policy Forum in New York on January 7, 2001, he apologized to this "pro-peace group," explaining his failure to deliver a settlement:

> The American Jewish community had been very good to me. Some, like my
> friend Haim Saban and Danny Abraham were deeply involved with Israel and
> had given me helpful advice over the years. Many others simply supported my
> work for peace. Regardless of what happened, I thought I owed to them to
> explain my proposal.[22]

A few years later, Eran, Barak's chief negotiator at the summit, explained what it would have taken to secure Israel's willingness to accept a freeze on the settlements. The Israeli Government, he noted, was dead-set against dismantling the Jerusalem settlements. Only an Arab gesture, such as recognizing Israel as a Jewish state, would satisfy the settlers. The old partial Arab conciliatory efforts have lost attractiveness a long time ago. Only a bold and stunning gesture such as a visit to Jerusalem by the head of the House of Saud or the President of Syria would shift Israeli public opinion to a different mode. He also belittled the positive impact of opening up semi-official Israeli offices in some Gulf capitals, like Doha.[23]

After the collapse of the talks, Arafat felt the ripple effect of Clinton's and Barak's negative campaign against him. Secretary of State Albright did better. She sent a special emissary, Ned Walker, to fourteen Arab and European countries to spread the American version of the Camp David II summit and Arafat's contribution to its failure. Barak paid a visit to Jordan, Egypt, and Turkey, while another Israeli emissary, former intelligence chief Danny Yatom, surreptitiously explained these events to leading Gulf states such as Qatar, Bahrain, Oman, and the United Arab Emirates. Another former Israeli intelligence chief turned foreign minister, Shlomo Ben Ami, toured North African and European countries. Also delivering the same message was Peres himself while on official visits to India and Indonesia. When the Islamic Republic of Iran expressed an interest in convening a special session of the OIC to defend Arafat's demand for full sovereignty over the holy places, it discovered that the Arab states, particularly Egypt which dominated the ALS, were not in support of this. Only King Muhamad VI of Morocco was prevailed upon as chair of the ALS' Jerusalem Committee to issue an affirmation of his Islamic role as the custodian over Jerusalem. Indyk added that even the Vatican, speaking through its Foreign Minister, Archbishop Jean-Louis Tauran, disapproved of ceding control of the Christian holy places to Arafat, preferring assigning them to an international regime. Lastly, the new Russian president, Vladimir Putin, objected to a unilateral Palestinian declaration of independence.[24] Barak topped this Arab and international wave of condemnation with an inflammatory rebuke of Arafat and his negotiating team in the *New York Review of Books.* Among his choicest words were the following:

> They [the Arabs] are product of a culture in which to tell a lie . . . creates no
> dissonance. They don't suffer from the problem of telling lies that exists in

Judeo-Christian culture. Truth is seen as an irrelevant category. They see themselves as emissaries of a national movement for whom everything is possible. There is no such thing as the truth.[25]

ARAFAT CORRALLED

In defense of Arafat's uncooperative and delaying tactics, it could be argued that the summit had a damaging impact on his own domestic constituency. Among the few voices which sought to exonerate him in the United States, however, was Deborah Sontag, American writer and peace activist who publicly regretted the simplistic analysis making the rounds in Israel, and even in the United States. She refuted the running narrative asserting that Barak made Arafat a very generous offer which the latter rejected, leading to another intifada. The real story was that all participants, the Americans, Israelis, and Palestinians contributed to the missteps and minor successes of the Oslo interim peace efforts, stretching to the Camp David II summit and the Taba meeting which it followed. Sontag was confident that Barak did not make a generous offer, he merely opened up for debate forbidden topics, like dividing up Jerusalem. Though displaying courage in the face of his weakening coalition cabinet, Barak's offer fell short of what the Palestinian expectations were for a state of their own. Arafat was also absolved of all blame for destroying the summit by Terje Roed Larsen, who believed that all sides contributed to the collapse of the Camp David II peace talks. Arafat was expected to demonstrate publicly his appreciation of the moderation of the Israeli negotiating team. Instead, he demonstrated good faith by authorizing his own team to participate in the follow-up talks at Taba, which he knew would be based on Clinton's parameters for peace. According to Ben Ami, the guidelines had already riled up Israeli public opinion at a time when elections were scheduled to take place, but the Taba meeting was held anyway.[26]

The strongest defense of Arafat was penned by two of the lesser known participants in the talks, Hussein Agha and Robert Malley. Agha was one of Arafat's assistants and Malley was an expert on Arab-Israeli affairs serving on the American team. Following the conclusion of the summit, they set out first and foremost to debunk the myth of Barak's generous offer to the Palestinians. They explained that the Israeli side brought three definitive ideas to the summit. First, it contributed a serious mistrust of the idea of incremental steps which characterized the Oslo talks, believing that partial withdrawal from Palestinian lands failed to guarantee any advantage to the Israeli side. Second, it held a firm conviction that the Palestinians would not come up with a grand compromise until all other options were exhausted. Thirdly, it believed that the Israeli public would only accept an agreement granting extensive concessions to the Palestinians if they were assured of the finality of such a deal and an end to the violence. Barak, additionally, was very conscious of the high price paid by Rabin for alienating the Israeli right, a dynamic which he did not wish to unleash. Barak also saw no harm in continuing to authorize the building of settlements or troop withdrawal from the three villages surrounding Jerusalem, or releasing Palestinian prisoners. Arafat, however, pleaded for more time before proceeding to the summit, complaining to Clinton that the Israeli Prime Minister had not carried out his side of the recent agreements.[27] The American president, it seemed, had expected a similar performance from Arafat as during the Oslo talks, when the clear absence of any alternate solutions forced the Palestinian leader to accept the deal. Perhaps the American team at Camp David II was obsessed with Sadat-like visions, dreaming of an Arafat replay of the Egyptian leader's eagerness to grasp the American deal, with no special sentiment or emotional attachment to Jerusalem. Arafat, however, proved to be the conscious bearer of a different historical legacy than that which motivated Sadat.

THE TABA CONFERENCE—A BACKGROUND

An Israeli-Palestinian committee began meeting in the Egyptian resort of Taba following the signing of the Declaration of Principles (DOP) to discuss the implementation of the agreement. At first, Nabil Sha'ath represented the PLO and Major General Amnon Lipkin-Shahak, the second top official in the IDF who also directed military intelligence, represented Israel. This was the first time the Israeli military were allowed to be involved in any meaningful peace negotiations, having been excluded from the Oslo talks. These included Barak, who was Chief of Staff at the time and propagated the notion that Israeli civilians gave away too much at Oslo. Initially, a Rabin move to allow the predominance of the military in these talks was intended to pacify them and to outflank Peres, preventing him from authorizing more concessions. The generals apparently aimed at putting the brakes on redrawing the occupation lines, feeling, as Barak had always claimed, that they would be held ultimately responsible for the security of the country. But after some delays, an agreement was initialed on February 9, 1994, at Cairo by Arafat and Peres. The agreement had prioritized Israeli security ahead of all other items, giving it total responsibility for safeguarding the occupied territories, including Gaza and its three Jewish settlements. The Israeli military were now officially allowed to ring the area designated for a future Palestinian state. The Palestinians presented the agreement to their constituency as the first step in the dismantling of Israeli civil administration in the territories. When an Israeli settler, Dr. Baruch Goldstein, opened fire on Muslim worshippers at the Ibrahimi Mosque at Hebron on February 25, 1994, the Palestinians suspended the talks and there was a loud cry within Israel to remove the four hundred settlers from the Hebron area. But Rabin objected, claiming that the Oslo Accords never called for the removal of the settlements during the interim period, leaving this decision to the final status agreement. Neither would he consent to putting the question of the settlements on the agenda of any peace talks until a three-year period had lapsed. The Israeli Government, however, launched a campaign against Kach, the extremist pro-settlement movement, and the PLO returned to the Cairo talks feeling somewhat vindicated.[28]

It was Clinton who presided over the signing of the Israeli-Palestinian Interim Agreement on the West Bank and the Gaza Strip on 28 September 1995, at Washington, in the presence of Arafat and Rabin. This came to be known as Oslo II, which concluded the first segment of the negotiations between Israel and the PLO, and which amplified the Gaza-Jericho Agreement. The Oslo II document was explained to the Knesset on 5 October 1995 by Rabin. His main selling points were maintaining a military presence in the Jordan Valley, preserving the large settlement blocks abutting the 1967 border, and keeping Jerusalem undivided, but with rights for followers of the various religions. He also emphasized that the Palestinian entity which would emerge from the agreements will be autonomous but remain a demilitarized zone.[29]

Clinton did not abandon the prospect of reaching a final agreement through diplomacy following the collapse of the Camp David II summit. Instead, he pushed the parties to resume their talks at Taba, which lasted through January 2001, but failed to deliver any results. Arafat's fears and concerns received much attention, but he never granted his final consent. Indyk felt that Arafat was simply a prisoner of the past, or the old Arab order, and was incapable of jumping at the opportunity offered by Clinton into the unknown. Reflecting the common American and Israeli view at the time, Indyk refused to acknowledge the enormous spiritual, historical and political significance of Haram al-Sharif sanctuary to the Palestinians, if not to all Muslims. Neither were subscribers to this view willing to concede the relationship of Palestinian sovereignty over the holy sites to the Palestinians' aspirations for statehood. Thus, the Camp David II negotiators were quick to accuse Arafat of blackmailing them with the threat of a widening intifada and to exploit Clinton's eagerness to add an Arab-Israeli peace agreement to his legacy. Indyk added that Arafat was assured of the consent of the Israeli right after his Kurdish-Iraqi economic adviser Ahmad Rashid entered into a secret dialogue with the leader of the Yisrael Beiteinu Party, Avigdor Lieberman, and Jerusalem's mayor, Ehud Olmert. Arafat was simply accused of misunderstanding where the center of Israeli decision-making was.[30] Indyk did not spare Clinton from any blame, although, like the rest of the American and Israeli teams, he saved his harshest words for Arafat:

> Clinton also repeatedly signaled Arafat that he was in a hurry. For the bazaar
> merchant, customers in a hurry are the most vulnerable to extortion, especially
> when he senses, as Arafat did, that time was on his side.[31]

Furthermore, any hope of receiving diplomatic assistance at a peace conference by a fellow Arab state was abandoned by the PLO a long time ago. Having given up on the Jordanians, Moroccans, and Syrians, Arafat had no expectations of Egyptian assistance either. Some of this may have resulted from past Palestinian reluctance to inform the Egyptians of the Oslo negotiations until some agreement was reached, fearing Cairo's coordination with Damascus. Any seepage of information to Syria might lead the latter to intervene and obstruct the talks. Not only did Syria have a lot at stake, but the regime of Bashar al-Assad enjoyed great access to Palestinian opposition factions within Syria's borders, which were capable of mobilizing against secret negotiations. Egypt was still held in reserve as a potential backer of another Oslo settlement, since its prestige allowed it to garner wider Arab support for a deal if it so wished. Not surprisingly, Israel held Egypt in great trust and wished to use it to overcome any disputes that might arise during the negotiations. Soon enough, President Husni Mubarak learnt of the secret track from Rabin. At one point, the Palestinian team at Oslo began to suspect the official credentials of their Israeli interlocutors, but were assured by the Egyptian president of Rabin's confirmation of the Israelis' official status. The Egyptians also dispatched a special envoy to Oslo, Ambassador Taher Shash, so as to verify all the documents upon the Palestinians' request. This visit coincided with Peres' arrival at Oslo for the same reason, before he departed to report to Christopher and the Americans about the main lines of the DOP. Often, Egypt was called upon by Israel to pressure the PLO, as when Rabin faced resistance when he preconditioned recognition of the PLO on the latter's amendment of the Palestinian Covenant. Eventually, Egyptian Foreign Minister Amr Mousa persuaded Rabin to accept such a commitment in a letter from Arafat, rather than insist on an amendment of the text of the DOP. All of this Egyptian intervention, which netted few gains for the Palestinians, worked towards the enhancement of Egypt's prestige within American and Israeli circles. But as to the Palestinians, they dug their heels demanding the return of the refugees and control over Jerusalem, all by themselves.[32]

THE ACHIEVEMENTS AND LIMITATIONS OF TABA

By the time the Taba talks commenced on January 21, 2001, pressure on the Palestinians to reach a settlement was rising. The only facilitators at the meeting were the EU's special envoy Miguel Moratinos and his aides. The Israelis arrived with a new map of Jerusalem, which superseded the

1949–1967 armistice borderlines with Jordan. Israel had already incorporated 4 out of the 9 percent of the West Bank already added to the area under its control by the "security fence" (the "Apartheid Wall" according to Palestinians) in its latest definition of Greater Jerusalem. The path of the fence had become the new border between Israel and the West Bank. The Israelis felt that postponement of any discussion of this enlarged Jerusalem was, therefore, meant to ease the Palestinians' pain. Neither was there any promise of freezing the settlements within this area. Israel continued to demand the placement of the Islamic holy places under the Muslim *awqaf*, but with a corridor or passage linking them to the projected Palestinian state. Any hope of gaining Palestinian political jurisdiction over these sites had now vanished.[33]

Yet, the Palestinians and Israelis were very close to a settlement, according to the EU's report on the Taba talks submitted by Moratinos. What emerged from it was that Taba achieved more results than the Camp David II negotiations due to the genuine and realistic suggestions presented by the Palestinians rather than satisfying themselves with critiquing American and Israeli proposals as happened earlier. This time, the Palestinians even presented maps. The leader of the Israeli team was veteran peace negotiator Yossi Beilin, who commended Moratinos on his meticulous reporting and his serious endeavor to seek comments on his report from both sides. The EU negotiator was apparently very conscious of each side's desire to come up with a settlement acceptable to their respective constituencies. Beilin believed that there was still time to finalize a settlement and that the meeting did not fall apart because it deadlocked. At the time of circulating the report, which Moratinos wished to remain a secret and to keep it hidden from the media and the general public on both sides, there was talk of setting up a meeting between Arafat and Barak. In the end, Beilin argued that the Israeli elections were responsible for killing the talks.[34]

He explained that the document revealed agreement over making the borderlines of June 4, 1967, the starting point for discussions on the final border, in accordance with Security Council Res. 242. Maps showing possible land swaps in order to deal with the issue of the settlements were exchanged. All discussion was based on the Clinton parameters devised during the Camp David II summit. Israelis argued that these allowed for the annexation of the settlement blocks, but the Palestinians disagreed. Israelis made the claim that there was a need to provide contiguity in order to connect the settlements together, with the Palestinians claiming that the interests of the Palestinian population in these areas would not be served. More importantly, the Palestinian negotiators insisted on maintaining the contiguity of the West Bank and Jerusalem and on keeping the latter's Palestinian villages within the West Bank. But in order not to repeat the unfavorable settlement of 1948 which separated populated Palestinian villages from their agricultural lands and relegated large swaths of territory to the strip of no-man's land separating the two entities, the Palestinians demanded the return of the La-troun area near Hebron.[35]

Discussions pertaining to Jerusalem also started from the Clinton parame-ters which recommended that each side exercise sovereignty over its own Arab or Jewish neighborhoods. Israelis, however, put in a bid for keeping their 1967 settlements in East Jerusalem and expressed willingness to ex-clude Jabal Abu Ghneim (Har Homa) and the Ras al-Amoud neighborhood. But the Palestinians did not concede Israeli sovereignty over any settlements within the Jerusalem metropolitan area, such as Ma'alet Adomim and Givat Ze'ev. Finally, they were satisfied with expressed Israeli willingness to open up the 1948 file of Arab property claims in West Jerusalem. Throughout these discussions, the Palestinians sensed that some progress had been achieved due to Israel's openness to negotiating sovereign Palestinian rights over the Arab neighborhoods of the Old City. The Israelis were also begin-ning to see some Palestinian willingness to grant sovereignty over the Jewish Quarter and a section of the Armenian Quarter. The Israelis returned again to the concept of the Holy Basin, hoping to declare this enlarged definition of the holy sites as an open city for all faiths, which would allow both Palestin-ians and Israelis to enter without having to go through checkpoints. The Palestinians, however, were not in favor of this definition, opting instead for the old boundaries of East and West Jerusalem. The Israelis, additionally, suggested more than one modality for municipal coordination between the two cities to deal with issues such as the infrastructure, roads, waste disposal, and the electrical supply. There was even some discussion of what would constitute a capital of the two states, with both sides willing to go along with the new nomenclature of al-Quds and Yerushalaim to distinguish one capital from the other. The Palestinian side was anxious to get a confirmation that a Palestinian state would be one of the outcomes of the talks. The concept of the Holy Basin, however, continued to alarm them. This was especially the case when the Israelis insisted on the inclusion of some areas within this enlarged territory. These comprised areas traditionally within Arab Jerusa-lem, such as the Jewish cemetery on the Mount of Olives, the City of David excavations and the Kidron Valley at the Arab suburb of Silwan. These sites which were mostly archeological locations lying outside the walls, were never part of West Jerusalem or under Israeli sovereignty before the 1967 War. Palestinians suspected that the principle of claiming sovereignty over recent excavations was simply a stepping stone to attaching additional terri-tory to areas under Israeli control.[36]

The widest gulf separating the two sides continued to be the future of the holy sites. There was no agreement over what section of the Western Wall, which Palestinians called the Wailing Wall, would be ceded to Israeli sove-reignty since the latter considered a segment of it known as al-Buraq Wall to be one of their holy sites. But as to the question of sovereignty over Haram al-Sharif, or Temple Mount, both sides acknowledged that major differences still existed. Here, the question of granting sovereignty to the five members of the Security Council and Morocco, with some Palestinians named as the Guardians, or Custodians, for the interim period was raised again. The two sides were expected to come up with a new solution at the end of that period or simply extend this plan for another period of time, but this issue remained unresolved. Another difficult question which re-emerged was the Palestinian demand for the return of the refugees, as was stipulated by General Assembly Res. 194. The Palestinians asked for the return of the refugees to the Israeli-swapped territory or to the future Palestinian state, with some being rehabilitated in another country. The Israeli side also suggested a joint narrative to expatiate the pain of the refugees, but no agreement was reached. But if a settlement was finalized, both sides agreed that UNRWA should be dismantled over a five-year period. The Palestinians, however, repeated the current Arab position which agreed that Jewish refugees should be compensated by the Arab states where they lived, not by the Palestinians. They asked that this issue should not be part of the proposed Israeli-Palestinian agreement. Finally, based on the parameters, the question of ending all claims by the Palestinians upon the implementation of the agreement was raised again.[37] But as was noted earlier by Beilin, what killed the Taba Summit was the Likud victory of the elections of February 6, 2001, which felled Barak's cabinet and brought Sharon to power. Failure to reach a settlement at the Taba summit, however, was considered to be the result of Arafat's betrayal by Clinton.

CONCLUSION

Having presided over the signing ceremony of the Oslo DOP, Clinton felt that the time was right to bring this conflict to a conclusion and that he had mastered the issue thoroughly. He was even convinced that he knew the location of the remains of the Jewish Temple, even when his advisers told him of the absence of such a position on the part of the American Government. Neither was there any appreciation of Arafat's reluctance to grant concessions in Jerusalem which could replicate Muslim loss of rights over access to Hebron's Ibrahimi Mosque.[38] But as always, Clinton entered this morass of conflicting passions and claims with great admiration for Israel's leaders, great contempt for PLO leaders, especially Arafat, and surrounded by advisers, all of whom held a deep and open attachment to Israel and its people. By mid-2000, Clinton felt that the time was right to pressure the Palestinians into participating in a new peace adventure, which, once more, was lacking any guarantees for a specific projected outcome. The Palestinians were also subjected to an Israeli psychological campaign by Prime Minister Barak, who planned to use his contacts with the Syrians as a tactical weapon with which to lead the Palestinians to the trough. Thus, he deliberately planned his delayed arrival at the summit while pursuing a peace deal with the Syrians. These theatrics were used as a threat to Arafat, waving the possibility of isolation and abandonment by Arab allies as a possible reaction to his reluctance to join the peace conference. Though nothing resulted from Barak's gamble to secure a Syrian deal, he continued to place his highest hopes in facilitating the orderly and speedy withdrawal of Israeli troops from southern Lebanon without any Syrian military retaliation.

Faced with the fallout of the Oslo concessions to Israel, Palestinian agitation in reaction to the tunnel incident and the prospect of another intifada on the eve of violence by Jewish settlers at Hebron's Ibrahimi Mosque, Arafat felt he was not yet ready for another peace summit. The Israelis, however, arrived at the summit fully prepared with maps and studies and a determination never to yield on the issue of Jerusalem or the Palestinian right of return. Most of the negotiations, therefore, centered on the issue of the settlements, with the Palestinians pushing for the dismantling of the larger blocks, or persuading the Israelis of the merit of concluding land swaps but without the loss of Arab populated villages as in the 1948 Israeli-Jordanian Armistice Agreement.

When the conference concluded, both Clinton and Barak circulated their views, both placing all of the blame for the summit's failure on Arafat's shoulders. After intense talks and several proposals regarding the future of Jerusalem, the summit ended with no settlement in sight. Arafat was accused of negative and obstructionist reaction to anything offered by Israel or proposed by the United States. The Palestinian team, which always deferred to Arafat, found itself unimpressed by Barak's alleged generous offer of massive territorial concessions to facilitate the creation of a Palestinian state, if that came at the expense of Arab concessions in the Jerusalem area. Intense discussions were held in order to bring the two sides together, but the gap between them remained unbridgeable. Israel's interpretation of the notion of ceding control over Jerusalem's Arab and Jewish neighborhoods to their respective majority communities was to exclude from this any Arab enclaves within the Old City. Clinton's solution for control over Haram al-Sharif/Temple Mount and the Western Wall area was to grant the Palestinians custodial rights, leaving meaningful political sovereignty to the Israelis. When his idea of granting control of the area beneath the Islamic holy sites to Israel aroused the Palestinians' suspicion, he seemed to be surprised. In desperation, he circulated his Egyptian adviser's idea of granting control over the holy sites to the five permanent members of the Security Council, who would then allow the Palestinians to assume control over these places. Arafat expressed hesitation before allowing these "Crusaders" to assume responsibility for the Islamic holy places, suggesting instead that the OIC and its Jerusalem Committee, of which he was the deputy chair, be in charge. Neither was there any agreement over making Jerusalem an open city, with no check-points, or accepting the new Israeli definition of the city's boundaries as encompassing the Holy Basin. This was a new concept asserting Jewish claims to all places of significance to Jewish history, even if located in Arab Jerusalem, outside the walls.

As the summit came to a conclusion and Clinton prepared to depart on his prescheduled East Asian trip, the drum beats against Arafat grew louder. He was publicly maligned by the American president, his secretary of state and most of his advisers for refusing to acknowledge the widely accepted location of Solomon's Temple as being beneath the length of Haram al-Sharif area, and suggesting inexplicably that it was located in Nablus. More significantly, Arafat was maligned before Arab and world leaders for promising Clinton to hand him a deal before the expiration of his presidential term of office. When the Taba summit of January 2001 also failed to produce an agreement despite the expert facilitation of Moratinos, the EU representative, Arafat again was singled out for blame. Clinton accused him of "lying," and Barak took to the pages of the American press to unleash a barrage of undiplomatic attacks on the Palestinians in general. Yet, as veteran Israeli peace negotiator Yossi Beilin admitted, there was no hope of concluding a peace settlement at the Taba Summit since the election of Sharon in early February 2001 ended all hope for achieving a historic compromise. But the shadow of the Jewish Temple which hung over the negotiations never faded away, and Arafat's "delusional" denial of its physical location was never explained.

NOTES

1. Michael Takiff, *A Complicated Man: The Life of Bill Clinton as Told by Those Who knew Him* (New Haven, Conn.: Yale University Press, 2010): 216.

2. Ibid., 216–8, 358–9

3. President Clinton, "Remarks to the Palestine National Council and Other Palestinian Organizations in Gaza City," December 14, 1998. FRUS, Vol. II, 2176.

4. Takiff, *A Complicated Man*, 385.

5. Dennis Ross, *The Missing Peace: The Inside Story of the Fight for Middle East Peace* (New York: Farrar, Straus and Giroux, 2004): 591–3.

6. Bill Clinton, *My Life* (New York: Alfred A. Knopf, 2004): 478, 912–6. See also: Aron Heller, "Khalil al-Wazir Death: Israel Admits to Assassination of Abu Jihad, Arafat Deputy in 1988," The World Post, 11/01/2012. www.huffingpost.com/.../khalil-al-wazir-abu-jha... Accessed 20/01/2016.

7. Clinton, *My Life*, 943–4.

8. Ross, *The Missing Peace*, 521–2, 601.

9. Ibid., 603–9.

10. Shlomo Brom, "From Rejection to Acceptance: Israeli National Security Thinking and Palestinian Statehood," United States Institute for Peace, Special Report, February 17, 2007. www.usip.org. Accessed 2/19/2007.

11. Ross, *The Missing Peace*, 623–4, 632–5, 643.

12. Ibid., 651–5.

13. Ibid., 655, 659–68.

14. Ibid., 673–6.

15. Ibid., 676–9.

16. Ibid., 679–83.

17. Martin Indyk, *Innocent Abroad: An Intimate Account of American Peace Diplomacy in the Middle East* (New York: Simon and Schuster, 2009): 346–51.

18. Clinton, *My Life*, 912.

19. Ibid., 924.

20. Ibid., 938.

21. Takiff, *A Complicated Man*, 387–9; Benny Morris, "Camp David and After: An Exchange (An Interview with Ehud Barak)," *New York Review of Books* (13 June 2002). www.nybooks.com/.../2002/camp-da...Accessed 5/9/2013.

22. Clinton, *My Life*, 946–7.

23. Oded Oran, "The US and Confidence-Building Measures, Arab Normalization Gestures to Israel," *Bitter Lemons*, July 23, 2009, www.bitterlemons.org. Accessed 7/24/2009.

24. Indyk, *Innocent Abroad*, 344–5.

25. Reported by Benny Morris in: "Camp David and After: An Exchange (An Interview with Ehud Barak)", *New York Review of Books* (June 13, 2002). www.nybooks.com/.../2002/camp-da... Accessed 5/9/2013.

26. Deborah Sontag, "Quest for the Mideast Peace," *New York Times* (July 26, 2001): 1 & A10. Reprinted in *Journal of Palestine Studies* (Autumn 2001).

27. Hussein Agha and Robert Malley, "Camp David: The Tragedy of Errors," *New York Review of Books*, August 9, 2001). http://www.nybooks.com/articles/archives12. Accessed 5/8/2013.

28. Avi Shlaim, *The Iron Wall: Israel and the Arab World* (New York: W. W. Norton, 2000): 523–5.

29. Ibid., 527–30.

30. Indyk, *Innocent Abroad*, 373–5.

31. Ibid., 376.

32. Mustafa Bakri, *Gaza wa Areeha: al-awraq al-siriyah*/Gaza and Jericho: The Secret Papers, 2nd Ed. (Cairo: Markaz al-Fikr al-Arabi lil-Dirasat wa al-Nashr, 1993): 163–8.

33. Menachem Klein, "Nothing New in Jerusalem, Jerusalem in the Current Final Status Talks," *Bitter Lemons*, September 10, 2008, www.bitterlemons.org. Accessed 30/9/2008.

34. Akiva Eldar, "'Moratinos Document'—The Peace that Nearly Was at Taba," *Ha'aretz*, February 14, 2002. http://www.peacenow.org./nia/news/haaretzspecial/0202.html. PDF. Accessed 8/2/2013.

35. Ibid.

36. Ibid.

37. Ibid.

38. Special Focus: The Closure of Hebron's Old City. www.ochaopt.org/documents/ocha-HUO7O5u.En. July 2005. PDF. Accessed 11/17/2013.

Chapter Nine

Conclusion

JERUSALEM: THE CORE ISSUE

Although the question of Jerusalem remains the core issue which still divides Palestinians and Israelis, it would be always difficult to disentangle it from the totality of the Israeli-Palestinian conflict. Yet, it was also capable of standing on its own as a supremely rich historical question beyond and above the subject of Palestinian statehood or modern Israeli nationalism. This inevitable interplay between its glorious past and its miserable and tragic present as a bargaining chip in the game of modern diplomacy would always challenge the skills and imagination of scholars and historians. How to balance its sanctity against its political reality, furthermore, had always required emphasis on various international players and their political agendas. In today's world, the international dimension of this conflict had always centered on the United States and its web of Arab-Israeli alliances. Since the American president is at the helm of the international system, as well as the chief executive in the domestic arena whose authority had long since eclipsed that of the State Department in matters of foreign policy, the impact of his decisions concerning the holy city cannot be overestimated.

The city's history as a national symbol, which always drew the great powers to its narrow streets, storied monuments, and religious places of worship, had resulted in many military confrontations since its religious affiliations always led to political confrontations. Throughout the centuries of Arab rule, the capital of the Palestine province was Ramla, not Jerusalem. Yet, the centrality of this holy city to the rest of Palestine was never eclipsed, granting it a status beyond that of a mere political or administrative capital. And while the city was always a religious center during centuries of Arab rule, it was the PLO which changed its status to that of a capital once the call for a Palestinian state was sounded. Yet, activities of the PA, the PLO's successor in Palestine, would never match the politicization of this city by European Zionists who utilized its religious credentials to fortify the secular nationalism of the state and convert it into their capital.

One of the most curious aspects of this Zionist transformation, ostensibly in order to draw Diaspora Jews to Israel, was the unconcealed contempt of early Zionist leaders like Herzl and Weizmann, and later Ben Gurion, for the Old City of Jerusalem. Reflecting their inescapable European cultural baggage, these and several others after them were content to gravitate towards the new city of Tel Aviv. This was the only Zionist center which they constructed. Like everything else in Palestine, it was built over Arab-owned land, in this case part of the Arab city of Jaffa. Yet, the lure of Zion, another name for Jerusalem, grew intensely once statehood became the declared objective of the Zionist generation of WWII.

Zionism was focused at first on the New City of Jerusalem, also heavily populated by Arabs, which euphemistically acquired the innocuous sobriquet of West Jerusalem so as to conceal its occupied status. The fate of East Jerusalem, or Jordanian Jerusalem later on, including the Old City, emerged as the most contentious issue preventing King Abdullah from entering into an open alliance with the Zionists on the eve of the 1948 War or after statehood was declared. This separated the Jewish state from the Wailing Wall which the Jordanians continued to guard and protect, claiming that it was the Buraq Wall which was administered by an ancient Islamic trust.

THE JORDANIAN BACK DOOR

Negotiations with Jordan over granting Jewish access and visitation rights to the wall quickly ran into obstacles such as Israeli rejection of the demand for compensating Arab property owners of West Jerusalem or allowing their return. Israelis persisted in painting the Jordanians as religious fanatics who refused to recognize the Jewish sanctity of the wall. As a result, the long sought-after peace treaty with Jordan never materialized. Yet, relations with Abdullah's successor, King Hussein, became friendly, especially as the latter assumed the role of the protector of the West Bank-Israeli border against the threat of frontline village infiltrators and guerrillas based mostly in Syria. But Israel did not hesitate to stage a massive attack on the Palestinian frontline village of Samu', as a lesson to infiltrators who attacked from Jordanian or Syrian territory. The disproportionate attack, which produced negative domestic results for Hussein, forced him to join the Arab defensive alliance and attack Israel as a bid to recoup some of his lost public support at home.

Hussein's armed forces and miniscule air power were met with stiff resistance by the IDF, which seized the opportunity to occupy all of the West

Bank and race to capture East Jerusalem. As efforts mounted at the Security Council to force Israel to fall back to the armistice lines of 1948, Hussein was given the clear impression by the United States that his support for Res. 242 would not go unrewarded. But following his endorsement of this seminal resolution which opened the way for similar steps by all the Arab antagonists of the 1967 War, Israeli hardliners led an iron-clad consensus against surrendering any territory, especially East Jerusalem, as a price of peace. There was some hope on Hussein's part that the Israelis would somehow retreat after teaching his government a lesson. But few people understood at the time the depth of Israel's dissatisfaction with the 1948 borders, believing that they made it vulnerable to attacks. Despite years of secret meetings with Israeli officials and demonstrating staunch fealty to the United States throughout the worst years of the Cold War, Jordan was always treated as a junior US ally worthy of little consideration. In the perceptions of most American presidents and their advisers, Jordan could never match Israel's strategic value to the West during the Cold War. The unspoken value of the latter to the United States was also its potential utilization to divide and disable the Arab World, a unique role which only the non-Arab state could play. No one understood Hussein's reluctance to extort strategic benefits from the United States in exchange for his proven loyalty to the West better than Kissinger, who wrote: "He [King Hussein] had the capacity neither for independent action nor for blackmail, which are the stuff of Middle Eastern politics."[1] The Jordanian monarch, furthermore, scaled back his demand for the retrieval of East Jerusalem, particularly after his disengagement from the West Bank in 1988, to a demand for custodial rights over the Muslim holy places. When he finally realized that the language of the Wadi Araba Agreement suggested that Israel was naturally endowed to cede these rights, he took steps to correct this flaw. It was his heir, King Abdullah II, who allowed these rights to revert to the PA.

THE UNITED STATES AND JERUSALEM

The United States remained within the international consensus on the Jerusalem question until the 1967 War. With the adoption of General Assembly Res. 181 in 1947, the city was expected to be governed by an international regime. Israel's unilateral decision to move most of its government offices to the Western part of the city in 1948, declaring this section the capital of the newly created state was met with a near-unanimous decision by the international community against extending recognition. Israel's move was readily seen not only as an annulment of the Israeli-Jordanian Armistice Agreement, but also as evidence of turning its back on Res. 181, the Partition Resolution. In order to break out of the straitjacket of international censorship and boycotts, Israel for a while floated the idea of functional internationalization which would have placed the Jordanian holy sites under international supervision and management. This attempt to ease the pressure on its Jerusalem policy, especially after the city was declared its capital, did not produce any results. Fearful of the kind of isolation imposed upon it by the Eisenhower administration following the Suez War, Israel adopted a strategy of preemptive attacks against Egypt and Syria. The response of the Johnson administration to these war preparations on the eve of the 1967 War was simply to caution the Israeli government against expecting automatic military support and be ready to fight alone. Actually, as early as 1964, Johnson planned to link US military assistance to Israel with a similar deal for Jordan in order to prevent any reliance on assistance from the Soviet Union. Ambassador Averell Harriman, who at the time was a member of the NSC, travelled to Israel in 1965 to convey these views. The United States asked that Israel acquiesce in the Jordanian arms deal, promise not to initiate a pre-emptive strike against any Arab state, refrain from using force against Syria's diversion plans of the Jordan River, and pledge itself against seeking nuclear weapons.[2]

But all of these were forgotten when Israel achieved a stunning military victory within a matter of days, demonstrating no interest in exchanging land for peace. US Jerusalem policy underwent a perceptible change following the war. Both the White House and the State Department began to call for keeping Jerusalem united, which amounted to acquiescing in Israel's annexation of East Jerusalem and uniting it with West Jerusalem. Since the United States never adopted the language of the UN, or Res. 242, which reiterated its Charter's call regarding "the inadmissibility of the acquisition of territory by war," no one was able to accuse the United States of sanctioning occupation or the annexation of territory. Not only did Israel defy the world community by ignoring this call, particularly as it applied to East Jerusalem, it also unleashed an irreversible trend of land annexation, resulting in the addition of 66 per cent of West Bank and East Jerusalem territory to its West Jerusalem land holdings.[3]

Had the Johnson administration or presidency really wished to force Israel to reverse course after the June War, it soon had a great opportunity to do so. Not only did the Israeli government embark on a policy of bulldozing the Arab quarters of East Jerusalem in full view of the world, reports of the destruction and looting of civilian property were received in Washington from the American Consul in the city on a daily basis. This stream of information, some of which was corroborated by international human rights' agencies, was never utilized to force Israel to comply with international human rights standards. With the passage of time, the silence of the United States made it an unwitting partner in these atrocities and sustained assaults on the Arab character of the city. Neither was this campaign of flagrant abuse of the human rights of an occupied population utilized to force the reversal of Israel's annexation of the city, thereby complicating any future opportunity for achieving a permanent Israeli-Palestinian peace. The Israelis simply refused to reverse course, with the Labor and the Likud prime ministers hardly differing on any points. Even when the Palestinians turned to peace-making, Israeli prime ministers remained as hawkish as ever, hardly interested in transcending their own terrorist past which pitted them against the British and the Palestinians. This intransigence, nevertheless, resonated with members of the Jewish American community. For instance, Prime Minister Shamir, who was in the words of Israeli professor Avishai Margalit, hardly the right material for a top executive office like that of prime minister, still received solid Jewish American support:

> Shamir's success with many American Jews seems based on their confidence that he is essentially a tough bargainer—a Jewish Assad. But Shamir is not a bargainer. Shamir is a two-dimensional man. One dimension is the length of the Land of Israel, the second, its width. Since Shamir's historical vision is measured in inches, he won't give an inch. He will not bargain about the Land of Israel or about any interim agreement that would involve the least risk of losing control over the occupied territories. [4]

THE INTERIM AGREEMENT

Palestinian delusions during the Oslo talks led them to believe that the mere placement of Jerusalem on the agenda was a victory of sorts and a promising beginning. Ignoring all signs to the contrary, they continued to disregard Israeli official statements promising never to surrender any part of Jerusalem. Although the United States left this phase of the peace process to the Norwegians, it was determined to sponsor the final agreement by itself. No American president was as eager as Clinton to preside over the signing ceremonies of the final agreement, but his distaste for Arafat and what he stood for became all too clear as he convened the Camp David II summit. The Oslo Accords, nevertheless, failed to stand in the way of Israel's open efforts to diminish the Arab presence in East Jerusalem and dismantle its institutions. Although the lead Palestinian representative in the city, Faysal Husseini, was known to the US Government as a moderate, no effort was made to protest his marginalization and the elimination of his headquarters at Orient House after his death. The United States could have easily invoked promises of non-interference in the status quo during the interim period after Oslo, but this pressure was never applied.

CLINTON: THE LAST IN THE CHAIN OF PEACE-MAKERS

Just as there were hardly any distinctions between one Israeli prime minister and the other when it came to their Palestinian policy, one can argue the same for most American presidents. Both the determined peace-makers and the ultra-nationalist presidents operated within known limits when confronting the Arab-Israeli conflict. This was clearly the case when it came to the Jerusalem question, and Clinton's highly publicized effort to midwife a final settlement between the Palestinians and Barak's Labor Government was a case in hand. Whenever the two sides drew closer to an understanding, the issues of the settlements, the return of Palestinian refugees and the question of Jerusalem intruded. Rather than breaking the logjam, Clinton followed a policy of brow-beating Arafat and intimidating the Palestinians. Clinton also constantly belittled the Palestinians' concern over losing their rights to the Muslim holy sites. Ignoring all the manifestations of the deep religious schism around him, and the dispute over archeological evidence and histori-cal precedents relating to the location of the Jewish Temple, Clinton behaved as if he was the final arbiter of this dispute who had all the answers. Even though he was president at the time of Netanyahu's authorization of the tunnel project, he pretended that no harm would come if the Muslim sites were to suffer from additional illegal archeological work. He even orchestrat-ed a diplomatic campaign to discredit Arafat and charge him with the total responsibility for the summit's failure. Following up the summit with another effort at the Taba conference, and a few years later when the Quartet was launched, additional developments materialized to narrow the margin of suc-cess of any peace settlement. One of these was President Grorge W. Bush's letter to Sharon defining he settlements as natural population centers. An-other development was Netanyahu's insistence on recognition of Israel as a Jewish state, which contributed to the demise of the Road Map.

The rise of Israel's status as a trusted and strategic ally of the United States acted as a limitation on the latter's ability to rein in its ally. An anecdote told by Peres' biographer illustrated this point. In the wake of the 1973 War, Peres was told by Kissinger to hold talks with Secretary of De-fense James Schlesinger for more weapons since the Secretary of State was leaving town. The shopping list presented by the Israeli official astounded Schlesinger. Peres requested the latest American weapons, such as Lances and Pershing missiles and Cobra helicopters in order to confront the Arabs' Scud and Frog missiles supplied mostly by the Soviet Union. Schlesinger objected mostly to the Cobra helicopters, stating that they were never used against "terrorist" attacks. He then calculated how much Peres' wish list was going to cost the United States, adding:

In the United States, we spend four hundred dollars per head on defense. If we agree to all your requests, we'll be spending six hundred dollars per head. Do you really expect us to spend more per head for Israelis than we do for Americans? [Peres replied:] "It depends on what heads we are talking about. The correct calculation is according to Arab heads—not Israeli ones. We need the weapons to use against the Arabs, not the Israelis."[5]

WHOSE RESPONSIBILITY IS JERUSALEM?

In a unique case argued before the US Court of Appeals for the District of Columbia Circuit in July 2013, a decision was handed down which confirmed that the President of the United States held the final responsibility for all decisions pertaining to Jerusalem. The case was brought on behalf of Menachem Binyamin Zivotofsky by his parents and guardians Ari Z. and Naomi Siegman Zivotofsky v. Secretary of State, Appellee. The ZOA, American Association of Jewish Lawyers and the ADL submitted *amicus briefs* in support of the appellant and others. The ruling was that the secretary of state can place the word "Israel" as the place of birth on an American passport of any citizen who was born in Jerusalem if that citizen or his guardians request such action. But the secretary of state refused to apply this decision, arguing that it was an infringement on "the president's exclusive authority under the United States Constitution to decide whether and on what terms to recognize foreign nations. We agree and therefore hold that section 214(d) is unconstitutional."[6] The suit by Zivotofsky's parents was initiated on 16 September 2003 against the secretary of state. The child was born a year earlier, and suits were made and decisions reversed or reinstated throughout the appellate court system. In 2004, the case was dismissed, prompting the government's counsel to declare that this was a confirmation of the absence of any authority which would have empowered the judiciary to exercise authority over the Executive Branch in matters of foreign policy. The conclusion was that this case was "nonjusticiable under the political question doctrine."[7]

As a background of this decision, the United States Government offered its own views on the most disputed issue in history. The statement emphasized that since the twentieth century, the United States has been in a neutral position, refusing to side either with the Palestinian or Israeli claims on who was sovereign in Jerusalem. When Israel declared its independence in 1948, it was promptly recognized as a "foreign sovereign" by President Truman. But neither this president nor any of his successors recognized any sovereign over Jerusalem. The US position was explained in a cable in 1948 when it declined an invitation to attend the opening ceremony of the Knesset in Jerusalem. The cable read that "the United States cannot support any arrangement which would purport to authorize the establishment of Israeli sovereignty over parts of the Jerusalem area."[8]

During the proceedings of the General Assembly following Israel's annexation of Jerusalem, the United States indicated that its policy continued to oppose any unilateral alterations of the status of Jerusalem without consultation with all sides. Reference was also made to the State Department's *Foreign Affairs Manual* which listed rules pertaining to passport administration, illustrating the US policy of neutrality. The rules stated that if an applicant was born in an area disputed by another country, the city of birth may be substituted for the name of the country. The manual called on consular officers not to write "Israel" or "Jordan" on the passport of any applicant who was born in Jerusalem. Additionally, the statement narrated the record of Congressional efforts to interfere with the consistent policy of neutrality adopted by the executive branch, beginning with the 1995 Jerusalem Embassy Act. This step specifically called for recognizing Jerusalem as the capital of the State of Israel and establishing a US embassy there no later than 13 May 1999. US Department of Justice also wrote an opinion to the White House counsel confirming that the constitution vests only the President with the authority to conduct the country's diplomatic relations with other states. The department warned that the proposed Congressional bill would simply diminish the constitutional authority of the president to chart out the nation's diplomatic relations. In the past, precedents confirming presidential policy on Jerusalem included those of President Reagan, who refused to relocate the embassy from Tel Aviv to Jerusalem in 1984. Yet, another instant which attempted to dilute the President's exclusive constitutional powers to oversee the country's diplomatic relations occurred during the term of office of George W. Bush. On 30 September 2002, he added his signature to the Foreign Relations Authorization Act (Fiscal Year 2003), known also as Public Law No. 107–228. Under Section 214 (d), it called for recording the place of birth when it is Jerusalem for passport purposes as Israel. Yet, even President Bush, who had established more than the usual friendly relations with Israel, attached a signing statement to this bill stating that "the Act contains a number of provisions that impermissibly interfere with the constitutional functions of the presidency in foreign affairs."[9]

By June 2015, the US Supreme Court provided the final disposition of this question. At issue was the definition of the perimeters of presidential, versus congressional, powers in setting foreign policy of the country and the exclusive power of the executive office to extend recognition to other states. The decision struck down the 2002 law, never applied, which authorized parents to list "Israel" as the birthplace of a child born in Jerusalem on a passport application. The justices voted 6–3 in favor of Presidents Bush's and Obama's rejection of this attempted infringement on their powers and those of their secretaries of state to determine the status of the holy city. Yet, in the dissenting opinion of Chief Justice John Roberts, a significant constitutional privilege had been breached, setting a dangerous precedent. He wrote that "Never before has this court accepted a president's defiance of an act of Congress in the field of foreign affairs."[10]

Every American president, therefore, was confirmed as fully in charge of the conduct of the nation's foreign policy, and in particular, of developing and following a specific policy of neutrality on Jerusalem. But this was only a legal and technical position regarding stamping American passports with the word Israel as a place of birth, and compelling the Chief Executive to recognize the status of Jerusalem as the capital of Israel. Barring this last step of recognition, which would have placed the United States outside the international consensus on the status of the city as occupied territory, the United States did everything in its power to support Israel militarily, economically and diplomatically over the years. What was lacking in this relationship was the application of pressure to deter Israel from pursuing its brutal policy of home demolitions, the destruction of historic areas, the eviction of Arab residents, tampering with the archeological remnants of ancient sites beneath the Noble Sanctuary and the creation of settlements on the outskirts of the Arab suburbs of the city. But who really shaped presidential policy on the city?

Ever since the Roosevelt administration during WWII, the institution of presidential advisers was gaining prominence, power, and effectiveness. Names like David K. Niles, who was chosen to maintain links to local organized voting groups, pioneered the role of the partisan adviser. Most of these subordinated American policy to Jewish American interests through influencing the chief executive, often to the detriment of State Department advise. Truman's decision to extend swift recognition to the new Israeli state in 1948 was certainly taken without the concurrence of this department. Increasingly, presidential advisers opened doors to Israeli officials through bypassing the appointed professional experts in charge of the nation's foreign policy. Insulated against oversight by other branches of government, the presidential advisers operated as the gate-keepers to the executive office and were unchecked or censored by any authority outside the Chief Executive's narrow circle of personally selected operatives. What was remarkable about some of these advisers, such as Walt Rostow, was that they often monopolized the shaping of foreign policy during periods of extreme presidential preoccupation with other foreign policy crises, such as the Vietnam War. Thus, they were often completely free to mold presidential policy unimpeded by other governmental influences. They were also able to forge links to organized voting blocks who were not necessarily representative of majority foreign policy views.

O'Connell, the CIA station chief in Jordan who enjoyed a close relationship with King Hussein in the 1950s and 1960s, became painfully aware of the close relationship of the advisers to the Israeli embassy in Washington during the George W. Bush presidency. At one point he requested a meeting with national security adviser Condoleeza Rice during the early years of the this administration in order to run by her one of his reports on the Middle East peace process, highlighting the Arab peace initiative of Hussein and Mubarak of Egypt. She declined this request on account of being over-whelmed with the duties of office, suggesting that he meet instead with her newly appointed aide on the Middle East, Bruce Riedel, a CIA officer inher-ited from the Clinton administration and now about to be replaced. O'Connell's meeting with Riedel yielded more than a reaction to his report. The latter approved the report, suggesting that only Rice could push it along and indicating that he was slated to return to the CIA soon. When O'Connell inquired as to whom his replacement might be, Riedel claimed to be totally in the dark. He did reveal, however, that Rice was running the names of every applicant for this position by the Israeli Embassy for its response. He added that when he voiced objection, Rice answered that if she did not get her final candidate approved by the Israelis, they would make her work difficult for her, so she resigned herself to accepting reality and yielding to their decision. The man who was eventually selected for this office turned out to be Elliott Abrams, who became a perennial appointee, serving several terms in this position. O'Connell claimed that it was Abrams who pushed the president to ignore Res. 242 in a letter to Sharon and to soften US condemnation of the settlements.[11]

WHO BEARS THE FINAL RESPONSIBILITY FOR THE FATE OF JERUSALEM?

Harold Saunders, former Assistant Secretary of State for Near Eastern and South Asian Affairs, founder of the International Institute of Sustained Di-alogue and the man who coined the phrase "Middle East peace process," had a front-row seat at the arena of presidential policy making. He complained in a speech in 1986 that American interests in the Middle East were not recog-nized broadly enough to compel American leaders to develop regional com-prehensive policies. The problem was a practical one, namely how to place the issue on the agenda of a president and a secretary of state. The challenge has always been getting their attention amid all the other crises which crowd their agendas. He questioned the wisdom of waiting for a crisis to emerge in the Middle East before developing a sustained policy for the area's prob-lems.[12] He wrote:

> How would you appeal to a president of the United States, six years in office and only occasionally deciding that the issues involved in the Middle East are sufficient to engage his personal and sustained attention?[13]

Saunders concluded that the challenge would always be how to define US interests in such a way capable of encouraging American presidents to risk embarking on a high-level quest for a comprehensive peace strategy in the Middle East.[14] Elaborating on the significance of prioritization to sustain the chief executive's attention towards this conflict, an author who examined fissures in the American–Saudi relationship prior to the Arab oil embargo of 1973, concluded:

> The president tends to set the agenda more than special interests or foreign governments. The priority assigned to the Arab–Israeli dispute by the president and his key advisors determines how U.S. Middle East policy is made.[15]

The role of the presidential advisers, therefore, cannot be exaggerated. They can inflate the power and influence of domestic constituencies favoring Israel, or they can magnify Israel's military achievement on the ground, thereby minimizing the impact of its human rights abuse of the Arab population. This was certainly the case of the Jerusalem issue, which was often misrepresented and downplayed over the years in order to belittle Palestinian and Arab rage over losing control of their holy sites. Presidential inaction in the face of Israeli intransigence which was transforming much of the Old City of Jerusalem into Jewish neighborhoods complicated, and finally defeated any American –sponsored peace–making endeavor. Much of the blame in this regard rested on the Johnson administration which permitted its client state to enjoy a free hand in the Palestinian territories in the wake of the 1967 War. That succeeding presidents, even Carter with his human rights'-centered foreign policy, failed to secure an equitable settlement in Jerusalem, and by extension the totality of the Israeli–Palestinian conflict, attested to the twisted priorities of most American chief executives and their dangerous subordination of foreign policy issues to domestic political considerations.

NOTES

1. Henry Kissinger, *The White House Years* (Boston: Little, Brown and Co., 1979): 362.
2. Dan Kurzman, *Soldier of Peace: The Life of Yitzhak Rabin, 1927–1995* (New York: Harper Collins, 1998): 200–1.
3. Nazmi al-Ju'beh, "The Colonizing of East Jerusalem," *Stone*, Issue 39 (Winter 2006): 10.
4. Avishai Margalit,"The Violent Life of Yitzhak Shamir," *New York Review of Books* 14 May 1992). Quoted in Avi Shlaim, *The Iron Wall: Israel and the Arab World* (New York: W. W. Norton, 2000): 464.
5. Motti Golani, *The Road to Peace: A Biography of Shimon Peres* (New York: Warner Books, 1989): 126–7.
6. www.cadc.uscourts.gov/internet/opinions. Nsf/.../07_5347_1447974. 23 July 2013. Accessed 8/22/2013.
7. Ibid.
8. Ibid.

9. Ibid.

10. David Savage, "Top Court Backs President in Jerusalem Passport Case," *Chicago Tribune* (June 9, 2015): 10.

11. Jack O'Connell, *King's Counsel: A Memoir of War, Espionage, and Diplomacy* (New York: W. W. Norton, 2011): 233–4.

12. Harold Saunders, "A Critical View of US Policy," *American–Arab Affairs*, No. 18 (Fall 1986): 48–9.

13. Ibid., 49.

14. Ibid., 56.

15. Lucia W. Rawls, "Saudi Arabia, ARAMCO and the American Political Process: Cause for Concern," in same as above, 100.

Bibliography

ARCHIVES

Lyndon B. Johnson Library, Austin, Texas.
Papers of the Special Committee (Control Committee) of National Security Council, 1967–1968.
Country File—Israel
Agency File—United Nations

OFFICIAL PUBLICATIONS

Foreign Relations of the United States (FRUS), 1953–1998
Israel Ministry of Foreign Affairs—Electronic Documents
Truman Presidential Library—Oral History Interviews

WORKS CITED

Abu 'Aliyah, Abd al-Fattah Hassan. *Al-Quds: dirasat tarikhiyah.* Riyadh: Dar Al-Marreekh, 2000.
Agha, Hussein, and Robert Malley. "Camp David: The Tragedy of Errors." *New York Review of Books* (9 August 2001). http://www.nybooks.com/Articles/archives12.
Albright, Madeleine. *The Mighty and the Almighty.* New York: First Harper Perennial Edition, 2007.
American Jewish Committee. "Interpretations of Jewish Commonwealth by Leading Zionist Personalities and Groups." www.bipa.org/Publications/downloadFile.cfm?FileID=1987.
Ami, Shlomo Ben. *Scars of War, Wounds of Peace.* Oxford: Oxford University Press, 2006.
Asad, Muhammad (Leopold Weiss). "Jerusalem in 1923: The Impressions of A Young European." In *My Jerusalem: Essays, Reminiscences and Poems.* Salma K. Jayyusi and Zafer I. Masri, eds. Northhampton, Mass.: Olive Branch Press, 2005.
Asali, Kamil J., ed. *Jerusalem in History.* Brooklyn, NY: Olive Branch Press, 1990.
Asfour, Hasan. "Ru'yah li-itifaq I'lan al-mabadi'". *Majallat al-Dirasat al- Filastiniyah,* No. 16 (Fall 1993).

Assi, Seraj. "Memory, Myth and the Military Government: Emile Habibi Collective Autobiography." www.palestine-studies.org/JQ-52-Assi- Me....

Bakri, Mustafa. *Gaza wa Areeha: al-awraq al-siriyah.* Cairo: Markz al-Fikr Al-Arabi lil-Dirasat wa al-Nashr, 1993.

Bard, Mitchell. "The Arab Lobby: The American Component." *The Middle East Quarterly.* Vol. XVII, No. 4 (Fall 2010). www.meforum.org/2773/ arab-lobby.

Bialer, Uri. "The Road to the Capital: The Establishment of Jerusalem as the Official Seat of the Israeli Government in 1949." *Studies in Zionism,* Vol. 5, No. 2 (Autumn 1984).

Bird, Kai. *Crossing Mandelbaum Gate.* New York: Scribner, 2010.

Booth, William, and Ruth Eglash. "At Temple Mount. Prayer Cuts 2 Ways." *Chicago Tribune* (13 December 2013).

Bowen, Jeremy. *Six Days: How the 1967 War Shaped the Middle East.* New York: St. Martin's, 2003.

Brom, Shlomo. "From Rejection to Acceptance: Israeli National Security Thinking and Palestinian Statehood." *United States Institute for Peace.* Special Report (17 February 2007). www.usip.org.

Carmon, Omer. "A Palestinian Village in the Heart of Tel Aviv." www. Zoghrot.org/en/content/Palestinian-village-heart-tel-aviv.

Carter, Jimmy, *Palestine: Peace not Apartheid.* New York: Simon and Schuster, 2006.

Christison, Kathleen. "U.S. Policy and the Palestinians: Bound by a Frame." *Journal of Palestine Studies,* Vol. 26, No. 4 (Summer 1997).

Clinton, Bill. *My Life* (New York: Alfred A. Knopf, 2004).

Cohen, Hillel. *The Rise and Fall of Arab Jerusalem.* (London: Routledge, 2011).

Committee on the Exercise of the Inalienable Rights of the Palestinian People. *The Status of Jerusalem.* New York: UN, 1997. http://Domino.un.org/UNISPAL.NSF/9a798adb.3/21/ 2005.

"Consulate General of the United States—Jerusalem." PDF.

Cook, Jonathan. *Blood and Religion: Unmasking of the Jewish and Democratic State.* London: Pluto Press, 2006.

———. "Canada Park and Israeli Memoricide." *The Electronic Intifada* (10 March 2009). http://electronicintifada.net/.../canada... Israeli.../8...

Davis, Rochelle. "Ottoman Jerusalem: The Growth of the City Outside the Walls." In *Jerusalem 1948: The Arab Neighborhoods and Their Fate In the War,* Salim Tamari, ed. Jerusalem: The Institute for Jerusalem Studies, 1999.

Dumper, Michael. *The Politics of Jerusalem since 1967.* New York: Columbia University Press, 1997.

———. *The Politics of Sacred Space: The Old City of Jerusalem in the Middle East Conflict.* Boulder, Colo.: Lynne Rienner, 2002.

Duri, Abd al-Aziz al-. "Al-Quds fi al-tarikh al-Islami." In *Al-Quds wa al-hal al-Filastini wa qira'at fi al-amn al-qawmi al-Arabi.* Tawfiq Abu-Baker, ed. Amman: Mu'assasat Abd al-Hamid Shuman, 1999.

———. Abd al-Aziz al-. "Jerusalem in the Early Islamic Period, 7th-11th Centuries AD." In *Jerusalem in History.* Kamil Asali, ed. New York: Olive Branch Press, 1990.

Eban, Abba. *An Autobiography.* New York: Random House, 1977.

Eldar, Akiva. "'Moratinos Document.'—The Peace that Nearly Was at Taba." *Ha'aretz.* (14 February 2002). http://www.peacenow.org./ Nia/news/haaretzspecial/0202.html. PDF.

Elgindy, Khalid. "The Middle East Quartet: A Post-Mortem." Analysis Paper No. 25. The Saban Center for Middle East Policy at Brookings (February 2012). www.brookings.edu/.../ 02 middle east-elgindy.

Eveland, Wilbur Crane. *Ropes of Sand: America's Failure in the Middle East.* New York: W. W. Norton, 1980.

"Factsheet: Resolution 242, Interpretation and Implications." http:// www.cjpme.org.

Farra, Muhammad Hussain al-. "Jerusalem and the Forgotten Documents." In *My Jerusalem,* Selma K. Jayyusi and Zafer I. Masri, eds. Northampton, Mass.: Olive Branch Press, 2005.

Feintuch, Yossi. *U.S. Policy on Jerusalem.* New York: Greenwood Press, 1987.

Fistere, John. "The Dome of the Rock, Jewel of Jerusalem." *Jordan,* Vol. 5, No. 3 (Fall 1980).

Franken, H. J. "Jerusalem in the Bronze Age." In *Jerusalem in History*, K. Asali, ed. Brooklyn, NY: Olive Branch Press, 1990.

Gelvin, James. "The Ironic Legacy of the King-Crane Commission." In *The Middle East and the United States*, David W. Lesch and Mark L. Hass, eds. Boulder, Colo.: Westview Press, 2012.

Golani, Motti. "Jerusalem's Hope Lies only in Partition: Israeli Policy on The Jerusalem Question, 1948–1967." *International Journal of Middle Eastern Studies*, Vol. 31, No. 4 (November 1999).

———. *The Road to Peace: A Biography of Shimon Peres*. New York: Warner Books, 1989.

———. "Zionism without Zion: The Jerusalem Question, 1947–1949." *The Journal of Israeli History*, Vol. 16, No. 1 (Spring 1995).

Gorenberg, Gershom. *The Accidental Empire: Israel and the Birth of the Settlements, 1967–1977*. New York: Henry Holt, 2006.

"Hadith li-rais al-hukumah al-Israiliyah fi ithri itifaq 'Gaza-Jericho First'." *Majallat al-Dirasat al-Filastiniyah*, No. 16 (Fall 1993).

"Hadith li-wazir al-kharijiyah al-Israeli bi sha'an itifaq I'lan al-mabadi'." *Majallat al-Dirasat al-Filistiniyah*, No. 16 (Fall 199

Hart, Alan. "What Really Happened in the 1967 Arab-Israeli War?" www.Redressline.com/.../what-really-happened-in-the-1967-arab-Israel . . .

Heikal, Muhammad Hassanein. *Kalam fi al-siyaseh*. Cairo: al-Sharika Al-Misriyah lil-nashr al-Arabi wa al-Duwali, 2000.

Herzog, Shira. "Discovering a Homeland Abroad: How the Six Day War In Israel Galvanized Canada's Jews." *Literary Review of Canada* (May 2011). www.reviewcanada.ca/magazine/.../discovering- a-h....

Hulme, David. *Identity, Ideology, and the Future of Jerusalem*. New York: Palgrave Macmillan, 2006.

Husseini, Faysal. "Al-Quds munthu Huzairan 1967." In *Al-Quds wa al-hal Al-Filastini wa qira'at fi al-amn al-qawmi al-Arabi*. Tawfiq Abu-Baker, ed. Amman: Mu'assassat Abd al-Hamid Shuman, 1999.

Indyk, Martin. *Innocent Abroad: An Intimate Account of American Peace in the Middle East*. New York: Simon and Schuster, 2009.

"Itifaqiyat Oslo: Muqabalah ma' Nabil Sha'ath." In *Majallat al-Dirasat Al-Filastiniyah*, No. 16 (Fall 1993).

"Jordanian-Palestinian Accord for Jerusalem Holy Sites." Ramallah: Anna Lindh Foundation. www.ansamed.infoANSAmedIsrael.

Ju'beh, Nazmi al-. "The Colonizing of East Jerusalem." *Stone*, Issue 39 (Winter 2006).

Judis, John B. *Genesis: Truman, American Jews, and the Origins of the Arab-Israeli Conflict*. New York: Farrar Straus and Giroux, 2014).

"Al-Kalimaat khilal al-ihtifal bi-tawqee' I'lan al-mabadi'". *Majallat al-Dirasat Al-Filastiniyah*, No. 16 (Fall 1993).

Kaplan, Neil. "Zionist Visions of Palestine, 1917–1936". *Muslim World*, Vol. LXXXIV, No. 1–2 (January-April 1994).

Kattan, Victor. "Competing Claims, Contested City: The Sovereignty of Jerusalem under International Law." Februay 2011. www.Qatarconference.org/Jerusalem/doc31.pdf.

Katz, Yossi, and Yair Paz. "The Transfer of Government Ministries to Jerusalem, 1948–49: Continuity or Change in the Zionist Attitude to Jerusalem." *Journal of Israeli History*, Vol. 23, No. 2 (Autumn 2004).

Khatib, Ghassan. "East Jerusalem is Crucial to a Two-State Solution." *Bitter Lemons*, 27 July 2009. www.bitterlemons.org.

Khatib, Rouhi El-. "The Judaization of Jerusalem and its Demographic Transformation." In *Jerusalem, the Key to World Peace*. Islamic Council of Europe. London: Islamic Council of Europe, 1980.

Klein, Menachem. "Nothing New in Jerusalem, Jerusalem in the Current Final Status Talks." *Bitter Lemons*, 10 September 2008. www. bitterlemons.org.

Kissinger, Henry. *The White House Years*. Boston: Little, Brown and Co., 1979.

Kollek, Teddy. "Introduction: Jerusalem—Today and Tomorrow." In *Jerusalem: Problems and Prospects.* Joel L. Kramer, ed. New York: Praeger, 1980.

Krystall, Nathan. "The Fall of the New City, 1947–1950." In *Jerusalem 1948: The Arab Neighborhoods and Their Fate in the War.* Salim Tamari, ed. Jerusalem and Bethlehem: Institute of Jerusalem Studies and Badil Resource Center, 1999.

Kurzman, Dan. *Soldier of Peace: The Life of Yitzhak Rabin, 1922–1995.* New York: Harper Collins, 1998.

Laqueur, Walter. *A History of Zionism.* New York: MJF Book, 1972.

Levine, Mark. "Framing Tel Aviv." http://english.aljazeera.net/focus/2009/09/20099892214748263.html.9/17/2009.

Levinthal, Louis E. "The Case for a Jewish Commonwealth in Palestine." *The Annals of the American Academy of Political and Social Science,* Vol. 240 (July 1945).

Lilienthall, Alfred. *The Zionist Connection: What Price Peace?* New York: Middle East Perspectives, Inc., 1979.

Lustick, Ian. *For the Land and the Lord: Jewish Fundamentalism in Israel.* New York: Council on Foreign Relations, 1988.

Manafeekhi, Bashar. "Min al-maqahi al-adabiyah fi al-'alam al-arabi; maqha al-sa'aleek fi al-Quds." *Al-Hurriyah,* No. 1224 (28 February 2009).

Margalit, Avishai. "The Violent Life of Yitzhak Shamir." *New York Review of Books* (14 May 1992).

Mattar, Philip, ed. "Jerusalem." *Encyclopedia of the Modern Middle East and North Africa,* Vol. 2. Farmington Hills, Mich.: Thomson Gale, 2004.

Mead, Walter Russell. "The New Israel and the Old: Why Gentile Americans Back the Jewish State." *Foreign Affairs,* Vol. 87, No. 4 (July-August 2008).

Mendenhall, George E. "Jerusalem from 1000–63 BC." In *Jerusalem in History.* Kamil J. Asali, ed. Brooklyn, NY: Olive Branch Press, 1999.

Montefiore, Simon Sebag, *Jerusalem: The Biography.* New York: Vintage Books, 2012.

Morris, Benny. *The Birth of the Palestinian Refugee Problem, 1947–1949.* Cambridge: Cambridge University Press, 1991.

———. "Camp David and After: An Exchange (An interview with Ehud Barak)." *New York Review of Books,* (13 June 2002). www. Nybooks.com/.../2002/camp-da….

———. *1948: The History of the First Arab-Israeli War.* New Haven, Conn.: Yale University Press, 2008."

Nakhleh, Issa, ed. *Encyclopedia of the Palestine Problem.* Vol. 3. New York: International Books, 1991.

Neff, Donald. *Warriors for Jerusalem: Six Days that Changed the Middle East.* New York: Simon and Schuster, 1984.

Nuseibeh, Hazem. "Al-Quds al-mu'asirah alati 'a'ref." In *Al-Quds wa al-hal al-Filastini wa qira'at fi al-amn al-qawmi al-Arabi.* Tawfiq Abu-Baker, ed. Amman: Mu'assasat Abd al-Hamid Shuman, 1999.

O'Connell, Jack, with Vernon Loeb. *King's Counsel: A Memoir of War, Espionage, and Diplomacy in the Middle East.* New York: W. W. Norton, 2011.

Oran, Oded. "The US and Confidence-Building Measures, Arab Normalization Gestures to Israel." *Bitter Lemons,* (July 23, 2009). www.bitterlemons.org

Peled, Alisa Rubin. "The Crystallization of an Israeli Policy Towards Muslim And Christian Holy Places, 1948–1955." *Muslim World,* Vol. No. 1–2 (January-April 1994).

Quandt, William B. *Camp David, Peacemaking and Politics.* Washington, DC: Brookings Institution Press, 1986.

———. *Peace Process: American Diplomacy and the Arab Israeli Conflict Since 1967.* Washington, DC: The Brookings Institution Press, 1993.

Raviv, Dan, and Yossi Melman. *Every Spy a Prince.* Boston: Houghton Mifflin, 1990.

Rawls, Lucia. "Saudi Arabia, ARAMCO and the American Political Process: Cause for Concern." *American-Arab Affairs,* No. 18 (Fall 1986).

Raziq, Adnan Abd al-. *Harat al-Yahoud fi al-Quds.* Nicosia: Al-Rimal, 2013.

Reich, Bernard, and David H. Goldberg. *Historical Dictionary of Israel.* Lanham, Md.: Scarecrow Press, 2008.

Rica, Simone. "Heritage, Nationalism and the Shifting Symbolism of the Wailing Wall." *Jerusalem Quarterly,* No. 24 (Summer 2005).

Roberts, Priscilla, ed. "Jerusalem." *The Encyclopedia of the Arab-Israeli Conflict,* Vol. IV. Santa Barbara, Calif.: ABC CLEO, 2008.

Rogers, William P. "A Lasting Peace in the Middle East." In *The Encyclopedia of the Arab-Israeli Conflict.* Priscilla Roberts, ed. Santa Barbara, Calif.: ABC CLEO, 2008.

Ross, Dennis. *The Missing Peace: The Inside Story of the Fight for Middle East Peace.* New York: Farrar, Straus and Giroux, 2004

Ryan, Rev. Joseph L. "The Catholic Faith and the Problem of Jerusalem." In *Jerusalem, the Key to World Peace.* London: Islamic Council of Europe, 1980.

Sabbagh, Karl. *Palestine: A Personal History.* New York: Grove Press, 2007.

Sa'adeh, Imad. "Al-Samiriyoun." *Tasamuh,* Vol. 3, No. 9 (June 2005).

Sassoni, Shomron and Osher. "The Samaritan—Israelites and Their Religion." www.shomronO.tripod.com/educationalguide.

Saunders, Harold. "A Critical View of US Policy." *American-Arab Affairs,* No. 18 (Fall 1986).

Savir, Uri. *The Process.* New York: Random House, 1998.

Segev, Tom. *1967: The War and the Year that Transformed the Middle East.* New York: Henry Holt, 2005.

Sela, Avraham. *Political Encyclopedia of the Middle East.* New York: Continuum Publishing Co., 1999.

Sheehan, Edward R. F. *The Arabs, Israelis, and Kissinger.* New York: Reader's Digest Press, 1976.

Shlaim, Avi. *The Iron Wall: Israel and the Arab World.* New York: W. W. Norton, 2000.

———. "Israel and the Arab Coalition in 1948." In *The War for Palestine: Rewriting the History of 1948.* Avi Shlaim and Eugene L. Rogan, eds. Cambridge: Cambridge University Press, 2001.

———. *Lion of Jordan: The Life of King Hussein in War and Peace.* New York: Alfred A. Knopf, 2008.

Skolnik, Fred, ed. "Jerusalem." *Encyclopedia Judaica,* 2nd ed., Vol. 10. Farmington Hills, MI.: Thomson Gale, 2007.

Smith, Charles D. *Palestine and the Arab Israeli Conflict.* New York: St. Martin's Press, 1988.

Sontag, Deborah. "Quest for the Mideast Peace." *New York Times* (26 July 2001). Reprinted in *Journal of Palestine Studies* (Autumn 2001).

Stettner, Ilona-Margarita. "Fact Sheet: Positions on the Legal Status of Jerusalem." Konrad Adenauer Stiftung. www.kas.de/Wf/doc/ kas_7186–1442–2-30.

Takiff, Michael. *A Complicated Man: The Life of Bill Clinton as Told by Those Who Knew Him.* New Haven, Conn.: Yale University Press, 2010.

Talhami, Ghada Hashem. "Between Development and Preservation: Jerusalem under Three Regimes." *American Arab Affairs,* No. 1 (Spring 1986).

———. "The Modern History of Islamic Jerusalem: Academic Myths and Propaganda." *Middle East Policy,* Vol. VII, No. 2 (February 2000).

Tall, Abdullah. *Karithat Filastin: Muthakarat Abdullah al-Tall.* Cairo: No Publisher, 1999.

Tibawi, Abdul Latif. "Jerusalem under Islamic Rule." In *Jerusalem: The Key To World Peace.* London: Islamic Council of Europe, 1980.

Tivnan, Edward J. *The Lobby: Jewish Political Power and American Foreign Policy.* New York: Simon and Schuster, 1987.

Wagner, Rev. Donald E. "The Mainline Protestant Churches and the Holy Land." In *Zionism and the Quest for Justice in the Holy Land,* eds. Donald E. Wagner and Walter T. Davis. Eugene, OR.: Pickwick Publications, 2014.

Wallach, Janet and John. *Arafat: In the Eyes of the Beholder.* New York: Carol Publishing Group, 1990.

Wasserstein, Bernard. "The Politics of Holiness in Jerusalem." *The Chronicle Of Higher Education,* Vol. 48, No.4 (21 September 2001). http://Search.ebscohost.com/login.aspx?direct=true&db=fsh&AN=5269861&site=ehost-live.

Zohar, Michal Bar. *Shimon Peres: The Biography.* New York: Random House, 2007.

Index

Abbas, Mahmoud (Abu-Mazen), 169, 180
Abd al-Shafi, Haider, 169. *See also* Madrid
    Peace Conference
Abdullah I (King of Jordan), 55, 57, 58,
    60–62; assassination, 66, 67
Abed-Rabbo, Yasir, 180
Abu-Dis, 180–181
Abu-Odeh, Adnan, 157
Abu-Sa'ud family, 167. *See also* Arafat,
    Yasir
'Administered Territories', 120
Agha Hussein, 187–188
Agha, Zakaria, 162
Agranat Commission, 147
Allenby, Edmund, 2, 3; Abd al-Latif
    Nuseibeh, 2, 3
Allon, Yigal, 86; Allon Plan, 141
American Federation of Labor (AFL), 4
American-Israel Public Affairs Committee
    (AIPAC), 149
American Jewish Committee (AJC), 4, 29
Ami, Shlomo Ben, 180, 186
Angleton, James, 134. *See also* Central
    Intelligence Agency (CIA)
Anglo-American Committee of Inquiry,
    39–41
Aqsa University, 9. *See also* Arab
    education before 1948; Arab and
    Jewish press, 8, 9
Arab city council, 110. *See also* Narkis,
    Uzi; Khatib, Rouhi; Salman, Ya'kov

Arab education after 1967, 164
Arab education before 1948, 9
Arab healthcare system after 1967,
    164–165
Arab Higher Committee (AHC), 8, 13. *See*
    also Anglo-American Committee
Arab oil lobby, 149–150
Arab strike and revolt, 1936-1939, 14–15;
    Qassam's revolt, 14–15
Arabian American Oil Company
    (ARAMCO), 101–102, 149–150
Arafat, Yasir (Qudwah), 180–187; Arab
    villages of Jerusalem, 180. *See also*
    Camp David II
Arlosoroff, Chaim, 22, 23
Armenian Quarter, 184, 192
Armistice Agreement, 1949, 60–62, 65
Asfour, Hasan, 169, 173, 180
Ashrawi, Hanan, 162, 168
Auster, Daniel, 6, 51, 68

Baker, James, 159, 162
Baker, Ray Stannard, 28
Balfour Declaration, 1–4, 29
Balfour, Lord Arthur, 29; and Hebrew
    University, 6
Barak, Ehud, 178–179, 187; view of Arabs,
    186–187; peace with Syria, 178–179,
    180. *See also* Camp David II
Barbour, Walworth, 83, 100, 123–124;
    treatment of churches, 109. *See also*

Eshkol, Levi; 'East Jerusalem' the term
Bayh, Birch, 117
Begin, Menachem, 140; Camp David
    Agreement, 157
Beilin, Yossi, 168, 180
Ben Gurion, David, 16, 30–31
King Abdullah's assassination, 66–67;
    Biltmore Conference, 21, 32–34;
    annexation of West Jerusalem, 51;
    return of West Jerusalem Arabs, 54;
    Irgun and Lehi militias, 52; United
    Nations Special Committee on
    Palestine (UNSCOP), 49; Suez War,
    75–76; Rafi Party, 97; Jewish Quarter,
    107; peace proposals, 1967, 132–133
Biltmore Conference, 32–34
Brandeis, Louis, 2, 29–30; *See also*
    Wilson, Woodrow
British census, 1922, 6
Bull, Odd, 97
Bundy, McGeorge, 129
Buraq Wall, 10–12, 104. *See also* Mohn,
    Paul; Wailing Wall
Burns, Findley, Jr., 81, 132
Bush, George H. W., 160
Byrode, Henry, 63, 65

Caradon, Lord (Sir Hugh Foote), 136, 138.
    See also Resolution 242
Camp David Agreement, 159
Camp David II, 181–187. *See also* Clinton,
    Bill (William)
Carter, Jimmy, 137
Cease-fire Agreement, 1948, 83. *See also*
    Jerusalem military parade
Central Intelligence Agency (CIA), 86, 96,
    130, 134. *See also* Helms, Richard;
    Refugees, 1967
. *See also* June War, 1967
Chief Rabbinate office, 6
Christopher, Warren, 169, 171. *See also*
    Madrid Peace Conference
Clinton, Bill (William), 177–180, 188. *See
    also* Camp David II
Clinton Parameters, 191–192
Control Committee (Special Committee) of
    National Security Council, 88. *See also*
    Johnson, Lyndon B.; Hussein, King
Corpus separatum, 63

Dayan, Moshe, 80. *See also* Mughrabi
    Quarter; Refugees, 1967
D Committee (Jerusalem Committee), 50
Deir Yassin, 60
Dov, (Bernard) Joseph, 51; military
    governor of Jerusalem, 54–55; looting
    Arab properties, 59

East Jerusalem, 170. *See also* Oslo Talks ;
    Camp David II
East Jerusalem, the term, 120
Eban, (Aubrey) Abba, 52–54, 95, 138–139,
    140, 143; West Jerusalem as Israel's
    capital, 63. *See also* Hussein, King;
    Refugees, 1967
Eran, Oded, 180, 186
Erekat, Saeb, 180, 182. *See also* Camp
    David II
Eshkol, Levi, 82, 97. *See also* Barbour,
    Walworth; Jerusalem military parade

Farra, Muhammad, 135, 139. *See also*
    Goldberg, Arthur
Faysal, King (Saudi Arabia), 101. *See also*
    Arab oil lobby
Forrestal, James, 42
Fortas, Abe, 81, 99
Functional internationalization, 51–52

Gazit, Mordechai, 81
Ghosheh, Sheikh Abdullah, 131
Glubb, John Baghot, 55–57. *See also* Tall,
    Abdullah
Goldberg, Arthur, 96, 135–136. *See also*
    Resolution 242; Hussein, King;
    O'Connell, Jack
Greater Israel, the concept, 133, 159

Hakham Bashi, 6
Harbi, Ghazi, 59
Hasan, Prince (Jordan), 66
Helal, Gemal, 183–184. *See also* Camp
    David II
Helms, Richard, 86
Herzl, Theodor, 71
Herzliya, 50
Herzog, Yaacov, 81, 133–134. *See also*
    Hussein, King
Higher Islamic Council (HIC), 164

Hirschfield, Yair, 168. *See also* Oslo Peace Talks
Holst, Johan Jorgen, 169
Holy Basin, 184–185. *See also* Taba Conference
Hurva Synagogue, 60
Hussein, King, 78, 80–81. *See also* Samu' ; Resolution 242 ; Allon Plan; United Arab Kingdom ; Rabat Resolution; Jordanian Option; disengagement from West Bank, 157; relationship to Jerusalem, 166
Husseini, Amin (Mufti), 10, 13. *See also* Islamic Congress, 1931; Arab strike and revolt, 1936-1939
Husseini, Faysal, 158, 160–165. *See also* Madrid Peace Conference; Orient House

Ibn Saud, King Abdul Aziz, 36–37
Ibrahimi mosque, 194. *See also* Camp David II
Indyk, Martin, 177–178, 189
Interim Agreement, 178
Interim settlement, 171, 172. *See also* Oslo Peace Talks
Internationalization of Jerusalem, 15; in Sykes-Picot Agreement, 15–16; in Peel Commission, 16–17
Iron Wall, 30
Islamic Congress, 1931, 13
Israeli settlements, 160, 186, 188, 192; and Rabin after Oslo, 188–189. *See also* Taba Conference

Jabotinsky, Vladimir, 10–11. *See also* Revisionist Movement
Jarring Mission, 139–140
Jerusalem Basic Law, 141
Jerusalem military parade, 83–85
Jerusalem municipal council, Mandate period, 5
Jewish Agency (JA), 6
Jewish commonwealth, 21, 33–35; Wilson's concept, 27–28. *See also* Biltmore Conference
Jewish cultural sites, 51–52, 58. *See also* Mt. Scopus; Rhodes Armistice Agreement

Jewish National Fund (JNF), 6
Jewish people concept, 19
Jewish Quarter, 57
Johnson, Lyndon B., 81–82, 129, 137–138. *See also* Jerusalem military parade; Control Committee; Resolution 242; Hussein, King; Samu'
Johnston plan (Jordan Valley Unified Water Plan), 79–80. *See also* Samu'
Jordanian option, 158, 174
June 4 lines, 97, 99, 102, 148. *See also* Eban, Abba; Nuseibeh, Anwar; Resolution 242
June War, 1967, 86, 88, 99. *See also* Hussein, King

Katznelson, Berl, 17
Kennedy, John F., ix, 97. *See also* Rafi Party
Khalidi, Hussein, 6, 67
Khartoum Conference, 103, 134. *See also* Nasser, Gamal Abdul
Khatib, Anwar, 113. *See also* Wilson, Evan M.
Katib, Rouhi, 109–110; infractions of international law, 142
King-Crane Commission, 2, 28. *See also* Wilson, Woodrow
Kissinger, Heny, 144–146, 159; 1973 War, 147–148. *See also* Hussein, King; Rabat Resolution; Meir, Golda
Knesset Israel, 6
Kollek, Teddy, 65, 142–143. *See also* Mughrabi Quarter; Khatib, Rouhi
Kook, Avraham Isaac, Chief Rabbi, 6–7
Krim, Arthur and Mathilde, 81–82, 99. *See also* Johnson, Lyndon B.

Lake, Anthony, 178
Lapidot, Ruth, 65–66
Larsen, Terje, 168. *See also* Norwegian Peace Research Institute (FAFO)
Latroun salient, 97
Latroun villages (Canada Park), 111–113, 136–137. *See also* Wilson, Evan M.
League of Nations Charter, 7; judgment of Wailing Wall Commission, 11–12
Levinthal, Louis F. (Judge), 33–34
Lincoln, Abraham, viii

Lipkin-Shahak, Amnon, 188

Madrid Peace Conference, 167–169. *See also* Arafat, Yasir
Malik, Charles, 64
Malley, Robert, 187. *See also* Camp David II
Mamilla cemetery, 52
Mandelbaum Gate, 73–74
Mehdi, Muhammad, 101
Meir, Golda, 17; Peel Commission, 17; relations with Kissinger, 145, 146; United Arab Kingdom plan, 146
Mohn, Paul, 131. *See also* Wailing Wall/Buraq Wall
Moratinos, Miguel, 190–191. *See also* Taba Conference
Morrison-Grady Committee, 41–42
Moshe, Eitan Ben, 105–106
Mt. Scopus, 58, 60; Rhodes Armistice Agreement, 72. *See also* Jewish cultural sites
Mubarak, Husni, 158, 190
Mughrabi Quarter, vii; background, 104; demolition, 1967, 104–106
Muslim holy sites, 157, 184. *See also* Hussein, King; Camp David II; Taba Conference

Nabi Musa festival, 9–10
Narkis, Uzi, 110
Nashashibi, Ragheb Pasha, 14
Nasser, Gamal Abdul, 102. *See also* Khartoum Conference
Niebuhr, Reinhold, 36, 40. *See also* Tillich, Paul
Niles, David K. (Neyhaus), 35, 37, 38–40. *See also* Roosevelt, Franklin Delano; Truman, Harry
Nixon, Richard, 144–145. *See also* Meir, Golda; Rogers Plan
Noble Sanctuary (Temple Mount), 5, 10–11. *See also* Muslim holy sites
Nuseibeh, Anwar, 117. *See also* June 4 lines

O'Connell, Jack, 81, 134, 136–137. *See also* Hussein, King; Greater Israel; Goldberg, Arthur; Resolution 242

Operation Sons of Light, 77
Operation Whip, 77
Organization of Islamic Cooperation (OIC), 183–185. *See also* Camp David II
Orient House, 160–162, 165. *See also* Husseini, Faysal
Oslo Peace Agreement, 171–173
Oslo Peace Talks, 168–169; Jerusalem in the peace talks, 169–170
Oslo II, 189

Palestine, ancient borders, 3; *See also,* Smith, Sir George Adam
Palestine Conciliation Committee (PCC), 52; Arab refugees, 54. *See also* Eban, Abba
Palestine Legislative Council, 14
Palestine Liberation Organization (PLO), 158–160; East Jerusalem, 160–161. *See also* Rabat Resolution
Palestine municipal boundaries, 5, 8
Palestine National Covenant, 158, 178. *See also* Clinton, Bill
Paris Peace Conference, 2, 3, 27–28
Peel Commission, 16–18
Peres, Shimon, 80–81, 168–171; provisional borders, 180–181
Pro-Jerusalem Society, 5–6
Protection of the Holy Places Law, 100. *See also* Status Quo Regulations

Qassam, Izz al-Din, 14–15
Quigley, John, 66
Qurei', Ahmad (Abu al-'Alaa'), 168–169, 181. *See also* provisional borders

Rabat Resolution, 147–148
Rabin, Yitzhak, 80. *See also* Samu'; Oslo Peace Agreement
Rafi Party, 97, 100
Ramla, 197
Rashid, Ahmad, 189
Reagan, Ronald, 160. *See also* Israeli settlements
Refugees, 1967, 117–120; 'administered territories', 119–120. *See also* Dayan, Moshe; Eban, Abba

Resolution 478, 141–142. *See also*
Jerusalem Basic Law
Resolution 242, 134–135, 140, 157–158.
See also Goldberg, Arthur; Caradon,
Lord; Hussein, King; Johnson, Lyndon
B.; O'Connell, Jack
Revisionist Movement, 11, 30. *See also*
Jabotinsky, Vladimir
Rhodes Armistice Agreement, 1951, 72
Rifa'i, Abdul-Mon'em, 135
Rifa'i, Samir, 72
rishon le zion, 6–7
Roach, Edward Keith, 11
Rogers Plan, 144
Ross, Dennis, 178–181, 182–185. *See also*
Camp David II
Roosevelt, Elinor, 37
Roosevelt, Franklin Delano, 31, 35–37;
Jewish New Dealers, 35
Rostow, Eugene, 109, 129
Rostow, Walt, 84, 88–89, 96, 140
Rusk, Dean, 88–89, 138
Rutenberg, concession (Pinhas), 8

Sadat, Anwar, 157, 173, 187
Safieh, Anton, 121
Salman, Ya'kov, 104–105, 109–110. *See
also* Arab City Council; Mughrabi
Quarter
Samu', 77–80; Israeli background, 82–83;
Johnson's reaction, 82–83
Samuel, Sir Herbert, 5
Saunders, Harold, 89, 135, 137. *See also*
Control Committee
Savir, Uri, 169. *See also* Oslo Peace Talks
Sha'ath, Nabil, 173, 188
Shamir, Yitzhak, 157–159
Sharett, Moshe, 48–49, 51
Sharon, Ariel, 159, 192
Shash, Taher, 190
Shaykh Jarrah (suburb), 162
Shultz, George P., 157–158
Shuqeiry, Ahmad, 78. *See also* Khartoum
Conference
Silver, Abba Hillel, 30, 33
Siniora, Hanna, 161–162; *al-Fajr*,
160–161
Solomon's Temple, 185. *See also* Camp
David II

Sontag, Deborah, 187
State Department Arabists, 38, 149
Status Quo Regulations, 8, 10–11, 52, 60
Suez War, 74–75
Supreme Muslim Council, 6, 13

Taba Conference, 188–192
Taft, Robert, A, 33
Tall, Abdullah, 52, 59–60; Mt. Scopus, 58
attacking West Jerusalem, 59–60
Tel Aviv, 4–5
Tillich, Paul, 37
Transfer Committee, 1948, 59
Truman, Harry, 37–39, 41–42

United Arab Kingdom plan, 146
United National Command (UNC),
159–162
United Nations Relief and Works Agency
(UNRWA), 193
United Nations Special Committee on
Palestine (UNSCOP), 49
USS Liberty, 102–103
Ussishkin, Menachem, 16–17

Va'ed ha-Kehillah, 6
Va'ed Leumi, 6
Vatican, 109. *See also* corpus separatum

Wailing Wall, vii, 10; Israeli claims, 1948,
57–58. *See also* Buraq Wall; Mohn,
Paul
Wailing Wall riots, 1929, 10–12
Waqf, Islamic, 10–13
Weiss, Leopold (Muhammad Assad), 10.
See also Nabi Musa festival
Weizman, Chaim, 1–2, 29, 30; Peel
Commission, 16–17; conflict with
Brandeis, 29–30
West Jerusalem, 49–60
Wilson, Evan M., 111, 114–115, 121. *See
also* Latroun villages; Mt. Scopus
Wilson, Woodrow, 2, 3–4, 27, 29–30
Wise, Rabbi Stephen, 31–32, 36
World Zionist Organization (WZO), 6
Wright-Compton Resolution, 33, 36
Wye River Conference, 178

Yitzhaki, Aryeh, 99–100

Zionist Executive (ZE), 6   Zivotofsky, Menachem Binyamin, ix, 174

About the Author

Ghada Hashem Talhami is D. K. Pearsons Professor of Politics, emerita, at Lake Forest College. She was born in Amman, Jordan, to Palestinian parents and received her early education in Jerusalem, Amman, and Surrey, Great Britain. She is a member of the board of editors of *Arab Studies Quarterly* and *Muslim World.* She participated in two conferences on Jerusalem convened by the World Council of Churches in Switzerland and Greece, and was a senior Fulbright scholar in Syria. She is the author of several books, including studies of Arab and Muslim women, as well as the policies of various Arab states towards the Palestine question, including *Palestine and the Egyptian National Identity, Palestine in the Egyptian Press*, and *Syria and the Palestinians: The Clash of Nationalisms*.

CPSIA information can be obtained
at www.ICGtesting.com
Printed in the USA
BVOW04*0841240417
480984BV00012B/10/P